# THE TAIPA
## HONG KONG'S MERCH

# THE TAIPANS
## Hong Kong's Merchant Princes

### COLIN N. CRISSWELL

*'Few of us can stand prosperity.
Another man's, I mean.'*

Mark Twain

HONG KONG
OXFORD UNIVERSITY PRESS
OXFORD  NEW YORK

*Oxford University Press*

*Oxford New York Toronto*
*Kuala Lumpur Singapore Hong Kong Tokyo*
*Delhi Bombay Calcutta Madras Karachi*
*Nairobi Dar es Salaam Cape Town*
*Melbourne Auckland*

*and associated companies in*
*Berlin Ibadan*

**First published 1981**
**Reissued in Oxford Paperback 1991**
**Second impression 1992**
**Published in the United States**
**by Oxford University Press, Inc., New York**

**ISBN 0 19 585373 3**

**Printed in Hong Kong**
**Published by Oxford University Press, Warwick House,**
**Hong Kong**

*To Charlotte and Rupert*

# Acknowledgements

I should like to thank Charles Buchanan Jardine for his assistance, especially in allowing me to make use of some hitherto unpublished family letters and for lending me some books from his collection, also numerous business houses in Hong Kong which gave me invaluable assistance, several old residents who prefer to remain anonymous, the staff of the University of Hong Kong library, the Royal Asiatic Society library and the Hong Kong Public Records Office, the Revd Carl Smith whose evening class on Hong Kong history gave me the idea for the book as well as some useful information, Diana Railton for finding an out-of-print book for me in England, Oxford University Press for their encouragement, and my wife for doing the typing.

## NOTE

The dollars referred to in the text are either trade or Hong Kong dollars unless otherwise indicated.

# Contents

# Plates

# Introduction

'All else —valour, a good name, glory, everything in heaven
and earth —is secondary to the charm of riches.'

Horace

TAIPAN means 'great manager' in Chinese and was the
sobriquet given by the Chinese in Canton in the eighteenth
century to the agents of the East India Company who together formed the Select Committee which supervised the
activities of the British traders there. After the East India
Company's monopoly ended in 1834, the word came to be
used of the leading merchants in the 'country' trade
between China and India—men like William Jardine,
James Matheson, and Lancelot Dent, who were partners in
the trading houses, or hongs, that succeeded the 'Honourable John Company'. These shrewd, hard-headed businessmen emulated the 'princely style of liberality' of their predecessors, 'the Select' as they ironically referred to them.
C. T. Downing in his book *The Fan Qui in China*, published in 1838, wrote of the taipans,

A few of the principals of the houses in Canton may well be
considered as merchant princes and actually live as such, keeping
open house for the gentry at the time in the place. It is very usual,
therefore, for them to invite people to come whenever they are not
otherwise engaged; and in this case it is not necessary for them to

send a note to express their intention, but merely to put their names on a large slate which is always kept at the door. . . .[1]

The merchant princes of India and the China coast were exotic examples of the financiers and entrepreneurs who, in the West, were rising to unparalleled prosperity on the swelling tide of industrialization. For centuries wealth and political power in Western Europe had been based upon the ownership of land. England, prior to the Industrial Revolution, was dominated by a small homogeneous group of landowning peers and gentry, comprising at the most 5 per cent of the population, in whose hands was concentrated almost all of the country's wealth and power. The great developments in textile and iron manufacturing, together with the rise of coal and steam power, were to change the traditional social pattern very rapidly, although the old upper class continued to set the tone of social life long after its real influence had waned. The first industrial peer, Edward Strutt, a textile millionaire, was not elevated to the peerage, as Lord Belper, until 1856. The Manchester *Examiner* observed 'It is something for those who claim to be regarded as descendants of the mailed barons of England to admit to their order a man who not only has made but is making his fortune by spindles and looms.' The landed nobility may have been slow to admit the plutocrats to their order but their sons were soon embracing the daughters of the newly ennobled industrial kings. The Duke of Norfolk, head of one of the oldest noble houses, who in lineage ranked with the ruling princes of Germany, married Edward Strutt's great grand-daughter. By the end of the nineteenth century, to paraphrase the words of Oscar Wilde's Lady Bracknell, land gave one position but prevented one from keeping it up. The early taipans, having made their fortunes, almost invariably returned to England to invest in land and live the life of country gentry, while later in the century, the Eastern merchant princes showed a preference for mingling with the raffish set of international financiers who surrounded the Prince of Wales and for participating in the ostentatious display of wealth associated with such circles.

Generally the first taipans came from the ranks of the middling gentry and, following traditions established in India in the eighteenth century, entered merchant houses in hopes of making a fortune from the expanding commercial dealings between Britain and the East. The speed with which this commerce grew in the nineteenth century was staggering. Britain's dominance of the world economy reached its peak around 1870, at which time her foreign trade figures almost equalled those of Germany, France, Italy, and America combined. A historian of the time wrote 'There has probably never been a period in the history of the world when the conditions of industry, assisted by the great gold discoveries in several parts of the globe, were so favourable to the formation of enormous fortunes as at present and when the race of millionaires was so great.' In the East, those with established positions in the Indian market were well placed to benefit from this upsurge. Some of Hong Kong's wealthiest taipans were of Parsee, Jewish, or Armenian origin and had links with merchant houses in Calcutta and Bombay. The First World War, which caused great rises in taxation and assisted the spread of socialist ideas, marked the end of the age of the plutocrats in Europe, although the breed survived in the East and other parts of the world. The hundred years preceding 1914 was an epoch in which those ready to seize the opportunities provided by the revolutions in technology and communications had a better chance to rise by their own individual efforts from poverty and obscurity to wealth and power than at any other time in history.

Of the merchant houses which developed in Canton before the foundation of Hong Kong, only the wealthiest of them, Jardine and Matheson, the 'Princely Hong', survives today. In the 1830s Jardine and Matheson controlled about one-third of foreign trade with China, which largely consisted of the illegal importation of opium from India into China. The opium trade was not mere small-time smuggling. Throughout the nineteenth century it yielded one-third of the total revenue of British India and has been described as 'the largest commerce of the time in any single commodity'. Jardine and Matheson and their smaller rivals such as Russell and Co. and Dent and Co. made a great deal of money. It was said that the head of Jardine's only needed to stay in the East for ten years before retiring home a rich man, while even a junior clerk kept a racing pony and was a member of three or four clubs. Looking back nostalgically to the good old days of the 1830s and 1840s, a writer in the *China Mail* in 1867 observed that 'the princely expenditure of leading Europeans was easily supported by their almost fabulous profits'.

William Jardine and James Matheson played an important part in the events which led to the Anglo-Chinese War of 1838 and the subsequent acquisition by Britain of Hong Kong. The first permanent building to be erected in Hong Kong early in 1841 was Jardine and Matheson's godown for storing opium. Jardine was in England at the time and Matheson wrote to him urging him to use his influence to ensure the retention of Hong Kong, adding prophetically 'Many prefer Kowloon but we ought to have both.' Jardine and his associate John Abel Smith, M.P., had the ear of Lord Palmerston, the Foreign Secretary, who wrote to Smith after the Treaty of Nanking in 1842, 'There is no doubt that this event, which will form an epoch in the progress of the civilization of the human races, must be attended with the most important advantages to the commercial interests of England.'[2]

England's commercial interests lost no time in expanding into China after the establishment of the colony of Hong Kong and the opening of the five Chinese 'treaty ports' to foreign trade. By 1844 there were nearly a hundred foreign firms operating along the China coast. About half of these were British and nearly a quarter were Indian or

Parsee. The largest hong was Jardine and Matheson with five partners and twenty assistants, followed by Dent and Co. with five partners and eight assistants, Russell and Co., an American hong, with six partners and eight assistants, and D. and M. Rustomjee with fifteen partners. Before long the hongs were followed by ships' chandlers, watchmakers, store keepers, doctors, and architects. In Hong Kong one of the earliest European owned retail shops was A. and S. Watson, established in 1841 as 'The Dispensary', a title still used by one branch of the company today.

The hongs acquired large plots of land, usually at least an acre or so, on which they established extensive buildings. These comprised offices, godowns, residential quarters, junior and senior messes, and stables. In the early days, there were few Western women in Hong Kong and the treaty ports and, apart from sport, 'Commerce was the beginning, the middle and the end of our life in China.' However this was the time before the telegraph when sail was still supreme and days of feverish activity when vessels arrived and departed, alternated with periods of idleness and leisure. The taipans and their assistants, who were known as 'griffins', apparently from the term used of new arrivals in India, made the best of it. As in the old Canton days, the taipans and griffins wined and dined extravagantly together in their baronial bachelor establishments. A Shanghai doctor of the time, in counselling moderation, advised a light breakfast consisting of 'a mutton chop, fresh eggs, curry, bread and butter, with coffee or tea or claret and water'. As late as 1875 a visitor to Hong Kong, J. Thomson, in his book *The Straits of Malacca, Indo-China and China*, commented that 'nothing surprised me more in Hong Kong than the expensive way in which English assistants were housed and the luxury with which they were indulged'.

The lack of civic amenities, the absence of family life, and the high death rate from disease, together with the belief that there were easy fortunes to be made, contributed to a general feeling of impermanence, and in some cases to a reckless determination to get rich quick at any cost. A Shanghai merchant wrote the British consul in the 1840s,

> In two or three years at furthest, I hope to realize a fortune and get away. . . . You must not expect men in my position to condemn themselves to prolonged exile in an unhealthy climate for the benefit of posterity. We are money-making, practical men. Our business is to make money, as much and as fast as we can— and for this end all modes or means are good which the law permits.[3]

By the 1860s the prevailing attitude and atmosphere was changing. Those merchants who had been dazzled by the prospect of the vast profits which could be made from the Chinese market were disappointed. Trade with China did not expand very rapidly. Chinese demand for opium continued to grow but this trade was dominated by the old-established hongs. The Chinese had little need for the textiles and other manufactured products that newcomers on the scene tried to sell. In the face of competition from elsewhere, the silk and tea trades declined. This, combined with a general world depression in the 1860s, caused the failure of many of the hongs, most sensational of which was the collapse and disappearance of Dent's in 1867. Men no longer believed that they could make a fortune in a few years and retire. They now resigned themselves to the prospect of a working lifetime on the China coast. The Hon. G. N. Curzon wrote in *Problems in the Far East* in 1894,

> Large fortunes are made with difficulty; the merchant princes and magnificent houses of an earlier day have disappeared; Messrs Jardine Matheson and Co. remain almost alone among the great houses whose establishments and operations a generation ago were the talk of the East. Men do not now expect fortunes; they are content with competencies. . . .[4]

1. C. T. Downing, *The Fan Qui in China*, London, 1838, I, 186.
2. M. Greenberg, *British Trade and the Opening of China*, Cambridge, 1951, 214–15.
3. J. K. Fairbank, *Trade and Diplomacy on the China Coast*, Harvard, 1964, footnote, 161.
4. Hon. G. N. Curzon, *Problems in the Far East*, London, 1894, 423.

# PART I

# A Most Gentlemanlike Speculation

'Let none admire that riches grow in hell:
that soil may best deserve the precious bane.'

Milton

# PART I

## A Most Gentlemanlike Speculation

# 1

# Early Days in Canton

It was not until the end of the eighteenth century that British merchants showed much interest in trade with China. Earlier, British adventurers attracted by the lure of the East had made for India where the East India Company, founded in 1600 and given a royal monopoly of all British trade in Asia, had established its headquarters. The Portuguese made their first voyage to China in 1513 and in 1557 were permitted by the local Chinese authorities to establish permanent buildings at Macau, a small narrow peninsula on the western side of the Pearl River delta. Although the Portuguese merchants were not allowed to go beyond the limits of the small settlement, for several decades they enjoyed considerable prosperity. Macau's close proximity to Canton enabled the Portuguese merchants to buy quantities of silk for resale to the Japanese from the Portuguese trading station at Nagasaki. After 1580, when Portugal became part of Spain, the Spanish, who had established themselves in the Philippines, used Macau as a terminal port for trade with Mexico via Manila. Next followed the Dutch, who in 1619 seized Jakarta in Java, which they renamed Batavia and used as a base to expand their activities throughout the Indonesian archipelago. However their attempt to establish trade with China was rebuffed by the Imperial authorities who dis-

liked their arrogant manners and their practice of raiding
Chinese and Portuguese ships in the China seas.

Early English attempts to open trade were no more
successful. The physical resemblance between the English
and the unpopular Dutch did not predispose the Chinese
authorities in their favour. In 1637 four English ships
commanded by Captain Weddell, who carried a letter of
introduction from King Charles I, arrived at Macau. One
reason why the Chinese had allowed the Portuguese to
establish a settlement was so that they could act as go-
betweens for other Western merchants, thus preventing
unwanted incursions by foreign barbarians into Chinese
ports. The Portuguese themselves did not want to encourage rivals and when Weddell wearied of their procrastinations and attempted to deal with the Chinese
directly, he was forcefully repelled. The Portuguese
bundled the English out of Macau and, exactly six months
after their arrival, they sailed away virtually empty-
handed, having been expelled 'outt off the Citty and the
Country, even by Fire and Sword as one May well say',
according to the rueful account of one of the merchants.

However Macau's boom days were over. In 1638 its
fortunes suffered a heavy blow when the Portuguese were
expelled from Japan on suspicion of involvement in a
rebellion by Japanese Christians. Its ruin was completed in
1640 when Portugal seceded from Spain and, as a result,
trade between Macau and Manila was prohibited. Such
local trade as remained was seriously disturbed by the
anarchic state of affairs that prevailed in South China
during the struggle between the decrepit Ming dynasty
and the Manchu invaders which ended with the victory of
the latter in 1644. Piracy on the South China Sea became so
rampant that in 1662 an imperial decree, from which
Macau was exempted, required the coastal population to
move several miles inland. When the East India Company's
ship *Return* visited Macau in 1673, the city was run-down
and impoverished. In spite of a stay of eight months, the

English did little trade, for the Portuguese merchants had only small quantities of goods for which they demanded exorbitant prices. The English view that there was little profit to be made from trade with China was confirmed.

In fact the low point in trade between China and the West had been reached. The K'ang Hsi emperor, who reigned from 1661 to 1722, was one of China's greatest and most powerful rulers. Intelligent and broad-minded, his attitude to Europeans in his youth was influenced by a Belgian Jesuit, Father Ferdinand Verbiest, who, in 1676, was appointed President of the Board of Astronomy, a position which frequently brought him into personal contact with the emperor. In 1685 the emperor declared that the ports of China were open to foreign trade. The motives behind this decree are not clear but the emperor may simply have wished to make some money from the dues which would be imposed on the foreign merchants. At any rate, Confucian philosophy rated commerce as a low and unworthy occupation and it is probable that the K'ang Hsi emperor did not regard the opening of China to Western trade as a very important matter. This change of attitude came at a propitious time for the British. The Portuguese empire had long since fallen into decay and decline, and the Dutch, although well established in the Archipelago, were not strong enough to challenge the British elsewhere. Nor were the French or the Americans serious rivals. In 1699 the East India Company ship *Macclesfield* made a successful trip to Canton selling a cargo of woollen cloth and buying in return silk, tea, porcelain, and oriental bric-à-brac. Each year thereafter at least one East India Company ship visited Canton. In 1719, when foreign traders were restricted to Canton for administrative convenience and to limit the disturbances of one sort or another which inevitably followed the arrival of a Western ship, the East India Company was already the principal European agency there.

In 1720 the Chinese official in charge of foreign trade in

Canton, called by Europeans the Hoppo, set up the Co-
Hong, a guild of Chinese merchants through which all
trade was to be channelled. The officials exacted large
amounts of 'squeeze' from the merchants of the Co-Hong
and they, in turn, took advantage of their monopoly rights
to charge the European traders whatever prices they liked.
The Europeans were expected to observe various other
restrictions which, in the season of 1760, were sys-
tematized in the form of the Eight Regulations. In the early
days of foreign trade with China, the European merchants
had arrived on the summer wind and had left some six
months later with the winter wind. Therefore the Chinese
had not envisaged that the merchants would want to take
up permanent residence in Canton. The Europeans were
allocated a section of the Canton waterfront opposite the
island of Honam and here they were permitted to rent
houses, which they frequently renovated and altered, for
their residence and for the storage of goods during the
trading season. However, as ships became larger and more
seaworthy, the merchants tended to leave later in the
winter season and arrive earlier in the summer season so
that the period when no foreigners were in residence
became shorter and shorter. Moreover a few foreign merchants ignored the disapproval of the Chinese officials and
contrived to stay on during the close season. It was to deal
with this situation and to curb the growing disorder caused
by disputes between the different European nationalities
and between the Europeans and the Chinese that the Eight
Regulations were framed.

In brief, all business was to be completed and all debts
paid by the end of the trading season and the Europeans
were not to live in their factories (warehouses) during the
close season, nor were they to bring their wives and
families with them. No arms were to be brought to the
factories and no European warship was to enter the Pearl
River. Chinese were not to be employed as servants in the
factories nor was any Chinese to teach his language to the

foreigners. Europeans were not to enter the city of Canton and were to remain within the immediate vicinity of their factories. All trade was to be carried out through the Co-Hong and any petitions from the foreigners to the Chinese officials had to be presented through the Co-Hong. Several of the lesser restrictions were not enforced by the Chinese officials, except at times when relations were bad, but they did insist that the foreign merchants were not to reside permanently in Canton.

The Senate in Macau, anticipating stricter measures by the Chinese authorities to clear Canton of foreigners during the close season had, in 1757, successfully petitioned the Governor to lift restrictions against foreigners residing there. Accordingly after 1760 the European trading companies began to rent houses in Macau. The East India Company did not take the lead for it did not permit the supercargoes, who travelled out with the ships to act as agents at the port of sale, to remain on the China coast between seasons until 1770. Three years later the Company moved into the first of four adjoining buildings which it came to own on one of the best sites in Macau. From the Praia Grande, a wide tree-lined boulevard bordering the crescent-shaped inner harbour, the houses mounted up to the Ridge, which runs like a spine through the small settlement. The President of the Select Committee, which supervised the Company's affairs in Canton and Macau, rented the finest house in Macau, now the Camões Museum. The extensive grounds of the house included Macau's principal historical monument, the Camões Grotto, commemorating the alleged visit of Luis de Camões, Portugal's most famous poet, to the settlement in 1557. The East India Company was the world's largest commercial organization at this time and the President of the Select Committee generally earned well in excess of £10,000 a year in commissions, equivalent to at least £200,000 a year today, so the grand manner and princely. style which its officers affected was not unfitting. In Calcutta a bachelor in the Company's employment might have forty or fifty servants and in Macau a household of twenty servants was not considered exceptional. Some of the British had sufficiently large wardrobes to enable them to send their laundry to Calcutta, a round trip of four months or more.

The merchants, cooped up in Canton for months at a time, sought 'gay and inspiriting amusements' in Macau and by all accounts social life there at the turn of the eighteenth century was a whirl of masquerades, musical parties, horse-racing, and amateur theatricals. One of the principal attractions was the remarkable superfluity of women. M. Greenberg in *British Trade and the Opening of China* notes that in 1822 there were 604 adult non-Chinese males as opposed to 2693 non-Chinese women. The British kept to themselves and maintained an attitude of aloof disdain to the Portuguese who generally lived a life of genteel poverty relieved only by occasional bribes. The remaining Portuguese merchant houses, with the exception of 'Widow Payva and Sons' and 'A. Pereira and Co.', had been taken over by merchants of other nationalities. At the same time the British were obliged to make liaisons with the local women for it was not until after 1800 that the East India Company was willing to allocate berths on China-bound vessels to women. Very few of these liaisons resulted in marriage for the unwritten code that no European should marry a Macau girl was strong. However, while they remained on the China coast, the merchants looked after their mistresses and bastards, remittances to them being entered in the accounts books as payments to pensioners. In some cases, when a merchant retired, his successor inherited his pensioner as well as his commercial position. Downing, in his memoirs published in 1838, makes it clear that liaisons were possible not only with Eurasian women but also with Chinese. The only Chinese women that the Europeans had the opportunity of meeting were the boat people who spent their lives afloat and were looked down upon by the average Chinese. Consequently they had fewer inhibitions about cohabiting with Europeans. Downing wrote of them with reference to his visit to Macau:

> They were good-natured, pretty looking young women, and smiled frequently, exhibiting beautiful teeth. One of them seemed to have taken a good deal of pains in adorning herself, and had arranged some artificial flowers in her hair. As I sat close to her, in trying to make myself understood, I happened to catch hold of her arm. This appeared to give her great uneasiness, as she immediately drew back and turned her eyes with much anxiety towards the shore, saying 'Na! na! Mandarin see, he squeegee mee! he squeegee me! Mandarin see!'. . . Squeegee means being put into prison, and a sum of money forced from them before they were liberated. Upon my inquiry whether the mandarins were always so strict, she replied with great expression 'Na! na! nightee time come, no man see!'[1]

Although the East India Company theoretically had a monopoly of British trade with China, in fact less than half of the British ships which visited Canton were owned by the Company. The majority were owned by private merchants engaged in the trade between China and India, this being known as the country trade. The Company found it very difficult to prevent interlopers entering trade in the East. Many were former employees of the Company who began to trade on their own behalf, if necessary using Portuguese companies as fronts. Around 1770 the Company decided to regularize the position by issuing licences at Calcutta to the country traders. From 1773 the traders in Macau and Canton were supervised by the Select Committee which ensured that they obeyed the Eight Regulations.

The Company kept the increasingly important trade in tea to itself while the country traders carried Indian cotton, pepper, and opium to Canton where they sold these items for silver. The Company had great difficulty in finding any British products to exchange with the Co-Hong merchants for tea since the principal British export, woollen goods, did not find favour with the Chinese. The country traders were forbidden by the Chinese to export silver so they gave it to the Company, getting bills payable in London in return. The Company then used the silver to pay for the tea.

The country traders in Canton generally formed themselves into partnerships and were linked with merchant houses in Calcutta and Bombay. Many of them had entered the trade as supercargoes and they usually continued to act as agents taking a percentage of the value of the cargoes which they bought and sold for others. As the agents acquired capital, they satisfied a local need by expanding into banking, insurance, and shipping. The Company saw that they left Canton in the close season, but some of them found a way of avoiding this. In 1776 France appointed a consul in Canton and although he was not recognized as such by the Chinese authorities, he was permitted to reside there permanently. A private trader named John Reid then got himself appointed as the Austrian consul and soon others followed his example and acquired consulships of various countries.

Initially the country merchants mainly handled cotton, spices, and indigo but towards the end of the eighteenth century the trade in opium became increasingly important. It had been used in China for centuries as a medicine but was not used there as a drug until the Dutch in Java popularized the practice of smoking it in the seventeenth century. Some opium was grown in Yunnan but the principal source of supply was Bengal. By 1729 the trade had become sufficiently important for an imperial edict to be issued banning its import but although the Company later complied with this and stopped carrying it, the Chinese officials made no real effort to impose the edict, regarding it as another means of extorting 'squeeze'. In India the administrative responsibilities of the Company were increasing rapidly and the need to find new sources of revenue became urgent. Accordingly the Company purchased the annual crop and auctioned it to the private traders, adopting the attitude that it was not the Company's responsibility to enforce Chinese regulations. Meanwhile the demand for opium in Canton increased rapidly and the private traders found themselves hard pressed to meet it. Even so, in 1818 the total amount of opium imported by China hardly exceeded 4000 chests, each chest weighing 140 pounds. However thereafter the amount increased considerably and by 1836 the value of imports reached $18 million, making it the world's most valuable single commodity trade. Between 1828 and 1836 $38 million worth of silver flowed out of China. The traders had at last found something the Chinese wanted to buy. One merchant wrote 'Opium is like gold. I can sell it any time.' There were some twinges of conscience but these were quickly suppressed. The general sentiment in England and among the merchants themselves was that the country traders were the epitomy of the values of self-help and commercial initiative which were the most prized of virtues in nineteenth-century Britain.

A disproportionate number of country traders were of Scottish origin. This was no accident. Education in Scotland was better than that in England at this time but the younger sons of the lower gentry had fewer opportunities to make an acceptable living in their own country than their counterparts in England. Some migrated to England but, although they prospered in many fields, their origins and their religion were disabilities to some extent, for example, in acquiring a living in the Anglican Church. Consequently many sought to make their fortunes abroad. The Scots are traditionally shrewd and they had fewer inhibitions than the English gentry against entering trade. Moreover in foreign lands the Scots, like the Jews, tended to form close-knit social and business communities of their own. In fact kinship linked many of the country traders. When the articles of partnership of Jardine and Matheson were redrawn in 1842, management was vested in the relatives of the two founders of the 'Princely Hong', William Jardine and James Matheson. However kinship without ability was not sufficient, for quick wits and sharp business acumen were essential to survival in the cutthroat conditions of trade on the China coast. Both Jardine and Matheson were partners of 'Holly' Magniac in their early days as traders. At a time when Magniac was still the senior partner, the agency was joined by one of his cousins, Francis Hollingworth. Although Francis was 'willing, well-disposed and desirous of making himself useful . . . Bell's "Life of London" was oftener in his hands than the Books'. Jardine, who could not abide idleness and incompetence, sent him home with a gratuity of £10,000. In 1830 Jardine wrote to his nephew, Andrew Johnston,

> You are aware that I have a strong objection to extravagance and idleness and trust you will impress on the minds of your young cousins—I never can consent to assist idle and dissipated characters however nearly connected with me but am prepared to go to any reasonable extent in supporting such of my relations as conduct themselves prudently and industriously.

He did in fact find positions for a number of his relatives and some of his surviving letters show that he gave considerable financial assistance to others. Neither Jardine nor Matheson spared themselves. Jardine wrote to Johnston on 3 December 1836, 'I have enjoyed good health since you left and continue to work until two or three o'clock in the morning as formerly. It is now two a.m. of the 4th and Mr Matheson and I are at our desks.'[2]

The principal ways in which men gained sufficient knowledge to venture into the country trade were through employment in an Indian-based country house or by service on the quarter-deck. In both cases they gained invaluable first-hand knowledge of Eastern produce and people, and established useful contacts. William Jardine came from farming stock and was born in 1784 at Lochmaben, Dumfriesshire. It seems likely that his father,

James, was the illegitimate son of a member of the local landowning family, the Jardines of Applegarth, which had been granted a baronetcy in 1672. He qualified as a medical doctor, not in those days a very highly esteemed profession socially, and joined the East India Company as a ship's surgeon, going to the East in 1802. Ships' officers were permitted to engage in a small amount of trade on their own behalf and Jardine did well out of several trips which he made between Bombay and Canton. In 1819 he left the service of the East India Company and went into business, acting as agent for the Bombay Parsee firm of Framjee Cowasjee. Later Jardine acted for another Parsee merchant, the euphoniously named Jamsitjee Jeejeebhoy, described by a contemporary as 'that prince of Eastern merchants'. Jeejeebhoy was an enormously successful businessman, renowned for his philanthropy. He was probably the first native of India to be created a baronet. The backing of the powerful Indian agency houses was to be invaluable to Jardine and the other country traders in the struggle which later developed to end the East India Company's monopoly. Jardine also had close links with Howqua, one of the Chinese Co-Hong houses. Foreigners used the term 'Howqua' to refer both to the merchant house and to two of its principals, Wu Ping-chan and his son Wu Yuan-hua. The former was estimated to be worth £4$\frac{1}{2}$ million in 1834. The Chinese called the house Ewo and this name was later adopted by Jardine's.

James Matheson came from more genteel stock than that of Jardine, indeed he was the first of the country traders to be the social equal of 'the Select' who comprised the East India Company's supervisory committee. Not that his antecedents were in any way exalted, for his family was one of clergymen and army officers, of some significance in their remote home county of Sutherland and sufficient for Matheson to be regarded as a gentleman, but of little consequence beyond the north of Scotland. Matheson graduated from Edinburgh University and in 1813 went to Calcutta to join his uncle's firm, MacIntosh and Co. One story relates that his uncle ordered him to return home after he had forgotten to deliver an important business letter. While making preparations for this ignominious trip, he was advised by a ship's captain to try his luck in Canton where he joined a partnership in 1819. By 1821 he had joined the Spanish firm of Yrissari and Co. and shortly after became Danish consul in Canton.

These two men were the outstanding personalities among the merchants on the China coast. Jardine's determined character earned him the Chinese nickname of the Iron-Headed Rat. This name referred to an occasion when Jardine continued imperturbably on his way after being struck on the head by bamboo while presenting a petition at one of the gates of Canton. Shrewd and sagacious, he concentrated his considerable energy and ability on making a fortune. In his office there was only one chair. Those who were granted an interview were obliged to stand. Jardine was a forceful man who did not tolerate fools lightly, yet at the same time he was described by Magniac as 'honourable and liberal beyond what we generally meet with in the general intercourse of business transactions'. Paradoxical though it may seem to us, Jardine and many of the other opium smugglers were men of principle with a contempt for what they regarded as deceitful business practices and a concern for the good of the communities they lived in. When a Company surgeon, Thomas Colledge, opened a free ophthalmic clinic in Macau in 1827, Jardine gave him his support and, to overcome resistance to treatment on the part of the poor Chinese for whom it was intended, paid the first patients operated on. Both Jardine and Matheson complained about those dealers who stooped to selling adulterated opium. Matheson wrote, 'I would in almost every case attribute it to disintegrity in the part of the agent . . . the article having for some time been attended with such large profits as to hold out more than common temptation to the weak passions of

our nature.'[3] When Matheson left Macau, he gave $5000 to
the Governor for charitable use. The money helped to
establish a school which still exists today.

Matheson was as enterprising and able as his partner and
had a rather more affable nature. One contemporary wrote
of him as 'a gentleman of great suavity of manner and the
impersonation of benevolence'. Jardine was respected,
even feared, while Matheson was regarded by many with
affection. When Matheson finally left Canton in March
1842 a local journal voiced a general sentiment when it
declared that 'the foreign community lost one of its most
enterprising, able and liberal members'. He was a man of
some taste and culture—he owned Canton's only piano
and, in 1827, supplied a small hand-press which enabled a
newspaper, the *Canton Register*, to be published for the
foreign community. Both partners had served a long apprenticeship in the country trade—the close attention
given to the market by Matheson is illustrated by a letter in
which he noted that blue bandannas 'with weaving white
lines sell for considerably more than if marked with round
white spots'.

1. Downing, *The Fan Qui in China*, I, 28–9.
2. Letters from Mr Charles Buchanan Jardine's collection.
3. Greenberg, *British Trade and the Opening of China*, 119.

# 2

# The Princely Hong and the End of the Canton System

THE origins of the Princely Hong can be traced back to James Cox, a maker of mechanical novelties who had a small family business in Shoe Lane, London. These novelties, known as sing-songs in China, were used to lubricate trade in Canton, being presented to Chinese officials and merchants on occasions such as Chinese New Year. In 1782 Cox came to Canton with a stock of these items and, after he had encountered some difficulty in collecting sums of money owed to him, he was given permission by the Select to stay in Canton between seasons. Some of his debtors subsequently paid in goods and so Cox began general trading. He went into partnership, first with John Reid, who headed the Austrian mission in Canton, and then with Daniel Beale, formerly a purser on an East India Company ship, who now held the Prussian consulship. This meant that he could not be expelled from Canton by the Select.

Most of the country merchants formed partnerships. This ensured continuity in the event of the death of one of the partners and increased the amount of capital available. However most partnerships were very loose affairs and the partners frequently had separate dealings on their own behalf. When a partner resigned he withdrew his share of the capital, although sometimes a partner returning to England might reinvest his capital in the London end of the agency. When a partner did resign, he was replaced by another and the agency continued under a new name. In the early days, the amount of capital required to join a partnership was not great for most of the business was done on a commission basis. In 1800 the capital of Reid, Beale and Co. was $120,000, each of the partners contributing $40,000. By 1837 the capital of the agency's successor, Jardine and Matheson, was estimated at over $2$\frac{1}{2}$ million.

Cox and his partners dabbled in a variety of items but the main business was opium. Cox was so successful in the opium trade that other merchants began to complain that he was putting them out of business, and so Cox was eventually obliged by the Select to leave Canton. However Beale remained and was joined by his brother Thomas who officially acted as secretary to the Prussian Consul. In 1797 Daniel retired to London where he joined Magniac and Company, a London firm dealing in sing-songs and controlled by three brothers. In 1801 one of the brothers, Charles, came to Canton and joined Thomas. He was followed in 1811 by another brother, Hollingworth.

In 1815 Thomas Beale, at this time one of the wealthiest and best established of the country traders, got into financial difficulties and was forced to leave the partnership. His fate illustrated some of the vicissitudes of trading on the China coast. In 1815 the Governor of Kwangtung suddenly arrested several opium dealers and ordered searches of all ships entering Whampoa, the port of Canton. The market collapsed and Beale was left holding large stocks of opium which, for the time being, were worthless and for which he had already drawn bills on the East India Company for about $800,000, cash to be paid in a few weeks' time. His partners refused to come to his aid and, as he could only manage to raise about half the sum owed, he was declared bankrupt. He lived on in his fine old house in Macau for many years, occupying himself with a little agency business and his renowned aviary and garden which contained over 2500 different plants. It was probably the largest collection of Chinese flowers ever made by a foreign individual and cuttings from it were sent to collectors in Europe. He remained dignified and courteous in spite of the persistent demands of his creditors, but he never managed to clear his debts and finally, in 1841, he committed suicide.

Magniac and Company prospered and by 1825 it was the most successful of the opium agencies. Having made their fortunes, Charles and Hollingworth wanted to return home and so began looking for a partner to join the remaining brother, Daniel, who had only become a partner in 1823. Jardine had arrived in Canton in 1822, living at first in property rented from Matheson, with whom he had become acquainted on an earlier trip. He quickly showed considerable flair for the opium trade. The money-making potentialities of the trade can be gauged from the fact that in his first year Jardine, working on commission, sold 649 cases for $818,000. On the strength of his rapid success, Jardine was invited to join Magniac's. Charles had already returned to England and Hollingworth followed him soon after, although he remained a sleeping partner until 1832. Before long Daniel was eased out. In defiance of the code of the time, he insisted on marrying his half-caste Portuguese pensioner by whom he had had two children. It was one of the paradoxes of the opium trade that the dealers in it took great pains to establish an aura of respectability. In the days when deals worth thousands of dollars were sealed by a handshake and a verbal promise, a sound reputation was of incalculable worth. Those who offended against the moral code of the tight-knit trading community could not expect to escape unscathed. With a ruthlessness which recalls the scant sympathy shown to Thomas Beale, Daniel was retired on a beggarly pension.

By this time Matheson had established a reputation as an astute businessman. In 1823 he had discovered the possibilities of the coast trade, that is, the direct smuggling of opium along the China coast. In two trips eastwards towards Fukien he had grossed over $200,000. He was not able to repeat his success, for when other agencies, among them Dent's, later to be Jardine and Matheson's greatest rival, tried to follow his example, the Chinese officials made difficulties and the coastal trade was given up for a time, to be revived later. When Matheson joined Magniac's in 1828, he brought with him a wealth of experience in the opium trade, capital of £20,000, and the flag of the Danish Consulate. In 1832, with the final retirement of Hollingworth, the agency was reconstituted as Jardine and Matheson. The two ablest men on the China coast had joined forces. They began to build up the most efficient selling organization on the China coast, in the process breaking the monopoly of the East India Company and shaking the Celestial Empire itself to its very foundations.

The 1830s were the heyday of the Canton system. In 1834 when the monopoly of the East India Company was ended there were sixty-six British merchants in Canton and thereafter the numbers rose rapidly, reaching more than a hundred and fifty by 1837. The foreign settlement stood outside the towering walls of the city of Canton, in the busy port area. The Western merchant ships did not use this port for they were obliged to anchor off the island of Whampoa, some thirteen miles downstream. Here they discharged their cargoes into barges, generally waiting another two or three months for the tea crop to arrive. During the trading season, sixty or more fine sailing ships would be anchored there. Downing described the scene,

. . . You have a view of a whole semicircle of shipping, drawn up and moored as if in the order of battle. . . . Cargo-boats and junks, some of them highly adorned, are seen winding their way with great skill between the Indiamen, while the whole surface of the water appears covered with an infinity of small craft, paddling about in every direction.[1]

The sailors were allowed to use two nearby islands for exercise and, in addition, were permitted to make excursions upriver in their ships' boats to the foreign settlement. Here the men would make straight for the drink shops in Hog Lane, a narrow alley bisecting the settlement, while their officers were entertained in a more decorous fashion in the factories. The offering of Hog Lane preferred by the sailors was a lethal mixture of alcohol, tobacco juice, sugar, and arsenic. Those who succumbed to the effects were likely to wake up a few hours later in the gutter with their pockets picked, while their stronger-headed companions engaged in fist fights with the resident Chinese riff-raff. Such proceedings were not likely to lessen the contempt in which most of the Chinese held the foreign devils, although the long-standing toleration by the authorities of the noisesome dens of Hog Lane indicates a degree of connivance between their proprietors and the officials.

There were no brothels in the settlement area but moored offshore near the outskirts of Canton there were elegant houseboats, euphemistically called Flower Boats, from which delicate, chattering girls nodded to the passing ships' boats. However these floating brothels were for Chinese customers and Europeans rarely ventured aboard. They had a bad reputation and Downing wrote,

A party of young men returning from town one night ran their boat alongside one of them. One, who was a little in liquor, jumped on board and was quickly assailed by eight or ten men, who seized upon him and were going to throw him into the water, and it was only by the greatest exertions of his mess-mates that he was rescued from their hands. One poor fellow, at another time, went on board by himself and insisted on penetrating into the interior. It was ascertained that he had gone in, but he was never heard of afterwards. [2]

However there was no problem about meeting girls at Whampoa and even in Canton it was not impossible for the merchants to make discreet assignations.

The factories themselves stood about fifty yards back from the water's edge. From the river they looked like a single row of houses built in European style, but appearances were deceptive, for each factory was a warren of rooms, offices, warehouses, and courtyards extending back to a depth of a hundred and fifty yards. Here the partners and clerks worked, ate, and lived together in an atmosphere of male camaraderie similar to that of an officers' mess. In front of the factories to the east there was a walled shrubbery known as the English Garden. West of this was Respondentia Walk, or Jackass Point, a square about a hundred yards across where the merchants could take a little light exercise. During the day, however, it was crowded with Chinese hawkers, beggars, and loungers who stared at or accosted those Europeans who walked among them. From time to time the Chinese were cleared away by the police but before long they filtered back into the square from Hog Lane and Old China Street. To the north, for a distance of about two hundred yards, stretched the suburbs of Canton, then came the city wall and Petition Gate where addresses to the Chinese authorities had to be presented. This area, with a frontage of not more than three hundred and fifty yards and a depth of about four hundred and fifty yards, comprised the world of the European merchants while they were in Canton.

In front of the factories, there were tall flagstaffs from which fluttered the flags of the different nationalities with representatives in Canton. The British predominated but there were also a number of American, French, Dutch, and Parsee merchants, each nationality occupying its own factory. At one time there had also been Swedish, Austrian, Danish, and Spanish companies but these had gone out of business by the 1830s. The factories formerly occupied by these companies were rented to the country merchants of other nationalities but they continued to be referred to by their old names. Jardine and Matheson leased the Greek Factory on the extreme east of the settlement. By far the

largest and most splendidly appointed factory was that of
the East India Company. The Company had a lordly way of
carrying on business and its generosity to its employees
was renowned. Each officer was allowed space on his ship
for private ventures and every man on the Factory staff was
allowed a share in the profits, amounting to as much as six
shillings in a hundred pounds in the case of the President.
This was in addition to salaries which in those days were
considered very handsome. The surgeon at the Factory
received £1300 a year while writers got between £400 and
£600. The celebrated Dr Robert Morrison, who served as an
interpreter in the last days of the Factory, received £1000.
Of the lesser members of the staff, the steward got $1100
and the butler $800.

The princely hospitality of the Company's Factory was
proverbial and to be asked to dine there was considered a
great honour for any newcomer. The guest, after passing
through the great outer gate, followed a broad paved walk
to a wide flight of stairs. At one side of the stairs stood the
chapel by whose chiming clock all the European residents
set their watches. Each guest was received by the President
in a reception room. When all were assembled, a dignified
English butler announced dinner and the tall folding doors
of the dining room were flung open.

> Their dining room was of vast dimensions opening upon a
> terrace overlooking the river. On the left was a library, amply
> stocked . . . on the right was a billiard room. . . . From the ceiling
> suspended a row of huge chandeliers, with wax lights; the table
> bore candelabra, reflecting a choice service amidst quantities of
> silver plate.[3]

Behind the President's chair hung a life-sized portrait of
King George IV, which had originally been intended as a
present from that monarch to the Chinese emperor. At the
opposite end of the room was a portrait of Lord Amherst
whose task it had been to take this gift to the emperor, only
to have it contemptuously spurned. As was the custom in

the East in those days, each diner brought his own servant to wait at table and look after his special needs. The servants stood in a line at one end of the room while the guests entered. Then, as each diner was seated, his servant silently stationed himself behind his master. The meal made no concessions to the climate and, in the old English fashion, consisted of numerous courses, in which roasted meats frequently featured, washed down with large quantities of claret and port. One qualification to be President must have been a strong head for, by tradition, he drank with each guest in turn. Few left the table with steady legs but, according to contemporaries, a decent decorum was nevertheless the rule.

During the First Anglo-Chinese War, the old home of the John Company was singled out for destruction by an angry mob.

Doors were knocked off their hinges; panels were burst in and windows burst out; fine oak staircases were hacked to pieces; stone floors were broken up and things smashed to atoms that one would have thought impossible to break ... beautiful cut-glass chandeliers were destroyed bit by bit, the great gilded looking glasses were brought down with a crash, the dregs of Canton scrambling for the pieces, and the large marble statue which stood in the hall was hurled on its side with every imaginable form of insult.[4]

The merchants, deprived of the distractions of female company and family life, and confined to the narrow limits of the settlement, did their best to make their lives as pleasant as possible, each factory seeking to outdo the others in hospitality and conviviality. Their other amusements were strictly circumscribed.

In the cool of the evening, when the sun has set, and the crowds of natives have somewhat dispersed, they usually take their exercise by walking to and fro before their factories, in that part of the Square which is called Respondentia Walk. .... The chief recreation of the younger residents is that of rowing and sailing on the

water. In fine weather . . . the Europeans take short excursions up
and down, occasionally landing at inviting spots and enjoying all
the luxury of a fete champetre. . . . However tempting the appearance of the country, few are foolhardy enough to venture but a
very short distance from the banks, as the same animosity towards
strangers exists here as lower down, and the adventurer would
probably be robbed and bambooed by the natives. . . .[5]

Some sport was provided by the Canton Regatta Club. An
old Chinese shipwright named Mo Pin ('no pig-tail') was
prevailed upon to build several schooners 26 feet long. The
first regatta was held in 1837. Ships' boats manned by
bluejackets kept the course and a Flower Boat was hired for
the committee, aboard which a lavish tiffin was served. The
first race was between two six-oared gigs, one of which
belonged to the American merchant, Warren Delano. The
small yachts covered a course downriver to the Tee To Tum
fort. The success of this occasion encouraged more competition. In 1838 two 34-ton cutters, Dent's *Gipsy* and
Forbes' *Atlanta* raced over a 35-mile course in the Macau
Roads. The winner, *Atlanta*, recorded an overall speed of
nine knots. A second race in the Macau Roads ended in
tragedy. Five yachts, Dent's *Gipsy*, Jardine's *Thistle*,
Campbell's *Dream*, Livingston's *Dragon*, and Raper's
*Fairy*, started in bad weather. The *Fairy* capsized and three
of her crew, including a Captain Haddock, were drowned.
The race continued and was won by *Gipsy* which com-
pleted the 25-mile course in four hours.

Life at Canton under the Eight Regulations was incon-
venient but the first generation of country merchants considered themselves fortunate to be there at all and were
content to put up with the restrictions imposed upon them
provided that they could make money. Besides it was possible to circumvent the system by bribery and smuggling,
and resort to such practices became increasingly common
after the turn of the century when opium became all-
important. Following the abolition of the East India Company's monopoly, the merchants became more numerous

and, encouraged by this first success of the new free-trade
ideas over the restrictive practices of mercantilism, they
began to envisage the immense possibilities for the expansion of trade that would follow the ending of the Co-Hong
system. This closely knit group had powerful allies in
India and England and was now led by Jardine and
Matheson, two men of forceful personality with a dominating position in the country trade. It was soon to prove
itself to be an irresistible force for change.

In the first years of their partnership, Jardine and
Matheson traded almost entirely in opium. It was, in
Jardine's opinion, 'the safest and most gentlemanlike
speculation I am aware of'. The fate of Thomas Beale indicates that the opium trade was indeed highly speculative.
To avoid gambling on the wildly fluctuating price of
opium, which in the case of Bengal opium might vary from
$550 to $1375 per chest, Jardine and Matheson worked on
commission except when they could buy opium very
cheaply. Their average profit was $20 per chest. By the end
of the 1830s they were handling over 6000 chests each
year, producing an annual profit of over $100,000. After the
ending of the East India Company's monopoly, they expanded into the direct tea trade to London. In addition, like
the other large agencies, they offered banking and insurance facilities. Insurance was of vital importance for those
who traded in the pirate-infested and typhoon-wracked
South China Sea. In 1805 a group of country traders formed
the Canton Insurance Company. It was managed alternate-
ly for periods of five years by Magniac-Jardine's and Dent's,
with the capital plus any profit being redistributed to the
shareholders at the end of each management period. After
1835 it remained in Jardine's hands and was reorganized as
Canton Insurance Limited. Dent's responded by establishing the Union Insurance Company of Canton which, in
1841, moved its headquarters to Hong Kong. It was liqui-
dated every three years until 1874 when it, too, was reorganized as a limited company.

In the early 1830s business with China was sharply divided into legal and illegal trade. The legal trade consisted principally of the import of Western products such as woollens, cotton goods, and furs, and the export of tea and silk. This trade passed through the port of Whampoa and paid duty there. In 1831 about five million dollars' worth of goods were imported legally. About two and a half millions' worth was handled by the East India Company, half a million's worth by British country traders, and almost all the rest by American merchants. These firms exported about eighteen million dollars' worth of goods, of which the East India Company handled about eight million, giving the Company alone an adverse trade balance of five and a half million dollars. This was made good by the opium traders.

In the same year, the British and Parsee country traders imported seventeen million dollars' worth of goods illegally into China, about eleven million dollars' worth being opium and the remainder cotton goods and spices. These goods were landed at the island of Lintin, the Solitary Nail, in the Pearl River estuary with the connivance of the Chinese officials who, in addition to bribes, received a duty on the opium imports equal to the official toll. These officials therefore conspired in the evasion by the traders of the official dues on the legal goods and in the furthering of the illegal trade in opium. The goods were carried to Lintin from Indian ports in fast armed clippers, and transferred there to anchored hulks. The Chinese smugglers who paid for the illegally imported goods in advance with silver at one of the Canton factories, collected their purchases in 40-oared galleys, crewed by ferocious Tanka fishermen and known as 'fast crabs' and 'scrambling dragons'. The opium was distributed by them through Triad receivers in numerous coastal villages. Fluctuations in the price of opium occurred when the market became temporarily saturated or if the Chinese officials made one of their short-lived attempts to interfere with the illegal trade. The silver obtained by the country traders was, as has already been indicated, passed to the legal traders in exchange for bills drawn on London, in order to make good their trade deficit without the risk and cost of importing silver from abroad.

Matheson's early success in his venture up the coast had not been forgotten and in 1832 the partners decided to send their ships north to the small coves and harbours on the Fukien coast from which they could sell opium directly to the distributors. Speedy ships were an important ingredient in the success of the enterprise for it would be necessary to evade pirates and interference by the authorities as well as to out-sail possible competitors. Already the American merchants in the China trade had shown the advantages of using small, fast Yankee clippers which could make two or three round trips between India and China a year and which could be sailed even through the monsoon season. The old East Indiamen, or country wallahs, were cumbersome teak vessels built to designs of the seventeenth century and displacing between 500 and 800 tons. They were built to last, and some continued to sail for over a hundred years but they could not beat up against the monsoon and generally took between two and three months to sail from India to Lintin. They were, none the less, handsome vessels. One captain wrote, 'The ships were kept in beautiful order, more like a man of war than a merchantman; the decks holystoned white; copper sheathing polished and oiled; yards all a-taunt-o; and the furled sails rolled up in snow-white sail covers.'[6]

One of the earliest opium clippers was the Red Rover built in Calcutta in 1829 to the design of Captain William Clifford, an ex-naval officer. The plans for the Red Rover were closely based on those of the famous American privateer Prince de Neufchatel which had been built in New York and was captured during the war with Britain in 1814. Clifford had promised the East India Company that he would build a vessel capable of sailing to China three times a year. On its first voyage this rakish vessel, which

displaced a mere 154 tons, did the round trip from Calcutta
to Macau in eighty-six days. She later established a record
of eighteen days for the voyage between Calcutta and
Lintin. The Red Rover was bought by Jardine's which, by the
late 1830s, had a fleet of over a dozen clippers, some on the
run from India, others working the coast trade. Many other
clippers were built on the same lines as the Red Rover.
Another much copied prototype was the Sylph which was
designed by Sir Robert Seppings, the Surveyor of the Navy,
for the leading Parsee shipowner Rustomjee Cowasjee, an
associate of Jardine's. The opium merchants also made use
of ex-naval vessels whose fire power was an effective deter-
rent to pirates and Chinese customs vessels. Matheson
bought H.M.S. Curlew, a brig of 18 guns, in 1823 and she
served as an opium runner for many years under the name
Jamesina.

The masters were mainly ex-naval or John Company
officers. After the end of the Napoleonic Wars and again
when the Company's monopoly ended, many officers
joined the country trade. The curious association between
opium smuggling and missionary activities is perhaps par-
tially explained by the fact that 'among the officers were
many sons of clergymen who, after a period of active service afloat, would retire to succeed ultimately to their fath-
ers' livings'. At first the crews were mainly Lascars,
Malays, and Filipinos but the winter passage up the China
coast was hard service and there was little comfort or rest
aboard a clipper. Consequently service aboard clippers
was not popular in spite of the extra pay. The term 'shang-
haied' probably originated from this fact. Later the captains
turned to deserters from the British and American navies
who could generally be found in the low haunts of Calcutta, Hong Kong, and Shanghai. One hand wrote,

> With her low black hull, tall rakish masts and square yards, she
> was a regular beauty, just such a vessel as it does an old tar's heart
> good to set eyes on—though for the matter of comfort, keep me out

of them, for what with their scrubbing and scouring in port and their carrying sail at sea to make a good passage and half drowning the crew, there's very little peace aboard them.[7]

It seems that the coastal trade had first been developed in the 1820s by Chinese merchants, for when the *Lord Amherst* had made a market survey up the coast on behalf of the East India Company in 1832, the officials and merchants as far north as Shanghai clearly expected the ship to have opium aboard which, in fact, it did not. It was plain to the leader of *Lord Amherst's* mission, Hugh Lindsay, that the great majority of the officials were only too anxious to participate in smuggling. He also learnt at first hand of the weaknesses of China's coastal defences, a point that was not lost upon those merchants who believed that China would never willingly agree to end the Eight Regulations. Aboard the *Lord Amherst* was the Revd Karl Gutzlaff, who was later to be employed in the same capacity by Jardine and Matheson. 'All of China's thousand war-junks cannot withstand one small frigate', he wrote.

The mission of the *Lord Amherst* encouraged Jardine to enter directly into the coastal trade and later in 1832 he decided to send the *Sylph*, a speedy 250-ton barque, up the coast as far north as the Gulf of Pechili, some 1600 miles from Canton, with a cargo principally consisting of opium. Business would be carried on by anchoring offshore of a port or natural harbour and waiting for the local dealers to make contact. A good interpreter was vital and Jardine resolved to enlist the services of Gutzlaff. The missionary was a well-known character on the China coast and one account describes him as '. . . a short square figure, with clothes that for shape might have been cut in his native Pomerania ages ago, a broad-brimmed straw hat, his great face beneath with a sinister eye'.[8]

In spite of his eccentricities, Gutzlaff was sincere in his desire to spread Christianity to the Chinese, and Jardine, who was a devout Christian, undoubtedly approved of his aim. At the same time, he had no scruples about using Gutzlaff's lack of funds for his missionary work, as a means to persuade him to sail with the *Sylph*. In October 1832 he wrote to Gutzlaff,

Though it is our earnest wish that you should not in any way injure the grand object you have in view by appearing interested in what by many is considered an immoral traffic, yet such traffic is so absolutely necessary to give any vessel a reasonable chance of defraying her expenses, that we trust you will have no objection to interpret on every occasion when your services may be requested. The more profitable the expedition, the better we shall be able to place at your disposal a sum that may hereafter be employed in furthering your mission, and for your success in which we feel deeply interested.[9]

On 20 October the *Sylph* weighed from Macau with Gutzlaff aboard. The missionary had experienced some mental conflict over Jardine's offer but his doubts were resolved when the ship survived a tremendous storm, '. . . God who dwelleth on high did not forsake us; and though often engulfed in the deep, His almighty hand upheld our sinking vessel'. The *Sylph*'s voyage was a commercial success and the coastal trade expanded rapidly. Gutzlaff saw the opium trade as a means of opening China to Christianity and Jardine, to do him justice, saw it as a means of opening China to more legitimate trade and to Western influence in general which, in his opinion and that of most of his contemporaries, was a laudable objective that could only be to the ultimate benefit of China.

Gutzlaff's talents were recruited by Jardine for the service of Mammon more than once. A few months after the *Sylph*'s return, he sailed with Captain McKay aboard the heavily armed *John Biggar*. Gutzlaff, by this time, had lost all sense of the incongruity of his position, handing out religious pamphlets to the villagers while the crew unloaded chests of opium. In a letter to Jardine, dated 2 January 1834, he observed unctuously:

At such a general prospect of increasing trade I heartily rejoice, but am equally grieved that the inhabitants of one village, with whom we have never had any (previous) communication showed themselves very hostile when our boat went on shore. This . . . gave us no favourable impression of the populace. We have in fact to deal with ragamuffins, the scum of the nation, villains by nature and habit. . . . May the Gracious God and Saviour protect you.[10]

Jardine's captains had a short way with any Chinese officials who seemed likely to interfere. On 8 June 1833 McKay noted:

The mandarins are not troubling as much but in harbour and on shore they are very vigilant. Shortly after we arrived a fleet of six of them anchored near us. Dr Gutzlaff (dressed in his best, which on such occasions is his custom) paid them a visit accompanied by two boats made to appear rather imposing. He demanded their instant departure and threatened them with destruction if they ever in future anchored in our neighbourhood. They went away immediately saying that they had anchored there in the dark by mistake and we have seen nothing more of them.[11]

The *John Biggar* returned from its mission with silver worth £53,000.

Another ship used by Jardine's in the coastal trade at this time was the *Jamesina* whose trading activities were under the control of the supercargo James Innes, a hard-bitten character who once settled a dispute with the Canton Hoppo by setting fire to his *yamen* with rockets. Like his employer, he found little difficulty in reconciling Christian principles with opium smuggling. In the log of his trading mission to Amoy in 1832 he wrote:

Dec 2. Employed delivering briskly. No time to read my Bible or to keep my journal.

Dec 5. Still delivering briskly. Today several small mandarin junks sailed round us once or twice, when some smuggling boats were alongside, but whether they did not like our look, or remembered the reception they got in this Bay from the little 'Kronberg', I know not. They gave us no trouble and the opium boats came and went easily close to them.[12]

The chests sold at about 50 per cent higher than the rate at
Lintin. Later, on 19 January, when a trip ashore was made
to obtain water, Innes took the opportunity to distribute
some religious tracts.

Familiarity with the Chinese officials bred increasing
contempt on the part of Jardine's captains. In 1835 the
Canton Register noted that when some government junks
anchored too close to Jardine's *Governor Findlay*,

> ... a jolly boat with an officer and four armed lascars was
> immediately dispatched to insist on their moving further off. As
> they appeared disinclined to acquiesce the officer boarded the first
> boat and seized the whole of her arms both large and small; then
> boarded the second boat, tumbled all the great guns overboard,
> seized the small arms, and made them both quit the Bay.[13]

Naturally Jardine's success in the coastal trade attracted
rivals. Principal among these was Dent's, another partnership that traced its origin to a Scotsman, W. S. Davidson,
who had gone to Canton as a naturalized Portuguese in
1811. Rivalry had begun early when both developed links
with London, Calcutta, and Bombay agents who were
already mutually antagonistic. In the establishment of
these links, kinship and old associations played a part.
Jardine's dealt mainly with Lyall, Matheson and Co. in
Calcutta and with Magniac, Smith and Co., and later
Matheson and Co. in London. The rivalry between Dent's
and Jardine's became a bitter feud after 1830 when Jardine
withheld correspondence from Calcutta brought in a
Jardine's clipper which bore news of the failure of Dent's
Calcutta connection, Palmer's.

In 1836 Captain McKay complained indignantly to
Jardine that Captain Thomas Rees of the *Lord Amherst*, by
this time operated by Dent's, was indulging in deceitful
trading practices. 'While under engagement to keep at
fixed prices, he sold his opium at the proper prices on
board and his chinamen on shore refunded to the pur-
chaser first four, then six and lastly ten dollars (a
chest). ....'

In reply Jardine expressed his regret 'that such mean acts should be resorted to by men placed in a respectable situation in life' and went on to advocate a price war, 'As you have more vessels than your opponents, how would it answer to place one of them alongside the "Amherst", and run prices down as low as they may think fit to go, while you keep prices up in the distant bays? Cured they must be of such evil practices, even at the sacrifice of reducing prices. . . .'[14]

Jardine's were well able to hold their own. They had a superior organization and greater experience and in general their ships were faster and their captains more ruthless than those of their rivals. By the late 1830s Dent's had begun to co-operate with Jardine's to squeeze out the other agencies. Usually it was sufficient to lower prices but on occasion arrangements were made for the Chinese authorities to act against the Chinese smugglers who patronized the small fry.

By the early 1830s, the country traders were more numerous, prosperous, and self-confident than ever before. They were impatient with the restrictions imposed upon them by the East India Company's monopoly and by the Eight Regulations and believed that if these restrictions were swept away an enormous expansion of the China trade would take place. Their links with the agency houses in India and England gave them allies but in any case the trend of opinion in Britain was moving strongly in favour of free trade ideas. Monopolies in general and that of the East India Company in particular were seen as being beneficial to the traditional ruling class and not to the emerging middle class of mill-owners, shippers, and merchants. Moreover, while the Company's monopoly imposed restrictions on British merchants, it did not curb the activities of the increasing number of Americans who were trading at Canton. Finally, the country traders had already acquired such a large proportion of the trade with China that it seemed pointless for Parliament to continue the monopoly of the Honourable John Company when it came up for renewal in 1833. Consequently, from April 1834, Parliament decreed that trade with China was to be opened to all British subjects although the Company was to retain its monopoly over opium sales in India.

Jardine's had led the campaign against the Company. Their employees had made no secret of their contempt for the once honoured privileges of the Select. One example followed the arrival of the Red Rover at Macau in June 1833 with mail from Calcutta aboard. Normally mail bags were handed over to the Company's steward who took them straight to the President. On this occasion the steward was not at the landing stage. The coolie with the mail bags found him in Marwick's tavern with James Innes and Jardine's marine superintendent, Captain Alex Grant of the Hercules. Grant seized the bags and calmly sorted out Jardine's mail. The Select Committee was furious and in retaliation refused to renew the trading licence of the Hercules.

Jardine and Matheson protested vigorously. The Select Committee complained to the Governor-General of the Council in Calcutta about 'the desire of Messrs Jardine, Matheson and Co. and of Captain Grant as Commanding their opium ships, to erect themselves into an authority independent of the Committee' but eventually it was obliged to climb down. Throughout the dispute, Jardine's had the backing of all the Parsees in Macau while Dent's remained aloof.

With the end of the monopoly, the first victory had been won. The next step was the destruction of the Co-Hong system. The issue of the 'Chinese Repository' published in December 1833 contained a lengthy article signed 'British Merchant' which, if not actually written by William Jardine, certainly put forward views which he agreed with. The writer began by pointing out that throughout the history of its dealings with the Chinese officials, the conciliatory attitude adopted by the Company had not suc-

ceeded in bringing about any significant improvements in
the regulations restricting trade and the life of the merchants while in Canton. In an infamous incident in 1784,
under threat of the stoppage of trade, the Company had
handed over to the Chinese a gunner aboard the *Lady
Hughes* who, on being ordered to fire a salute, had accidentally killed a Chinese boatman nearby. After a secret
trial, he had been strangled. 'Has not the Chinese commerce of Great Britain been purchased with the blood of the
gunner of the "Lady Hughes"?' asked the writer indignantly. He went on to state unequivocally that with the
dissolution of the Select Committee, a representative of the
Crown should be appointed to supervise trade and to deal
with the Co-Hong merchants and the Chinese officials.
This representative would have to be prepared to use the
same methods employed by the merchants engaged in the
coastal trade, namely the threat of force, for only this would
persuade the Chinese officials to relax the trade restrictions. The threat alone would probably be sufficient for

It is well known that the Tartar dynasty floats upon a smooth but
dangerous sea, and that its existence depends upon the habit of
tranquil obedience to its authority. Sensible of this, the high
authorities view with abhorrence anything that savours of per-
turbation. . . . The only thing that has raised our character above
its abasement and created an influence with the Chinese is the
conduct of our men-of-war. They indeed have established a character which makes the Chinese tremble at the knowledge of their
approach.[15]

Anticipating the acquisition of Hong Kong, he advised that
the navy should establish a base in the China seas where it
could pose a constant threat to the Chinese government.
'By bold demonstrations' the Chinese authorities might be
persuaded to negotiate with the representative of the
Crown and 'the basis of the new commissioners demands
should be open trade with China'.

These views were undoubtedly those held by most of the
British merchants in Canton. To some extent, it might seem

strange that they were so dissatisfied with the existing situation. The illegal trade in opium had circumvented the Eight Regulations and the merchants were prospering on it. The evidence hitherto was that there was little demand in China for Western manufactured products. However the merchants did not accept that this would always be the case. They believed that if China was opened to Western influences, demand for Western products would follow. The Manchester mill-owners assured each other that just one more inch on every Chinaman's shirt-tail would give the mills enough work for decades. Moreover they were not willing to see the situation whereby trade with China was based principally on opium smuggling continue indefinitely. The shrewder among them realized that, however they might justify the carrying on of the opium trade to themselves, there was a body of opinion both in Britain and China that regarded it as an immoral business. The opium trade was acceptable as a lever to open China to legitimate trade, Christianity, and other Western influences but not as the permanent basis of relations between China and the West.

The Act of 1833 which abolished the East India Company's monopoly also provided for the appointment of a British superintendent of trade at Canton, as Jardine and the British merchants wished. The first superintendent was Lord Napier, a humourless Scotsman with little knowledge of Eastern affairs whose main interests were the navy and sheep-farming. The Foreign Secretary, Lord Palmerston, had no desire to provoke a war with China and Napier was instructed not to endanger Britain's existing relations with China and to 'cautiously abstain from making any appeal for the protection of our military or naval forces'. At the same time Palmerston added, almost as an afterthought, that 'Your lordship will announce your arrival in Canton by letter to the Viceroy'. This was quite contrary to the tenor of the rest of Napier's instructions, for direct contact between the Chinese officials and the foreigners was forbidden by the Eight Regulations. Napier was set on a collision course before he left England, a collision, moreover, which he could not emerge from victorious for he had been forbidden to call upon military aid.

When Napier arrived at Macau aboard H.M.S. *Andromache* on 15 July 1834, Jardine and Matheson, the leaders of the British community, both happened to be in Canton but they had made arrangements for his reception and a member of their staff, A. Robertson, offered him the use of a house belonging to the firm which he accepted in preference to the spacious quarters belonging to the East India Company. This was symptomatic of events to come as, for the short period before his death on 11 October, Napier fell under the influence of the 'forward' group of merchants headed by Jardine and Matheson.

Napier arrived at Canton on 25 July and was greeted by Jardine. They dined together on the evening of 26 July. Jardine, the Iron-Headed Rat, was well aware that the Chinese authorities would not accept Napier's letter, which was presented the following day, but Napier had his orders and anyway Jardine was not averse to making Napier immediately aware of the intransigence of the Chinese officials. Once Jardine and Matheson realized that Napier's instructions fell far short of what they had hoped, their policy was to encourage him to take a hard line. This, they knew, could only lead to his humiliation but the result would be to convince the British government that only force would bring the Chinese authorities to reason. If Napier persisted in trying to deal with the Chinese officials on terms of equality, this might lead to the stoppage of trade at Canton, as had previously occurred on several occasions. However this would not greatly affect Jardine and Matheson for their main involvement was now with the coastal trade which was beyond the influence of the officials of Canton. In the event of a more widespread disruption of trade resulting from a war, they were better equipped than their rivals to ride out the storm and to benefit from the better conditions that would follow.

Napier, rebuffed by the Chinese officials, and baffled by the intricacies of Chinese diplomacy, relied increasingly on the advice of Jardine, who saw him almost daily. Within three weeks of his arrival, he was writing a despatch home which repeats almost verbatim the known views of Jardine.

Disclaim every view of conquest; disturb not the passage of their vessels or the tranquillity of their towns; only destroy their forts and batteries along the coasts, and on the river sides without interfering with the people. Three or four frigates or brigs, with a few steady British troops, not sepoys, would settle the thing in a space of time inconceivably short.[16]

The Governor-General, Lu K'un, requested Napier to leave Canton and, when he refused, trade was halted and supplies to the factories were cut off, although the factories were well provisioned and fresh food could easily be obtained with a little bribery. It seems a reasonable presumption that Jardine played an important part in Napier's decision to stay in Canton and in his request that two British frigates lying in the Pearl River estuary should force their way up to Canton to relieve the foreign community there. Napier was seriously alarmed for the safety of the merchants but Jardine knew that there was no real danger. Blockades had occurred before and the last thing that the officials in Canton wanted was a serious incident which would put them in bad odour with the authorities in Peking. Clearly Jardine's view must have been either that the frigates would frighten the Governor-General into making concessions or, more realistically, that they would be stopped on the way up the Pearl River and the consequent humiliation would anger Parliament. It is interesting to note that at this point opposition to Napier's Jardine-inspired line developed among some of the merchants. A few of them, led by Jardine's great rival Lancelot Dent, who did not have the reserves to endure a lengthy interruption to trade, urged Napier to withdraw to Macau, but in vain. In the event, after fighting their way past the Bogue forts, the frigates were trapped in the Pearl River by barriers and block ships.

Napier now had no option except to bow to the wishes of the Governor-General. He was already suffering from the fever that was soon to kill him and the negotiations with regard to the details of his withdrawal and that of the frigates took place principally between Jardine and Howqua. Napier left Canton on 21 September. Worn out and dispirited he died at Macau on 11 October. Prominent among the mourners at his funeral were William Jardine, James Matheson, and James Innes, the opium runner.

The merchants at once tried to make capital out of Napier's humiliation. A petition urging that a powerful naval force be sent to demand free trade was addressed to King William IV and signed by sixty-four merchants. Matheson returned to England with Napier's widow and children to lobby support for it. The Duke of Wellington, who was Foreign Secretary in Peel's short-lived administration of November 1834 to April 1835, was not sympathetic. He was more concerned that the tea trade which yielded substantial revenue should remain undisturbed. Matheson wrote indignantly to Jardine that he was a 'cold blooded fellow . . . a strenuous advocate for submissiveness and servility'. The hopes of the 'forward' party were raised when Lord Palmerston returned to the Foreign Office. Palmerston was more sympathetic to the idea of forceful support for the interests of the China coast merchants and he was under increasing pressure from the Lancashire cotton manufacturers. The main obstacle to action was the fact that opium smuggling made up the major part of Britain's trade with China. Public opinion would need to be aroused by a more emotive *casus belli* before the government could venture to support the opium traders. Palmerston was content to wait. Matheson wrote sarcastically to Jardine that '. . . the people appear to be so comfortable in this magnificent country, so entirely satisfied in all their desires, that so long as domestic affairs, including markets go right, they cannot really be brought to think of us outlanders. . . . Lord Palmerston means to do nothing'.[17] However, as a consequence of their success in rebuffing Napier, the Chinese officials had become dangerously over-confident. Palmerston did not have long to wait.

The officials at Peking were becoming seriously concerned by the increase in the opium trade. The drain of silver helped to increase the value of the silver tael in relation to copper cash. One tael was supposed to equal 1000 cash but by 1838 it took 1650 cash to buy a tael. This was causing discontent among the farmers because the land tax was assessed in silver but was usually paid in copper. A more important reason for the devaluation of cash than the opium trade was a decline in the production of copper in China which had caused the government to mint debased coins. However the officials placed the blame entirely on the adverse balance of silver payments.

Another consideration was the spread of addiction. It is unlikely that more than 1 per cent of the population of China were addicts, but since opium smoking was an expensive habit requiring leisure time, it tended to be found particularly among government officials. Moreover the habit must have been more widespread and obvious in the coastal towns and along the principal trade routes, than in the rural interior. Moralists saw opium as an agent of barbarian aggression which would dissolve the observance of Confucian ethics and encourage in its place a selfish and debased languor. Furthermore the great increase in opium smuggling was leading to the widespread corruption of government officials. In Kwangtung special patrols had been established to catch smugglers but within a few months they had been bought off for 36,000 taels a month. Even the commander of the fleet, Rear-Admiral Han Shao-ch'ing, had taken a cut. Consequently the patrols had been abolished in 1832.

In May 1836 a debate on the question of the opium trade

had been started in the highest court circles by a memorial to the Tao-Kuang emperor from an official named Hsu Nai-chi, proposing that it should be legalized, thereby eliminating corruption and enabling the state to derive revenue from the trade. This pragmatic view was countered by those who took a moral stance, arguing that legalization of the trade would spread the habit even further. What was needed was a determined effort to stamp it out. The emperor, who modelled himself on the sage rulers of the past, sided with the moralists, seeing the elimination of opium smuggling as part of a general moral regeneration of China. The officials in Canton were ordered to take more vigorous action against native smugglers and dealers and these instructions did have some effect. Thousands of dealers were arrested and as a result the trade had practically come to a standstill by early 1837. However the moralists saw this as only a temporary success. As soon as the local officials relaxed their efforts, which they undoubtedly would as demand and the consequent size of bribes mounted, the trade would revive again. In July 1838 one of the most able, efficient, and incorruptible of the Chinese officials, Lin Tse-hsu, Governor-General of Hupei and Hunan, proposed the final and obvious solution. Foreign smugglers must be treated in the same way as native smugglers. Only in this way would the evil be permanently eradicated. The emperor was impressed. Lin was summoned to court and was granted the exceptional total of nineteen personal audiences. On 31 December 1838 Lin was named imperial commissioner in Canton and was instructed to 'reverently obey Our order to exert all his strength to resolve this matter [opium smuggling] . . . he must, according to the place and circumstances, radically sever the trunk from the roots'. Lin had little practical knowledge of the Westerners. There is little doubt that he was convinced that the foreign barbarians would be frightened into obedience by a firm stand, as they had been in the Napier affair. It might be necessary to use some force but the possibility of war, much less defeat, never crossed the mind of this zealous and righteous official.

Meanwhile, the superintendents of trade who had succeeded Napier, John Francis Davis and his successor Sir George Robinson, in the absence of any instructions had followed, to quote the former, a policy of 'absolute silence and quiescence', the main object of which was to keep trade going without interruption. At the end of 1836, Robinson was replaced by Captain Charles Elliot, R.N. Elliot attempted at first to improve relations by adopting a conciliatory attitude. After submitting a petition to the Viceroy, Teng T'ing-chen, he was recognized as being the spokesman of the merchants, although not the representative of the British Crown, and was permitted to go to Canton. However when Palmerston learnt of this he peremptorily ordered Elliot to communicate with the Chinese officials directly and by means of letters, not petitions. The Viceroy, as might be expected, refused to accept this and Elliot was obliged to retire to Macau. Subsequently he tried to remove a cause of friction with the Chinese officials by asking the British merchants to stop shipping opium directly to Whampoa. They had begun doing this when the Viceroy, who himself was known to be extorting squeeze from the dealers, started taking action against Chinese smugglers, in accordance with instructions from Peking. The British merchants did not have a great deal of time for Elliot, who was known to be personally opposed to the opium trade and the majority, led by Jardine, ignored his request, thereby illustrating Elliot's complete inability to control the smuggling.

The news of Lin's appointment reached Canton in late January. Opium prices fell to rock-bottom and trading virtually came to a standstill. Even before his arrival in Canton on 10 March, an investigation had begun into the extent of official involvement in the smuggling of opium and a number of arrests had been made. His entry into the city by water was watched by thousands of Cantonese, for once awed into silence, as well as by some of the foreign merchants. Wells Williams wrote,

Of all the Chinamen I have ever seen, Lin was decidedly the finest looking and the most intelligent. He was indeed a very superior man, and if only he had been better informed he might have brought the difficult business entrusted to him to a much more creditable issue than he did; but this his ignorance and the conceit that accompanies ignorance prevented. . . . [18]

Lin wasted no time in beginning his cleansing of the Augean stables. On 18 March he told the Co-Hong merchants that they had three days to persuade the foreigners to hand over their stocks of opium and to sign a bond that they would never deal in opium again. If the foreigners refused, some of the Co-Hong merchants would be executed and all would lose their property. The foreign merchants had not yet grasped the nature of the new Commissioner and, as if to propitiate him in the time-honoured way, they offered to surrender a token 1037 chests. At this point the merchants in Canton had no generally accepted leader. Elliot, the Queen's representative, was in Macau. Whether by luck or judgement, Jardine had retired on 30 January and had set sail for England where he was able to exercise a far more decisive influence on the coming course of events than if he had stayed on the China coast. His place in Canton had been taken by Matheson who, on learning of Lin's edict, had at once prudently sent a message to Lintin instructing that all Jardine and Matheson's stocks there be sent up the coast. However the most prominent individual in Canton was Lancelot Dent, who was rumoured to have a stock of 6000 chests. On 22 March Lin summoned him to an interview and threatened to execute two Chinese merchants if he did not come. Dent, like most of the foreign merchants, was on good terms with his Chinese counterparts and he expressed his willingness to go, but the other merchants prevailed upon him first to request a safe-conduct.

The following day, Saturday 23 March, Howqua and Mowqua, another Hong merchant, appeared at Dent's house, stripped of their buttons of rank and with iron chains around their necks. They glumly told the foreigners that Lin had degraded them because of Dent's refusal to obey his summons and that two of their number would be killed if Dent did not obey at once. Dent again volunteered to go but was restrained by his friends. Some discussion followed in the course of which Dent's brother emotionally told the other merchants, 'If you let him go, I will lay his death at your door.' Finally it was agreed that John Inglis, a partner in Dent's, who was reasonably fluent in Chinese, should go and explain to the officials that Dent would obey the summons if his safety was guaranteed. Inglis was sharply told by the officials that if Dent did not come of his own volition, he would be taken by force. However, as the 24th was a Sunday, a day's grace was graciously granted in deference to the foreigners' religious susceptibilities and Dent was now ordered to present himself at 10 a.m. on the 25th. On Sunday the foreign community attended church twice. Significantly the texts of the sermons were 'What is our life?' and 'We must all appear before the judgement throne of Christ'.

At 6 p.m. on the 24th, about the time of evening service, Elliot arrived in Canton post-haste from Macau in a small ship's boat. The gallant captain was certainly courageous if rather inclined to self-dramatics. Noticing that the flag was not flying outside the British factory, he immediately ordered one hoisted. He wrote to Palmerston that '. . . I well knew, my Lord, that there is a sense of support in that honoured flag, fly where it will, that none can feel but men who look upon it in some such dismal strait as ours'.[19] The following day, on learning that Dent was due to go and see Lin, he exclaimed that all must stand together and that no one should be a scapegoat for the rest. Somewhat to Dent's embarrassment, Elliot insisted on taking him by the arm and leading him to his own apartments 'where by God's gracious mercy he still remains'.

Elliot was now obliged to share the blockade that was imposed upon the foreign community. No foreigners were to leave Canton, servants were withdrawn from the factories, and supplies of food and water were cut off. The river was blocked by armed junks and the streets around the factories were patrolled by armed men. The situation seemed menacing and Elliot, who was already in an overwrought state, became seriously alarmed. The threat was more apparent than real. The factories were well stocked with food and the servants of the Co-Hong merchants smuggled fresh supplies in daily, probably with Lin's knowledge. Elliot, however, was convinced that 'the safety of the great mass of human life hung upon my determination'. When Lin made it clear that the merchants would be released after all the opium was handed over, Elliot instructed the merchants to surrender their stocks to him, promising at the same time that they would be indemnified for the loss by the British government. The merchants were delighted. The season had been a bad one with hardly a chest sold for several months. The representative of the Crown was guaranteeing them the cost of all the remaining stocks. The merchants responded by pledging him 20,283 chests valued at $9 million. This was actually 500 more chests than were in stock but the balance was made up by the arrival of the first of the next season's crop. The chests were handed over to the Chinese officials who, on Lin's instructions, began their destruction.

Lin now demanded that each merchant sign a bond promising on pain of death never to smuggle in future. Elliot refused to sanction this and although some American merchants did sign the bond he was backed wholeheartedly by the British merchants. For the time being Lin agreed to compromise. The merchants did not sign, but sixteen of them including Dent and Matheson, had to sign a guarantee that they would never return to China. This they did with full mental reservations.

Matheson was already planning to move the receiving
station for the coastal trade from Lintin to Manila. His main
concern was that Elliot would agree to co-operate with the
Chinese authorities in controlling the trade. A note in the
firm's private letter book dated 16 October 1839 reads,

> We shall modify the arrangements of our firm so as to prevent
> our drug operations at Manila being interfered with by Captain
> Elliot's views, should they be carried into effect—which however
> we much doubt. We cannot believe that the British Government
> will adopt the novel and unheard of principle of acting against its
> own subjects to enforce the fiscal regulations of a foreign
> power. . . .[20]

Matheson was sufficiently convinced that the coastal trade
would continue as before to buy up stocks of opium at
depressed prices, instead of acting on commission, thereby
enabling the firm to reap large profits in the near future by
selling at virtually monopoly prices. Throughout the negotiations between the British and Chinese authorities in
1842–3, Jardine's main concern was to avoid the legalizing of the trade which would subject it to controls and
probably lead to increased competition.

The blockade was ended and by 4 July the entire British
community had moved to Macau. Since they fully intended to continue the opium trade, and indeed the new
season's crop had already been purchased in India and was
on its way, they did not wish to remain at risk within the
Commissioner's jurisdiction. Lin was pleased with the
results of his efforts and, for a time, he basked in imperial
favour. 'This affair has been well-managed', wrote the Tao-
Kuang emperor.

In reality Lin had played right into the hands of the
opium merchants. The question of the opium trade was a
delicate one in England. A significant body of opinion
deplored it on humanitarian grounds and even men who
were deeply involved in the trade, like Jardine, would have
conceded that trade between China and Britain could not

1. The Praia Grande, Macau, in the eighteenth century (*Mansell Collection*)

2. The Factories, Canton, in the 1840s (*National Maritime Museum*)

3. Opium ships at Lintin, 1824

4. Whampoa Anchorage (*MacPherson Collection*)

6. William Jardine (*Jardine, Matheson and Co. Ltd.*)

5. Howqua, the senior Hong merchant and close associate of William Jardine (*Tate Gallery*)

7. Sir James Matheson (*Jardine, Matheson and Co. Ltd.*)

8. The *Falcon*, pride of Jardine, Matheson's fleet in the 1830s

9. Clippers in Hong Kong harbour, 1847

10. The Hong Kong waterfront in the later nineteenth century (*Hong Kong Land Co. Ltd.*)

11. The old Hong Kong Club, illuminated for a visit by the Duke of Connaught in 1870 (*Mary Evans Picture Library*)

12. The Hong Kong Cricket Club's grounds about 1880. The central building in the middle distance belonged to Butterfield and Swire's for a time. (*Government Information Services*)

13. Sir William des Voeux, Governor of Hong Kong, 1887–1891 (*Hong Kong Electric Co. Ltd.*)

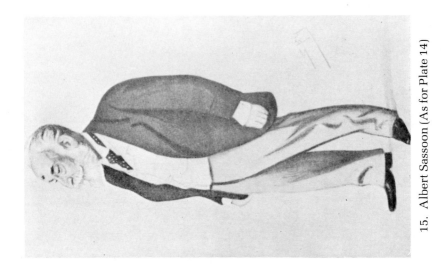

15. Albert Sassoon (As for Plate 14)

14. David Sassoon (From oriental merchants to members of Britain's high society in two generations: taken from Roth, *The Sassoon Dynasty*)

17. J. S. Swire (*Liverpool University Press*)

16. Reuben Sassoon (As for Plate 14)

18.  Butterfield and Swire's staff in Hong Kong, 1892 (*Liverpool University Press*)

19. *Changsha I* was with Swire's fleet from 1886 to 1912. She was especially built for the Japan-China-Hong Kong-Australia route bringing raw sugar for the Hong Kong refinery on the northward run. (*John Swire Co. Ltd.*)

20. Happy Valley in the late nineteenth century (*Hongkong and Shanghai Banking Corporation*)

21. The Governor's Box, Happy Valley, about 1890 (*Hong Kong Museum of Art*)

22. The Hong Kong Hotel opened for business in 1866 in a building
formerly owned by Dent's (*Hongkong and Shanghai Banking Corporation*)

23. The old Hongkong and Shanghai Bank building: it was replaced by
a Corinthian-style building in 1886. The Town Hall is on the left.
(*Hongkong and Shanghai Banking Corporation*)

24. The Peak Tram, opened in 1888 (Hongkong and Shanghai Banking Corporation)

continue indefinitely on the basis of opium smuggling. In theory it would probably have been possible for the imperial authorities to have come to an agreement with the British government whereby, in return for free trade, the opium traffic would have been brought under control. However for the Universal Emperor to treat with barbarians in this way was unthinkable and the worthy Lin, ignorant of the West and its superior technology, believed that the foreigners, like other rebels in the past, could be brought to heel by a display of imperial determination. In fact Britain was the strongest nation in the world at this time and her people, conscious of this fact, were not prepared to be browbeaten by an administration whose pretensions were much greater than its power.

Only an incident was needed to start a war. On 7 July a fight had taken place on the Kowloon peninsula between a mob of drunken sailors and some local peasants and as a result one of the Chinese, Lin Wei-hsi, died. Commissioner Lin demanded that the guilty man be handed over to the Chinese authorities but it was not clear which of the many sailors was responsible. Anyway the memory of the *Lady Hughes* gunner was still fresh and Elliot made it clear that he had no intention of handing over an English seaman to the processes of Chinese law. Lin was irritated by Elliot's refusal and wanted to resolve the question of the bonds so that legal trade could be resumed as normal. Accordingly he decided to repeat the seemingly effective tactics he had employed in Canton and cut off supplies to Macau, simultaneously moving two thousand troops to the border. The British quit Macau and anchored their ships in Hong Kong harbour. Tension rose higher as war-junks attempted to prevent the British landing to get fresh provisions. Late in October a Chinese war fleet began to assemble near the Bogue, probably with the intention of boarding one of the British ships and seizing a hostage for the killer of Lin Wei-hsi. At the same time Lin issued a warning that if all the British merchants did not sign the bond, the ships in

Hong Kong harbour would be attacked. Elliot, who had at his disposal two British warships, sailed upriver on 2 November and demanded the withdrawal of Lin's threat. On the following day fighting broke out between the British and Chinese ships and after a short engagement, the Chinese fleet was scattered. The First Anglo-Chinese War had begun.

News of the Canton crises reached London in the early autumn. William Jardine at once busied himself lobbying support for a 'forward' policy. He backed a pamphlet which depicted the 'siege in the factories' as a second Black Hole of Calcutta and helped to organize petitions from over 300 firms asking Palmerston to intervene in Canton. At the same time he did not wish to embarrass the Foreign Secretary for, with his usual shrewdness, he appreciated that Palmerston was not averse to taking action provided that it could be presented to the public and to Parliament in an acceptable light. In 1835 Hollingworth Magniac had formed an agency house with John Abel Smith, member of a banking family, an M.P. and an acquaintance of Palmerston's. Jardine himself joined this agency on his return to England and later bought Smith out. Meanwhile Abel Smith, on Jardine's behalf, solicited Palmerston for a personal interview. At first he was unsuccessful. Jardine bided his time. 'We prefer doing things quietly if possible', he noted, 'though the delay is very provocking.' As the petitions from the solid Midlands textile firms began to arrive, Palmerston felt that he had some basis on which to act. On 27 September he granted Jardine an interview. The latter arrived well equipped with maps and charts and for some time 'The extent of armaments, number of troops necessary, number of shipping etc were all discussed'. The Foreign Secretary made no definite avowal that he would intervene, for the Cabinet had not yet been consulted, but Jardine wrote confidently to Matheson that he did not believe that the government would swallow the insult.

It was soon confirmed to Jardine that the Cabinet had

decided to act. Accordingly he sent Palmerston 'a paper of hints' in which he outlined the need to blockade China's ports and to seize some offshore islands in order to obtain an equitable commercial treaty, compensation for the surrendered opium, and the opening of four more ports to trade. Further consultation took place between Palmerston and Jardine in the early weeks of 1840 and on 20 February Palmerston formally appointed Captain Elliot and his cousin Admiral George Elliot as plenipotentiaries to head a British expedition. They were instructed to obtain terms on the lines of those indicated by Jardine. Parliament had not yet been consulted and on 7 April a debate took place on an Opposition motion of censure on the conduct of affairs leading to the war. Gladstone, then a Tory, stated for the Opposition,

A war more unjust in its origin . . . I do not know and I have not read of. The right honourable gentleman opposite spoke of the British flag waving in glory at Canton. That flag is hoisted to protect an infamous contraband traffic; and if it were never hoisted except as it is now hoisted on the coast of China, we should recoil from its sight with horror. [21]

However, in answer, Palmerston denied that the government wished to protect the opium trade and insisted that its aim was to guarantee the safety of British citizens and their right to trade. The Opposition motion was defeated by five votes.

Jardine bought land in Perthshire and elsewhere in Scotland and in 1841 became Whig M.P. for Ashburton, thus fulfilling an ambition to have a political career which he had made no secret of in his Canton days. He wrote to Matheson that it gave him much pleasure to confound Dent who had often derided this ambition in the past. [22] In a letter to Abel Smith in November 1842, Palmerston paid tribute to the accuracy of Jardine's advice 'which was embodied in the instructions which we gave in February 1840' and declared that 'To the assistance and information which you, my dear Smith, and Mr Jardine so handsomely afforded us, it was mainly owing that we were able to give our affairs, naval, military and diplomatic, in China, those detailed instructions which have led to these satisfactory results'.[23] Jardine died shortly after the war was over, in 1843, in his fifty-ninth year.

The opium trade continued while Britain and China were officially at war. Matheson's astuteness in buying up stocks worth £40,000 at depressed prices in 1839 enabled him to reap rich profits averaging 200 per cent in the following season. The other merchants were encouraged to emulate his example and by the spring of 1840 competition was such that Matheson reverted to his usual practice of selling on commission. Two other merchants who did well were the sea captain brothers, Joseph and Henry Pybus. As soon as Lin's destruction of the opium stocks at Canton had become known, the price on the China coast had risen as high as $3000 a chest, while in Singapore holders were glad to get rid of chests at $150 each. Joseph beat down to Singapore against the south-west monsoon in his schooner *Time*, not leaving the deck for six weeks. On his arrival he immediately bought 300 chests at an average of $250 each. Pausing only to cover his leaking schooner with one-inch teak planking, he returned to the China coast where he sold his cargo at $2500 a chest. His brother Henry was equally enterprising and in a voyage up the coast with a full cargo a few months later he netted a profit of £50,000. With the proceeds of these ventures, the brothers had three schooners and a brig, *Harlequin*, *Clown*, *Columbine*, and *Pantaloon*, built in India. These were used to provide a regular service on the route between Calcutta and Singapore carrying mail, passengers, and occasionally opium. Later they extended their run to Macau. The brothers retired in 1843. The hazards of the China coast are indicated by the fact that by the mid-1850s the *Columbine*, *Pantaloon*, and *Harlequin* had all been lost at sea.

Jardine and Matheson's fleet of a dozen or more clippers

gave them a great advantage over their rivals. Like the East
Indiamen in earlier days, they were superbly equipped and
heavily armed. The flagship *Falcon*, which had been originally built for the Commodore of the Royal Yacht Squad-
ron, carried yards and spars equal to those on a ship twice
her capacity, all her metal fittings including the belaying
pins were of brass and copper, and the skylights, coamings,
and stanchions were of mahogany. One of the mates of the
*Falcon* was inspired to write:

Nothing in still life could be more picturesque than her sails
which, unfurled at anchor or in a calm, fell in full heavy graceful
folds from her yards and booms. Nothing could confer so strik-
ingly the same triumph of art, when the same sails were filled and
trimmed. . . . It was on the 'Falcon' that I began to comprehend a
singular belief that prevails among seamen. She appeared to
resent every neglect of her handling and rebel at once against any
over pressure or any tampering with her trim, so that our common
expressions, that she was complaining or sulking or huffed or
offended, seemed to us rightly applied. 'She can do everything but
speak' was a common remark among the crew.[24]

On occasion during the war the clippers came into
conflict with the Chinese authorities. In May 1840 when
the *Hellas* was becalmed off Swatow she was attacked by
several armed junks. The junks came up astern so that
Captain Jauncey was unable to bring his guns to bear.
When the junks got close enough, their crews hurled
burning oil pots onto his deck. Some of his crew tackled the
blaze, while others boarded the junks and engaged the
Chinese in a fierce hand-to-hand struggle. After four hours,
a breeze sprang up and the *Hellas* managed to escape, not
without injuries, for Jauncey had lost an eye and twenty-
five of the crew were wounded.

In June 1840 the British expeditionary force, consisting
of twenty-seven transports and 4000 troops, arrived. Elliot
had always hoped that the threat of force alone would
persuade China to negotiate, thereby increasing the low

esteem in which he was held by the merchants. Matheson thought that the more tender Elliot showed himself to be, the more obstinate the Chinese would become. Elliot's efforts to reach an agreement without open conflict were fruitless and, on 7 January 1841, the British warships seized the Bogue forts, opening the way to Canton. Two weeks later, the Convention of Chuenpi was signed by the Chinese plenipotentiary Ch'i-san and Elliot. By it, Hong Kong was to be ceded to Britain, there was to be official intercourse on a basis of equality, China was to pay an indemnity of $6 million, and trade was to be reopened at Canton. Elliot was pleased that he had secured all that he believed necessary without undue bloodshed. When Palmerston heard the terms, he was furious. He agreed whole-heartedly with Queen Victoria who wrote of 'the unaccountably strange conduct of Charles Elliot . . . who completely disobeyed his instructions and tried to get the lowest terms he could'. Elliot was replaced by Sir Henry Pottinger, who had served as a political agent in India for many years and was therefore presumably experienced in the extraction of satisfactory terms from wily Orientals. He was given explicit instructions which included obtaining a higher indemnity, the abolition of the Co-Hong, and the opening of more ports to trade. The Chinese plenipotentiary's acts were also repudiated. The emperor considered he had given away too much. His property was confiscated and he was sent into exile in chains.

Matheson's first reaction to the Convention of Chuenpi was favourable. He was pleased that the opium trade had not been mentioned and saw Hong Kong as a safer and more convenient centre for the storage and distribution of the drug. Palmerston, on the contrary, thought that 'it seems obvious that Hong Kong will not be a Mart of Trade, any more than Macao is so'. When Matheson learnt of Palmerston's objections to Hong Kong he wrote to Jardine urging him to use his influence '. . . if not for its retention, at least for the retention of some place near this river where alone the British people are known and multitudes of natives are ready to become our subjects and trade with us'.[25]

Meanwhile Matheson had acted with his usual speed to take advantage of the acquisition of Hong Kong. In February 1841, one month after the island's occupation by British troops and prior to any official land sales, he erected a matshed godown on the centre of the northern shore, a little below the present site of Flagstaff House. It was quickly rebuilt in a more permanent fashion and fittingly Matheson's godown was the first stone building built by the British in Hong Kong.

The first official land sale took place on 14 June 1841. Originally two hundred lots had been advertised but preparations were inadequate and in the end only about fifty were put up for sale and these were inaccurately measured and, in some cases, so undesirable that no one bid for them. However bidding for the better sites, exclusively by Europeans and Parsees, was vigorous and Elliot later denied to Matheson and Dent that he had restricted the number of lots in order to force the prices up. Captain William Morgan, a ship's captain, acting on behalf of Jardine's, bought the lots on which the already erected godown stood and also a large area at East Point which later became the Company's headquarters. Matheson intended the headquarters to be on the Central site and on high ground behind the godown he erected a bungalow of which the *Canton Press* caustically remarked 'On entering the harbour, you perceive the most commanding site, disfigured by a hybrid erection, half New South Wales, half native production'. However the military had acquired most of the land in the vicinity and early in 1842 Jardine's were offered cash compensation and the choice of lots elsewhere if they would move out. They obligingly agreed, choosing instead two lots in West Point. Matheson now decided to develop the East Point site and Pottinger wrote of it in mid-1842 as having been

. . . one chaos of immense masses of granite and other rocks, that it
was hardly accessible by person or on foot, either on the side of the
water or the land, that the firm in question, by the application of
science and extra ordinary labour and by an expenditure of about
£100,000, have not only made it available for their vast mercantile
concerns, but have rendered it a credit and an ornament to the
Colony.[26]

However Jardine's in common with most of the merchant
houses did not finally move their headquarters from Macau
until 1844. A sketch of about 1843 shows that, as well as
several godowns, two fine houses had been built at East
Point by this time. Robert Jardine, William's nephew,
wrote home in 1849,

> You will like to know who have got the nicest houses here. As
> you are aware the Governor and the General have generally the
> finest, here it is not so, 'Who then?'—Jardine's—their house is
> separate from the others and is situated on a Point which over-
> looks the greater part of the Town, the Rooms here are much larger
> than in most houses.[27]

In the first land sale Dent's bought an extensive lot in
Central on the north side of Queen's Road, in the vicinity of
Pedder Street. Not long after they bought another lot on the
opposite side of the road where a sumptuous residence
known as Green Bank was built. The Revd James Legge
described Hong Kong in 1843 and wrote 'All the space
between Wyndham Street and Wellington Street was
garden ground with an imposing flat-roofed house (Green
Bank) on it built by Mr Brian of the firm of Dent and Co.'

The bungalow built by Matheson was used later in 1842
by Lord Saltoun, Commander of British Forces in China.
Presumably its distinctive architecture did not appeal, for
it was later demolished by the military and the site used for
the present Flagstaff House, until recently the residence of
the Commander of British Forces in Hong Kong. Saltoun
left an interesting account of life in the new colony at this
time:

I have secured a house. . . . I am to pay 1000 dollars for furniture and pictures and forty dollars a month rent. The plan here is to engage a man, they call him a compradore, a major domo in fact. He finds cook and helper, wine coolies, table decker etc etc and these worthies cost about sixty dollars a month. . . .

We breakfast at eight, lunch at one and dine at half past six, and, not much liking to lead a hermit's life, we generally sit down eight or ten to dinner. . . .

Amongst other things we have a sheep club; that is a certain number of us subscribed and sheep are brought from Bengal and also from Sydney in Australia. We graze them here on the hill and feed them with grain, which makes them very fat and good. They kill a sheep for each four members, and at one killing you get a hindquarter, at the next a forequarter. . . .[28]

Pottinger was appointed to replace Elliot in May 1841 and he arrived in Hong Kong in August. He had been well primed before his departure. Jardine wrote to Matheson, 'I have had two or three conversations with him of a very satisfactory nature, and he has spared no trouble to gain information.' He travelled from Bombay to Hong Kong with Alexander Matheson, James's nephew, and James's house was one of the first that he entered in Hong Kong. Matheson, who had disliked Elliot's conciliatory attitude to the Chinese and his opposition to the opium trade, found Sir Henry more to his taste. After further hostilities, the Treaty of Nanking was signed by British and Chinese representatives aboard Pottinger's vessel, H.M.S. *Cornwallis*, in August 1842. The new peace terms included an indemnity of $21 million, the opening to trade of the ports of Canton, Amoy, Foochow, Ningpo, and Shanghai, official intercourse on an equal basis, British consuls at each treaty port, the abolition of the Co-Hong and confirmation of the cession of Hong Kong. As in the earlier convention, there was no mention of the opium trade.

The attitude of the British government to the opium trade was set out in a despatch to Pottinger in January 1843, 'HM Government . . . have not the power to put a stop to this trade ... but they may perhaps impede it to some degree by preventing the Island of Hong Kong or its neighbouring waters from being used as the point from whence British smugglers shall depart on their illegal adventures'. It was hoped that the Chinese would agree to legalize the trade so that it could be regulated by taxation. The British authorities would then help to stamp out any smuggling. However in the treaty negotiations the Chinese made the stock statement that the emperor's decision to prohibit the trade could not be reversed. The Chinese representatives did give Pottinger a guarantee that they would not take action against foreign merchants but only against Chinese subjects.

Pottinger for his part made some effort to control the British merchants. In November 1842 he issued a proclamation that no British merchants were to trade in the four new treaty ports until they had been officially opened with consuls installed. He followed this in January 1843 with a declaration that in future British merchants would not be allowed to trade outside the treaty ports. These actions caused some consternation among the opium traders— James Matheson wrote in December 1842,

> Uncertainty prevails as to opium. Sir Henry Pottinger thinks it must be legalized eventually but when it is impossible to say. Meanwhile it is evident that the new system will tend materially to increase the difficulties under which the coast trade is carried on.... Under these circumstances we consider it extremely hazardous to purchase drug at high prices in India and imprudent to hold a large stock in hand here.[29]

In fact there was considerable doubt not only among the opium traders but also the British officials as to whether under British law, Pottinger's proclamations could actually be enforced. Moreover, in spite of widespread hostility to the opium trade in Britain, illustrated by a petition from two hundred merchants denouncing it as a rival to legitimate trade presented to the government in July 1842, the trade had become too important as a source of official revenue to be lightly abandoned. After reflection, Matheson summed up the views of the opium traders: 'The plenipotentiary has published a most fiery proclamation against smuggling, but I believe it is like the Chinese edicts, meaning nothing and only intended ... for the gratification of the Saints in England. Sir Henry never means to act on it, and no doubt privately considers it a good joke.'[30] Meanwhile the opium trade continued to flourish. Receiving ships had been anchored off the treaty ports for some months. As a precaution, Matheson did purchase three American clippers which continued to trade under the U.S. flag. It was evident to Pottinger that this expedient would be widely adopted if he made any serious effort to control the British opium traders.

If the British merchants did not take Pottinger's proclamations very seriously, Captain Charles Hope, senior British naval officer at Chusan, did. He could not 'for a moment suppose that a British minister would issue proclamations without he intended to act upon them'. Accordingly, in April 1843, finding some British vessels, which included Jardine's Vixen, off Shanghai, which had not yet been opened for trade, he ordered them to leave within twenty-four hours. The result was a significant object lesson. A few days after the Vixen's return to Hong Kong, Pottinger was presented with a petition from all the principal merchants remonstrating against Hope's action. Pottinger promptly disavowed this attempt to enforce his proclamation. Both the captain and the Shanghai taotai (Chinese port official) who had co-operated with him were recalled by their respective superiors. The Royal Navy henceforth was to ignore the existence of the opium trade. Matheson was concerned about the unpopularity of the trade in England and therefore wished to keep it 'as quiet and as much out of the public eye as possible'. He instructed his principal captain not to flaunt this 'victory' over the Navy and to avoid trouble with the Chinese officials by 'moving from one anchorage to another when they require it and not approaching too near to their towns'.

Pottinger now maintained that it was up to the Chinese officials to prevent their own people from trading with the opium merchants. From this he logically concluded that it was 'neither desirable nor necessary to exclude our opium trading ships from Hong Kong harbour'. Furthermore he made it clear in a proclamation on 23 October 1843 that, although his earlier prohibition on British ships trading outside the treaty ports still stood, nonetheless it would not be contrary to this prohibition 'should British vessels approach and anchor for safety . . . near the coast of China'. Alexander Matheson noted gleefully that all hopes of legalizing the drug trade had ended. Jardine's now moved a large receiving ship, the *Bomanjee Hormusjee*, into Hong Kong harbour where the protection afforded to it by the guns of the Murray Battery enabled some of the crew to be dispensed with, saving $2000 a month in wages. Dent's established an opium godown on shore and Jardine's later followed suit, employing Sepoy guards to protect it.

James Matheson finally left Hong Kong, probably in late 1842, satisfied that he had left the partnership well established in the new conditions of trade. On his return to England he was elected to the seat at Ashburton left vacant by Jardine's death. He held the seat until 1847, after which he sat as member for Ross and Cromarty until 1862. In 1844 he purchased the island of Lewis, spending well over half a million pounds on the purchase price and subsequent improvements which included the construction of Stornoway Castle. In 1851 he was created a baronet for his work in relieving famine there. He died in Mentone in 1878 aged eighty-two.[31] He was succeeded as head of the firm by Alexander who had started with Lyall, Matheson and Co. in Calcutta, becoming a partner in Jardine and Matheson in 1835.

The life style of the opium merchants and their attitude to the problem of opening China to international trade were derived from Britain's experience in India. The Honourable John Company was the epitome of Anglo-Indian attitudes and the agency houses in Canton that eventually replaced it were, in most cases, offshoots of the East Indian houses in Calcutta, Bombay, and London. The leading opium merchants came from this background and they maintained and developed their connections in the close-knit world of the Anglo-Indian business community. The victory of a small nation of 22 million over an empire of 400 million is partly explained by the fact that the merchants came to China convinced that they were an élite, the 'select', a conviction inspired not only by Britain's rapidly developing industrial strength but also by the success of British arms and the consequent extension of the British administration in India. Their arrogance and self-confidence was matched by that of the Chinese officials but the latter were unaware that technological developments had given their opponents all the aces when it came to war.

Britain's victory in the First Anglo-Chinese War ensured the continuation of the opium trade well into the twentieth century. The trade itself, described by one historian as 'the most long-continued and systematic international crime of modern times',[32] did much to ensure the success of Britain's invasion of China. The opium merchants suggested aims to the British government and gave it the necessary intelligence on which to base strategy, leased ships to the fleet, provided pilots, and gave hospitality to British officials, while the exchange of silver from opium sales for bills on London helped to meet the military expenditure. The crux of the matter was that the opium trade, for which the British government disclaimed any responsibility, for many years provided revenue essential to the British administration in India.

1. Downing, op. cit., I, 77.
2. ibid., I, 243–4.

3. W. C. Hunter, *The Fan Kwae at Canton before Treaty Days*, Shanghai, 1938, 18.

4. B. Lubbock, *The Opium Clippers*, Glasgow, 1933, 220.

5. Downing, op. cit., III, 201.

6. Lubbock, op. cit., 15.

7. ibid., 20.

8. Harry Parker, quoted by M. Collis, *Foreign Mud*, London, 1969, 81.

9. ibid., 82.

10. Fairbank, *Trade and Diplomacy on the China Coast*, footnote, 70.

11. ibid., 70.

12. ibid., 69–70.

13. *Canton Register*, 14 April 1835.

14. Fairbank, op. cit., footnote, 71.

15. See Collis, op. cit., 107–8.

16. ibid., 142.

17. ibid., 184.

18. A. Coates, *Prelude to Hong Kong*, London, 1966, 183.

19. Collis, op. cit., 223.

20. Fairbank, op. cit., footnote, 134.

21. Collis, op. cit., 280.

22. In *Sybil* Disraeli gave an indication of the attitude of the Tories to Jardine,
'You had a formidable opponent, Lord Marney told me' said Sir Vavasour 'Who was he?'
'Oh, a dreadful man! A Scotchman, richer than Croesus, one Mr Druggy, fresh from Canton, with a million in opium in each pocket, denouncing corruption and bellowing free trade.'

23. Greenberg, op. cit., 214–15.

24. Collis, op. cit., 290–1.

25. Greenberg, op. cit., 213.

26. Quoted in *Journal of the Royal Asiatic Society, Hong Kong Branch*, vol. 8, 1969, 149.

27. Buchanan Jardine Letters.

28. J. M. Braga, *Hong Kong Business Symposium*, Hong Kong, 1957, 34.

29. Fairbank, op. cit., footnote, 136.

30. ibid., footnote, 137.

31. His estates were inherited by his nephew Donald Matheson who had been in China for a few years in the 1840s. He was a devout and philanthropic Presbyterian and in 1892 he became Chairman of the Executive Committee of the Society for the Suppression of the Opium Trade.

32. J. K. Fairbank, ed., *Cambridge History of China*, Cambridge, 1978, 10, 213.

# PART II

## Between the Two Wars

'Get place and wealth, if possible, with grace,
If not, by any means, get wealth and place.'

Pope

# 3

# Anglo-Chinese Relations

BRITISH foreign policy in the middle decades of the
nineteenth century was characterized by a remarkable
homogeneity, a major reason for this being that it was
guided by one man, Lord Palmerston, who was either
Foreign Secretary or Prime Minister for two-thirds of the
period from 1830 to 1865. Continuity of policy was regarded as a virtue within the Foreign Office so that, even
when he was out of office, the main trend continued,
although the emphasis might change. Palmerston had a
typically Victorian belief that right and justice were on his
side and, strengthened by this conviction and by Britain's
unchallenged dominance of the sea, his main aim was to
assert, by force if necessary, the right of British citizens to
trade throughout the world under the protection of law. To
Palmerston, and to men like William Jardine and James
Matheson, this was a policy of enlightened self-interest.
The expansion of British trade would assist the spread of
civilization throughout the world, and the rule of law,
albeit based upon British principles of jurisprudence, was
assumed to have universal validity. The treaty port system
in China set up after the Treaty of Nanking reflected this
aim. It was intended by Palmerston to safeguard established trade interests, seemingly threatened by China's

arbitrary actions prior to the outbreak of war, and to afford the opportunity for further expansion, especially in those fields which would be likely to benefit constituents in Britain, within the context of mutually accepted rules. Thus Palmerston intended that the treaties which resulted from the First Anglo-Chinese War would be a charter of rights for the merchants.

The aims of the Chinese officials were very different and, in time, it became clear that they were not compatible with those of the British. The Manchus were skilled in dealing with troublesome non-Chinese on the borders of their empire and to them the British were just another barbarian tribe with temporary and local military superiority, whom it was necessary initially to appease and ultimately to mould into the traditional posture of a tributary state. The stated British aim was trade and thus, as a gesture from the Celestial Emperor to the outer barbarians, trade concessions would be granted but, at the same time, limits would be set to ensure that trade and the inevitable contact which it involved would be kept on the periphery of the empire. The military superiority of the barbarians would be neutralized by winning their friendship and by emphasizing China's cultural superiority. Accordingly the imperial clansman Ch'i-ying, who handled the new treaty relations from 1842 to 1848, acted in the great Manchu tradition of personal diplomacy and set out to bind the British headmen with friendship. His subordinates attempted to keep the foreigners in an inferior position by imposing their own interpretations on the terminology of the treaties and by continuing to treat them as tributaries. When obliged by the barbarians' superior military power to act otherwise, they represented any concession as an act of benevolence and not a recognition of foreign rights. This policy contained two fatal flaws. The Chinese officials did not appreciate the nature of Britain's industrial development and the consequent expectation on the part of the British merchants that trade would steadily expand. Nor did they realize that Britain's military superiority was such that she could, if need be, impose her aims on the central government in a way that would permit no alternative interpretations.

Ch'i-ying's policy in action was demonstrated by the visits which he made to Hong Kong in 1843 and 1845. On the first occasion Pottinger wrote that the Manchu diplomat 'embraced me with all the warmth and sincerity of an old friend and was even visibly affected by the strength of his emotion at our meeting again'. Ratification of the Treaty of Nanking followed and tariff negotiations proceeded. At the series of banquets which were held, Ch'i-ying was the life and soul of the party, singing songs, playing 'guess fingers' and plying Pottinger with expressions of affection and esteem. He declared a wish to adopt Pottinger's eldest son and, having obtained a miniature portrait of him, then requested one of his mother as well. He explained later to the emperor that 'the English barbarians think much of women and little of men'. Pottinger informed Lord Aberdeen, the Foreign Secretary, with a touch of gratified amazement, that Ch'i-ying's visit had 'thrown a perfectly new light on the character and habits' of the Chinese officials. Ch'i-ying found it more difficult to make a 'yin-ti-mit'e' friend of Pottinger's successor, Sir John Davis, who confessed to finding his long-winded interpretations of minor treaty points 'tiresome' and 'childish'. Nonetheless his visit to Hong Kong in 1845 made a good impression on the British residents. The *China Mail* felt that 'nothing could exceed the affability and good humour of Keying, accompanied by the highest tact and good breeding. He was jovial at dinner but without excess . . . but for his dress and language he might have been taken for a fine specimen of an old English gentleman of the highest class.'[1] The Manchu diplomat enjoyed a temporary vogue with the merchants. The building in which he stayed on Queen's Road became known as Keying House and the Chinese junk which sailed to Britain in 1846 was named after him.

However his efforts seem to have been in vain for there is no evidence that his professions of affection had any effect at all on British policy.

Far more significant from the British point of view was the failure of the treaty settlements to bring the expected results. Legitimate trade expanded very slowly. The merchants believed that this was due to obstruction by the Chinese officials and the taxation imposed on imports in the interior. Convinced that their interests were national interests, they pressed the British government to act on their behalf. If more ports and the major rivers were opened to British traders, the corrupt administration reformed, and a more modern system of communications built, then demand would be sure to increase. The Foreign Office realized more than they did that such pressure might result in the collapse of the Manchu government with injurious consequences to British interests but, at the same time, it did want to secure the charter of merchants' rights which it was clear in practice had not been obtained in the settlements of 1842–3.

Canton was a particular point of friction. The merchants were still confined to the old factory area and the refusal to permit them entrance to the city, contrary to the treaty arrangements, became a symbol of Cantonese defiance. The hostility of the Cantonese and the arrogance of the foreigners led to many incidents. Palmerston joined Davis in condemning the young British merchants who 'amuse themselves by kicking over fruit stalls and by making footballs of the Chinese' but there was little either of them could do to stop it. The rioting which followed the Compton incident in 1846 caused damage estimated at $46,000. Joseph Jardine, a nephew of William Jardine, who was in Canton at the time, wrote to his brother Andrew, 'Two unfortunate sailors were lately inveigled into one of the back streets and very narrowly escaped being made mincemeat of. One found refuge in a shop and the other took to the river, but they were cut and hacked with hatchets and other sharp weapons in a most horrible manner.'[2]

In 1847 the Canton British Chamber of Commerce was formed with David Jardine, another of William's nephews, as its first chairman to promote British interests there. It began pressing, under treaty rights, for the lease of more land for godowns and the improvement of navigation on the river from Whampoa. After the stoning of British merchants making excursions outside the confines of the factory area, Davis, in April 1847, resorted to gunboat diplomacy. Within thirty-six hours, British warships captured the Bogue forts, spiked the guns there, went up to Canton, and occupied the factories. Ch'i-ying was conciliatory but all he could promise was that the city would be opened in two years' time. Eight months later, after six Englishmen on an excursion were killed, Ch'i-ying sent troops to the village concerned and punished the inhabitants. However Peking now feared, correctly, that his attitude of appeasement would lose the dynasty the support of the local people. Therefore in 1848 he was recalled and his successor, Hsu Kuang-chin, adopted a hostile anti-foreign policy. The British government was not yet ready for another war and so the demand for entry to Canton was dropped for the time being, thereby convincing the Chinese officials that intransigence paid.

Another problem was that the increase in the opium trade, together with the decline in the authority of the government in Peking, led to a sharp rise in piracy and banditry. Many of the Chinese hustlers and racketeers involved in the drug trade acquired British nationality and, by the simple device of adopting foreign dress, became immune from the control of the Chinese officials, at least within the treaty ports. The same Chinese became leading figures in the thriving new industry of shipping cheap contract labour to South-East Asia and South America. Unscrupulous British merchants like James Tait of Amoy, who was protected by extraterritoriality as a British subject and was also consul for Holland and Spain, helped to organize it. The growth of lawlessness threatened legal trade. Chinese shipowners began to hire armed vessels. One such was the *Spec* which was owned by William Davidson of Ningpo and had an English master, mate, and gunner. The armament of this 105-ton schooner consisted of 9 guns, 23 muskets, 5 pistols, 10 cutlasses, 4 pikes, and 5 spears. With the best will in the world, the masters of such vessels found it difficult to differentiate between pirates and honest fishermen and frequently the will was lacking. They became involved in Chinese feuds and frequently their activities were little short of privateering. One prominent Chinese businessman in Hong Kong, Loo Aqui, was accused of piracy in 1860 after he had hired the steamer *Jamsetjee Jeejeebhoy* to raid Hakka villages which he claimed harboured pirates.

That the treaty port system would have to be revised was clear by 1850; the accession to the throne of the anti-foreign Hsien-feng emperor in that year made it almost inevitable that revision would be imposed by force of Western arms. The young emperor, supremely ignorant of the outside world, was impressed by Hsu Kuang-chin's success. He dismissed those officials who had urged a conciliatory line and supported Hsu and his close colleague the Governor of Kwangtung, Yeh Ming-chen, in their refusal to avoid having discussions with Western envoys. British and French attempts to open negotiations for a treaty revision in 1854 failed and the following year the return to power of Palmerston, who had been out of office since 1851, encouraged the British activists in China.

War was precipitated by Sir John Bowring, who became Governor of Hong Kong as well as Plenipotentiary and Superintendent of Trade with China in 1854. An economist, former M.P., and radical Whig, he had become interested in China after his son obtained a position with Jardine's. He became consul at Canton in 1849 and served as Superintendent of Trade in Bonham's absence. In many

ways a very gifted man, he claimed himself that he 'spoke
with ease and fluency French, Italian, Spanish, Portuguese, German and Dutch', had a 'fair acquaintance with
Danish and Swedish . . . a book knowledge of Russian,
Servian, Polish and Bohemian . . ., studied Magyar with
some success . . . learnt a little Arabic . . . and mastered a
good deal of that difficult language Chinese', he was
nonetheless conceited and self-important. In the words of
one historian, 'he had come back big with the fate of China
and himself'. Bowring was a classic example of the strange
contradictions which could beset a progressive liberal
following the Palmerstonian line of thought. Prior to his
consular appointment, he had been the president of a Peace
Society which advocated the non-violent settlement of
international disputes, and as Governor of Hong Kong he
generally adopted a humane attitude to the Chinese population. Yet his experiences in Canton had convinced him
that the revision of the treaties, with all the benefits which
would, in his opinion, accrue to the Chinese as well as to
the British merchants, would only be brought about by
force. In October 1856 the *Arrow*, a Chinese-owned vessel,
registered in Hong Kong and entitled to fly the British flag,
was seized in Canton on a charge of piracy. The British
consul in Canton, Harry Parkes, had just returned from
England where Palmerston had agreed that Britain must
take a 'high tone' and demand redress for the slightest
insult. He was backed enthusiastically by Bowring and,
after some unsatisfactory negotiations with the Chinese
officials, a British naval force yet again attacked the Bogue
forts, sailed to Canton, and bombarded Yeh's *yamen*, so
beginning the Second Anglo-Chinese War. Bowring, with
his belief in the inevitable triumph of 'commerce and
Christianity in natural and necessary alliance', had observed earlier that 'I could hardly terminate my public life
more honourably or more happily than by opening wider
and wider the gates of access to this extensive Empire'.
　　The first phase of the war, in which Britain was joined by

France on the grounds that a French missionary who had trespassed into the interior had been executed, ended in 1858. Treaties were signed at Tientsin with Britain and France and also with the United States and Russia who had not taken part in the fighting. Difficulties arose over the ratification of the treaties and fighting broke out again, to be ended in 1860 by the Convention of Peking. By these treaties fresh ports and the River Yangtse were opened to foreign trade and foreigners, including missionaries, could travel in the interior. Under the new tariff regulations, the opium trade was legalized. Kowloon, on the mainland, was added to the colony of Hong Kong. In future foreign powers were to have the right to station diplomatic representatives in Peking who would deal with Chinese ministers on equal terms. The British government was satisfied that it had at last obtained a charter of rights for the Western merchants and for some years to come was to adopt a co-operative attitude towards the Chinese authorities. Britain had already got by far the largest share of China's trade and stood only to lose if China's government was overthrown internally as a result of external pressure from the foreign powers. Moreover the principal British negotiator during the war, Lord Elgin, had become convinced while in the East that China's commercial self-sufficiency made the merchants' hopes of a great trade increase quite illusory. So it was to prove. Trade increased slowly after 1860 and, although between 1885 and 1894 British trade with China doubled, the volume was still relatively small. The more realistic and adaptable taipans came to believe that their best opportunities for profit lay in the role of privileged foreign participators in the modernization of China, a notion which, more than a hundred years later, is once again enjoying a vogue.

1. Fairbank, *Trade and Diplomacy on the China Coast*, footnote, 270.
2. Buchanan Jardine Letters.

# 4

# Trade with China

THE period immediately following the Treaty of Nanking was the time when the opium traders reaped their greatest profit. One estimate states that between 1827 and 1847 the partners of Jardine and Matheson shared £3 million, the greater part of it being accumulated in the last ten years. In spite of this, one of the partners, William Jardine's nephew David, wrote in 1844, 'I am not quite clear that with the new system of things and steam communication that a partnership in J. and M. will continue to be so desirable an object as it has hitherto been.' In 1845 Jardine's had fourteen receiving ships along the coast with four clippers carrying supplies to them. The annual cost of maintaining this system was around $300,000. Such high overheads drove out the small agencies which had proliferated during the war and in the later 1840s Jardine's and Dent's shared a virtual monopoly of the coastal trade. Between them they also handled most of the insurance business on the China coast, and this enabled them at times to withhold insurance from competitors' ships. During this period Jardine's opium trading activities followed a routine which varied little. Each fortnight two clippers left Hong Kong, one to the north and one to the south, to deliver opium to the receiving ships. It was estimated in 1849 that three-quarters of the shipments from India were distributed from

Hong Kong. On the return journey, the clippers would collect the proceeds in the form of silver or gold coins, part of which was sent to India from Hong Kong and part of which remained in China to finance legitimate trade. The trading operations of the receiving ships were directed by monthly instructions from the company's headquarters at Hong Kong. On average sales totalled about 600 chests monthly, more than half of which was from the receiving ship at Woosung, near Shanghai, from where the opium was distributed to hitherto relatively undeveloped markets up the Yangtse.

Retail sales within Hong Kong amounted to about 250 chests monthly, most of which went to the Chinese consuming public. The drug passed successively through the hands of licensed merchants, brokers, refiners, and finally opium den owners. In 1844 the government sold the exclusive right to retail opium for one year to the highest bidders, George Duddell and Alexander Martin Mathieson of the firm of McEwen and Co. However the monopolists could not enforce their privilege because it was difficult to prove that other merchants with stocks in hand were not intending to sell it outside the colony. In 1847 a licensing system was instituted instead. The British mania for regulating vice manifested itself in provisions whereby opium den operators were required to display their licences, sell opium only for money, keep out armed persons, and close their premises by 10 p.m. The big agencies restricted their sales to retailers in Hong Kong in order to develop the trade elsewhere. Chinese smugglers on occasion bought their supplies in Hong Kong in hopes of getting a better price than that offered by the receiving ships. In order to discourage this practice, Jardine's and Dent's would cut their prices at the receiving ships as soon as the smugglers had left Hong Kong.

Another advantage which Jardine's and Dent's had over their smaller rivals was their close connection with the big Indian houses. Even in the 1830s, Jardine's joint account with Jeejeebhoy's of Calcutta averaged over £1 million annually. Jeejeebhoy's, together with Remington and Co. of Bombay and Jardine, Skinner of Calcutta, dominated the Indian end of the opium market for more than thirty years. Their agents sent in detailed reports on the expected yields and market trends from all over the growing areas, thus enabling Jardine's to build up or run down stocks in advance of predicted changes in supply. Generally the Indian houses did not buy opium themselves but instead canvassed opium exporters for consignments using their superior shipping and insurance services and their ability to handle large quantities as inducements.

In the 1840s Jardine's and Dent's paid the crews of their clippers more than twice the rates on a first-class merchantman. As a result only the Royal Navy could match their smartness and efficiency. One writer commented,

When lying at anchor in Hong Kong harbour or the Shanghai River, they fairly shone as the rays of the sun sparkled on their brass guns and glinted off the bright metal of their rails and deck fittings. It was the day of shining black topsides, burnished copper, gold streaks and much ginger-bread scroll work and carving at bow and stern. Belaying pins were mostly of copper, ropes were all pointed or else brass capped, and Flemish coiled on the snow white decks. What wonder if these little schooners were the pride of their officers and the delight of their owners.[1]

Among the fastest schooners of this time were Dent's *Zephyr* and Jardine's *Mazeppa*. The former, built in Boston to a pilot boat design, carried nine 18-pound cannons and one 68-pounder. Another heavily armed vessel was Jardine's *Lanrick* which was reputed to have carried a cargo of opium worth £200,000 on one occasion. The *Mazeppa* was commanded for a time by Alex Ryrie, whose brother John was also employed by Jardine's. Another brother, Phineas, was employed by Turner and Co. and later became a prominent businessman in Hong Kong. Alex wrote to his mother in 1850,

Jardine's and Matheson's employ is far before any other in
China, but I am afraid I shall have to wait sometime before I am
promoted to Captain. However I don't mind that when I know that
they always promote their own servants to that rank in preference
to giving it to strangers.[2]

Alex was lost at sea in 1855 on the Shanghai–Hong Kong
run while in command of *Audax*.

The 1850s saw the last great era of the sailing ship. By
then the pride of the rival fleets were the big Yankee
clippers, displacing a thousand tons or more. These were
used on the tea run from Canton to London. The first tea
race was in 1850 when the *Oriental* (1003 tons) reached
London in 97 days compared with the 110 days or more of
the smaller clippers. Big clippers like the *Oriental* or the
famous *Sea Witch* could command £6 a ton freight against
the usual £4. The most famous of the tea races was that in
1860 between Gilman's *Taeping* and the *Ariel*. Although
the *Ariel* was the first to get a pilot off Dungeness, 99 days
out from Foochow, the *Taeping* secured a tug in the
Thames ahead of its rival, and docked twenty minutes
before the other vessel. The captains agreed to share the
prize money.

Jardine's and Dent's opium clippers set high standards of
efficiency and elegance. Moreover, in the early days of the
treaty port system they provided an essential link with
Hong Kong, India, and from thence Europe for the consuls
and merchants along the China coast. In spite of his official
disapproval of the opium trade, Pottinger in 1842 used the
*Cowasjee Family* to forward despatches to India and in
1843 used the *Red Rover* and the *Petrel*. However the
captains of the clippers only took government mail by
courtesy and at their own convenience. In 1843 Dent's
clipper *Zephyr* left Bombay ahead of schedule before
despatches for Pottinger had been put aboard. A government mail boat pursued the clipper for some distance but
was disregarded. Pottinger suspected that the captains
sometimes deliberately avoided carrying official mail so

that information they were carrying for their owners should arrive first. Nonetheless the service provided by the clippers was indispensable. The British consul at Amoy explained in 1844 that he was obliged to make use of the clippers because they called once or twice a week while regular mail arrived at intervals of up to a month. The consul at Ningpo in 1847 asked that government despatches be sent to him through Dent's office in Hong Kong. The opium merchants also provided the consuls with banking facilities. The consul at Ningpo noted in 1850 that all the consulate's cash was supplied by Dent's receiving ship twelve miles down river. Naturally Her Majesty's Consuls, isolated, far from home and frequently in ill health, appreciated these services. Alexander Matheson wrote to his agent in Shanghai, 'Captain Balfour, the consul for Shanghai, and Mr Thom, the consul for Ningpo, are particular friends of ours and will give our vessels as little trouble as they can. . . . You will of course oblige Captain Balfour and Mr Thom by cashing their bills or otherwise.'[3]

In the early 1840s sailing ships using the route around the Cape still took about four months to reach Hong Kong from England. Government despatches were sent by the overland route across the Isthmus of Suez and took about three months. The Peninsular and Oriental Company's paddle steamers had already established a service between Southampton and Ceylon taking thirty-five days. This was extended to Hong Kong in June 1845 by the *Lady Mary Wood*, a steamer of 553 tons. Shortly after, a regular service between Southampton and Hong Kong was begun on a fifty-four day schedule, making use of the overland route. The service was operated by using two or more vessels in three sections: Hong Kong to Ceylon, Ceylon to Suez, Alexandria to Southampton. A gentleman's berth in the general cabin, including food, cost £185. The steamship service was not sufficiently frequent to render sailing ships obsolete and the latter remained numerous on the run to England until the opening of the Suez Canal in 1869. The

arrival of the P. & O. steamers on the China coast fore-
shadowed the end of the almost complete dominance
which Jardine's and Dent's had established over the coastal
trade. In the 1840s the only rival of any substance was the
American firm of Russell and Co. whose Yankee clippers
enabled it to maintain a share of about 10 per cent of the
opium trade. However in 1850 the *Lady Mary Wood*
inaugurated a steamer service between Hong Kong and
Shanghai. The P. & O. never became directly involved in
the sale of opium but the smaller agencies now began to use
its steamers to transport both opium and legitimate goods.

The 1840s and 1850s were prosperous years for the
opium traders but legitimate trade grew only very slowly.
The merchants had believed that the abolition of the Co-
Hong system would lead to a great increase in the demand
for foreign imports. Alexander Matheson had headed a
committee of merchants which made recommendations
about the proposed new tariff system and the details were
actually worked out by Robert Thom, formerly one of
Jardine's agents, and later, as we have seen, British Consul
at Ningpo. The tariff rate was low by any standard and the
special fees and perquisites that had comprised a major
part of the system of 'squeeze' were swept away. However
'free trade' had not been imposed upon China since the
British could not prevent the taxation of goods once they
had left the treaty ports. Basically there was little demand
in China for foreign goods. The merchants persisted in
believing that there was. Some blamed the opium trade for
absorbing too much cash, others blamed the treaty port
system. Both came to believe that only further modifications of the system established after the First Anglo-
Chinese War would increase legitimate trade. Their views
were expressed by the *Shanghai Recorder*, a journal
founded and financed by Jardine's, which persistently
urged the abolition of all tariffs and the removal of the
remaining trade restrictions.

In 1851 Chinese imports consisted of £6 million worth of

opium, £11½ million worth of British manufactures, and £1½ million worth of other goods, principally from India. Although imports of legitimate goods increased very slowly, exports of Chinese goods like tea and silk were rising. There were about two hundred-odd foreign firms in Hong Kong and the treaty ports at this time, of which about half were British and a quarter Indian or Parsee. Many were small concerns, such as ships' chandlers, architects, and doctors, who served the needs of the expatriate community. Legitimate trade was dominated by the big hongs which were divided into departments dealing with tea, silk, piece goods, shipping, insurance, and miscellaneous Chinese goods, known as 'muck and truck'. There were, of course, many newly established agencies whose partners had been lured to the China coast with hopes of emulating the example of William Jardine and James Matheson. Modest fortunes had been made even by assistants in the agencies. Temple Hilliard Layton had joined the East India Company in 1832 as a tea-taster or 'expectorator'. He was paid a salary of £500 a year, provided with accommodation in Canton and Macau and given an allowance of £10 a month and a seat at the Company's table. After 1834 he remained in the Company's Canton agency, his salary rising to £2400 a year. He was comfortably off when he retired in 1839, and later became vice-consul at Ningpo.

The main imports into China were raw cotton from India and cotton and woollen goods from Britain. They were sent out on consignment. The big hongs took a 3 per cent commission and bartered them for tea or silk if they were unable to sell them. British manufacturers began to view the Chinese market as very much of a gamble and it was disconcerting not to know whether to expect a shipment of tea or a bill drawn on Matheson and Co., London, in return for their goods. After the trade slump of 1846–7, they became increasingly unwilling to send goods in consignment.

Influential officials in Britain were already inclining to

the view that the prospects for legitimate trade with China
were not very good and that to support the demands of the
merchants would only lead to expensive, unnecessary, and
unproductive disputes with the Chinese authorities. Some
officials viewed the legitimate traders with as much dis-
favour and suspicion as they did the opium traders. Louis
Mallet, under-secretary at the Board of Trade, wrote in
1862,

> The class of Britons who press into this new and untrodden
> field of enterprise is mainly composed of unscrupulous and reck-
> less adventurers who seek nothing but enormous profits on partic-
> ular transactions and care little for the permanent interests of
> commerce—still less for the principles of truth and justice. These
> men always cloak their injustices under the guise of patriotism
> and civilization. . . .[4]

The principal partners in Jardine and Matheson in the
period between the two Anglo-Chinese wars were Alexander Matheson and four Jardine brothers, Andrew, David,
Joseph, and Robert Jardine, nephews of William Jardine.
Another nephew, Andrew Johnston, who had started his
career, like his uncle, as a ship's surgeon for the East India
Company, was a partner from 1835 to 1836, although he
had begun trading on his own account as early as 1824. He
bought a large estate at Halleaths, Dumfriesshire, and led
the life of a country gentleman until his death in 1857. He
was a great sportsman and won the Goodwood Cup in 1841
with Charles XII for which he had paid the then unheard of
sum of 3000 guineas. Andrew Jardine retired in 1843 and
he too purchased a country estate at Annandale, Lanark. In
1854 he bought another estate for his brother Joseph at
Castle Milk, Dumfriesshire. On Joseph's death in 1861 the
estate passed to his brother Robert.

Alexander Matheson remained as head of the firm until
his retirement in 1852, although he left China in 1846.
There was some friction between him and David and
Joseph Jardine when the latter wanted to make their
brother Robert a partner as well. David wrote to Andrew in

1846, 'The object he has in view is evidently to make the Matheson side of the house supreme in the control of affairs here and to attain it I believe he will attempt to assume authority and adopt every means in his power although they may be at variance with what is just.'[5] However the matter was settled amicably and when Alexander suggested on his retirement that the name Matheson should be dropped from the style of the firm, David Jardine refused saying 'that so long as I am connected with it, it would be with great regret and remonstrance that I consented'.

Shortly after Alexander's return from China, the City of London was swept by a great economic crisis and many reputable firms went bankrupt. Jardine's London agency, Magniac Jardine and Co. was threatened but Alexander and Andrew Jardine between them met its liabilities. The firm was then wound up in 1847 and a new agency, Matheson and Co., was started on the same premises with Alexander Matheson, Andrew Jardine, Hugh Matheson, and William Fraser as partners. Alexander wrote confidently that it 'ought to be the strongest financial house in London'.

In 1851 Alexander bought extensive estates in Ross-shire at a cost of £773,000. He represented Inverness Burghs from 1847 to 1868 and then succeeded to Sir James Matheson's seat, the county of Ross, holding it until 1884. He was made a baronet in 1882. In the last years before his death in 1886, he suffered some heavy financial losses and was forced to sell a large part of his estates but his son, Sir Kenneth Matheson, retained Lochalsh and Attadale.

---

1. Lubbock, The Opium Clippers, 340.

2. ibid., 330.

3. Fairbank, 170.

4. N. A. Pelcovits, Old China Hands and the Foreign Office, New York, 1948, 170.

5. Buchanan Jardine Letters.

# 5

# Hong Kong Affairs

THE Governor, Sir John Davis, who arrived in Hong Kong on 7 May 1844 soon made himself unpopular with the taipans. Such was the odium in which he came to be held by the horse-racing fraternity, that when he presented the Plenipotentiary Cup in 1848, not a single horse was entered in the race. Not long after his arrival, he wrote to the Colonial Office that 'it is a much easier task to govern twenty thousand Chinese inhabitants of this colony, than the few thousands of English'. Part of the trouble was the obvious disdain which the haughty and scholarly Governor had for the philistinic fortune-seeking merchants. Davis had long experience of China. In 1813 at the age of eighteen he had been appointed to the East India Company factory in Canton. Unlike most other foreigners in Canton he quickly developed a great interest in the Chinese language and within two years had published the first of many translations of Chinese literary works. He was also an able official and was to be the last chairman of the Select Committee. When this post was abolished, he accepted the position of Second Superintendent of Trade under Lord Napier and succeeded the latter as Chief Superintendent after his death in 1834. However he resigned after a few months, later giving as one of his reasons that he had too little power to control 'the ill-conduct of British subjects in China'. He undoubtedly disliked both the new free trade regime and the 'unscrupulous and reckless adventurers' which it attracted to Canton.

His brief as Governor was to increase revenue, since the Colonial Office adhered to the principle that colonial governments should as far as possible be self-supporting. Hitherto no one in the colony had paid any taxes, nor were they inclined to do so. The merchants argued that the colony was principally a naval and military station to control and defend trade with China. Since this trade benefited the home country, it was proper that it should contribute towards the cost of the colony's administration. Davis could not raise revenue from customs duties because Hong Kong had been declared a free port. He anticipated that the major source of revenue would be land rents and commenced their collection, at the same time ruling that the leases already granted would be for seventy-five years only, although the merchants claimed that Elliot had promised perpetuity of tenure. Monopolies for the sale of opium and salt and the quarrying of stone were created and each market was made a monopoly and was let. Pawnbrokers, auctioneers, billiard table proprietors, and those selling wines and spirits were required to have a licence. A property tax was introduced in 1845 to pay for the cost of a police force, but such was the storm of protest that Davis was obliged to reduce the assessments by 40 per cent. He also failed earlier to get the Legislative Council to agree to a tax on wines and spirits although the Governor pointed out that this was the only tax which the wealthier merchants would have had to pay. Revenue rose from £22,242 in 1845 to £31,078 in 1847 but there was still a deficit of £31,000 in that year which the home government had to make good. A Colonial Office official commented that 'This promises to be a very expensive colony'.

Davis further offended the susceptibilities of the merchants in his attempt to impose some law and order on the colony. Pottinger had suggested that a system of registration would be a check on Chinese criminal elements and Davis now proposed to implement his proposal, but to make it more acceptable to the Chinese, extended it to cover all residents, both European and Chinese. The former were to pay five dollars annual registration fee and the latter one dollar. There were angry protests from both communities. The European merchants sent in a memorial which was so disrespectfully worded that the Governor refused to accept it. Two amended versions were also rejected. The Chinese closed their shops and threatened to leave the colony. Davis complained about 'ill-conducted opposition' but was obliged to give way. The registration ordinance was modified so that it only applied to those who could not produce $500, mainly Chinese, and the registration fee was cancelled.

The incensed merchants sent a memorial to the home government in 1845 which ranged over a wide field of grievances. They complained that the rates ordinance was illegal and that, having been encouraged to move to Hong Kong from Macau with the promise that they could have perpetuity of tenure, seventy-five-year leases had now been imposed on their land purchases. Furthermore the colonial government had 'aggravated the evils' since every type of trade and commerce was 'a subject of taxation, a source of revenue or of monopoly'. They argued that since the colony of Hong Kong, which was 'never really required by the British merchants', was designed to serve the treaty ports, the British residents in those ports should contribute towards the cost of the administration. Finally they demanded a municipal body 'with power to decide on the appropriation of monies raised'. W. E. Gladstone, then Secretary of State, rejected the memorial and, as a mark of the government's confidence in him, Davis was created a baronet. However the intemperate ire of the merchants was partly caused by the failure of trade with China to expand after the ending of the Co-Hong system. The merchants had influential supporters in Parliament, headed by James Matheson and shortly to include Alexander Matheson. This pressure group succeeded in getting Parliament to set up a Select Committee on trade with China in 1847 which was to vindicate the merchants' views in a number of ways.

Meanwhile Davis's tenure of office was cut short by an unsavoury and notorious dispute with the Chief Justice, J. W. Hulme, which helped to establish the view expressed by The Times in 1859 that 'Hong Kong is always connected with some fatal pestilence, some doubtful war or some discreditable internal squabble'. Hulme was a bibulous, convivial man who had been chiefly attracted to Hong Kong by an annual salary of £3000, a princely sum in those days. Ill-feeling between the two officials had begun on the voyage out to Hong Kong. They had travelled together to Bombay where, much to his annoyance, the judge and his numerous family were left to find their own passage because there was insufficient accommodation aboard the warship which was sent to bring the party to the colony.

The ill-feeling evolved into an open dispute when the Governor objected to Hulme awarding himself a six-month vacation when drawing up the rules for the Supreme Court. Davis referred the matter to the Legislative Council and there the matter became personal with Davis refusing to address Hulme as 'Your Lordship' and Hulme denying the title of 'Your Excellency' to the Governor. Another issue soon arose. A merchant in Canton called Compton started a riot there by assaulting a Chinese hawker and was fined £100 by the consular court. Compton appealed to the Hong Kong Supreme Court where Hulme quashed the sentence and passed strictures on irregularities in the consular proceedings. Davis was furious. A matter of principle was at stake, as the Governor felt that the British merchants in China could not be controlled if strong administrative action could not be taken, free from judicial interference. He complained to London that, as long as Hulme was at his post, the British in Canton would feel 'they can shoot the Chinese with impunity'.

When Hulme defied the Legislative Council over the matter of his vacation, Davis officially requested his dismissal, at the same time sending a personal letter to Lord Palmerston alleging that Hulme was a habitual drunkard. The result was not to the Governor's liking. The Secretary of State, Earl Grey, refused to agree to Hulme's dismissal and criticized the Governor's treatment of him. Palmerston had passed the personal letter to Grey who treated it as an official communication and insisted that a public inquiry into the charge should be held. Davis tried desperately to avoid an inquiry but, when Grey remained adamant, he resigned. Nonetheless he was obliged to preside over the inquiry held before the Executive Council. Hulme was accused of specific instances of drunkenness and, in spite of his defence that his unsteady gait in public was caused by varicose veins, was found guilty on one charge and was dismissed. The Chief Justice was much more to the taste of the merchants than the cultured and disdainful Governor and they took the opportunity offered by Hulme's departure to display their feelings. He was showered with testimonials and left amidst exploding firecrackers and much rather inappropriate drinking of champagne. In contrast, when Davis left a few months later, in March 1848, not a speech or banquet marked his departure. A local newspaper, *The Friend of China*, commented scathingly, 'Never surely, in the Heavens above, or in the earth beneath, did there ever exist, embodied or disembodied, such a pleasant little gentleman as Sir John Davis.' Hulme subsequently had his appeal upheld and returned to Hong Kong vindicated, to the great satisfaction of the colony's expatriate community.

Davis was succeeded as Governor by Sir Samuel George Bonham, a youngish man, still in his forties, affable and tactful. His father had been the Captain of an East Indiaman and he himself had joined the East India Company, obtaining a post at the Company's factory in Sumatra in 1827. Three years later he became assistant to the Resident at Singapore and in 1837 became Governor of the Straits Settlements. Ten years of successful administration in this post made him the obvious choice for the Governorship of Hong Kong. Lord Palmerston had resolved to avoid the friction with the merchants and the disputes between officials that had characterized Davis's troubled period of office. The report of the 1847 Select Committee, in which Alexander Matheson played an important part, had largely upheld the merchants' view and its recommendations were to form the basis of the home government's policy towards Hong Kong for the next few years. Palmerston chose Bonham principally for his 'practical common sense' and because it was believed that he had the right personality to establish a rapport with the taipans. After Davis, anyone was sure of a welcome from the merchants and Bonham was greeted on his arrival by cheering crowds. He was able to capitalize on this goodwill and, over the six years of his term of office, established an easy relationship with Hong Kong's commercial aristocracy. Eitel, in his *The History of Hong Kong*, published in 1895, wrote, 'From the very commencement of this administration, Hong Kong society began to take its tone from, and was henceforth held together by, the spirit that prevailed at Government House.' To put it another way, Hong Kong for the first time had a governor who was prepared to devote himself to the interests of the merchants. Not surprisingly, after his departure, he was hailed as a 'model governor'.

The Select Committee recommended that a share of the government of the colony should be given to British residents and that some form of municipal government be set up to deal with local affairs. It criticized the 'system of monopolies and farms and petty regulations' and agreed with the merchants' contention that the cost of maintaining the colony should not be thrown entirely on the residents, at the same time arguing that the colonial admin-

istration should cut its expenditure. Bonham faithfully set
out to implement these proposals. He began the practice of
consulting informally the fifteen leading merchants who
made up the bench of local justices and of publishing
ordinances in draft so that the local community could
make representations on them before they became law. In
1849 he proposed that the two unofficial members should
in future represent the community on the Legislative Council and invited the Justices of the Peace to elect two of their
own number. The justices nominated David Jardine and
another merchant, J. F. Edger. David Jardine remained on
the Legislative Council until his retirement from China in
1856, after which he was succeeded by his brother Joseph.
It would seem that David found attendance at the Legislative Council an unwelcome distraction from business
affairs for Sir John Bowring, who became Governor in
1855, wrote that he attended only infrequently and indeed
'had ceased to attend because his time was too valuable to
waste on trivialities'. The proposal to create a municipal
council foundered when Bonham made it clear that self-
government would have to be self-financed. The merchants, in any case, had been satisfied by having representatives on the Legislative Council; there was always the risk
that they might not be able to control a municipal council.

The home government had decided to make a flat annual
payment to Hong Kong of £25,000. Bonham, rather than
take the unpopular step of increasing revenue by creating
additional taxation, drastically pruned expenditure, on
one occasion balancing his budget by delaying payment of
his own salary until the following year. He reduced the
estimates for 1849 to £39,000 from actual expenditure in
1848 of £62,000. Fortunately revenue was increasing without any new taxation and this enabled the parliamentary
grant to be reduced. In 1855, for the first time, Hong Kong
became self-supporting, except for military expenditure.
Naturally, since retrenchment was the theme there were no
great projects during Bonham's administration, but the

merchants were not dissatisfied provided that taxation remained low.

The new Governor, Bowring, was to prevail over the Chinese Empire but he suffered a notable defeat at the hands of the taipans. The Governor's enthusiastic plans for liberal reforms in Hong Kong antagonized the conservative merchants, and indeed it was true that his schemes were very numerous and were proposed in a precipitate fashion. Even Russell, the Colonial Secretary, felt obliged to note that Bowring 'was rather wild on all subjects'. One of his key proposals, which constitutional reformers in Hong Kong are still vainly proposing, was that the Legislative Council should have some elected members. He wanted to make the Legislative Council the agent of his reforms and therefore wished it to be more representative. He complained to the Colonial Office that under Bonham it had become a nullity since the Governor had not consulted it on financial matters and David Jardine, 'the only non-office holder of weight', had ceased to attend. The merchants some years earlier had sought more say in the colonial government but they did not like Bowring's suggestion that the Chinese and the Europeans should have the vote on the same terms. Nor did Labouchère, the Secretary of State, who minuted Bowring's proposal 'I have no wish to try the experiment'. Labouchère noted that 'great commercial interests and the future progress of civilization throughout the East are to a great extent involved in the maintenance of British rule and of orderly government in Hong Kong', sentiments with which the merchants heartily agreed. The proposed elections were dropped, but Bowring did add two more officials and one unofficial to the existing three officials and two unofficials. Later in 1858 and 1859 two more officials were added, to the annoyance of the unofficials who wanted their own numbers proportionately increased. The unofficials continued to be chosen by the bench of justices of the peace.

In 1858 Bowring submitted to the Legislative Council an

ordinance to give the government compulsory powers to repurchase marine lots in Central District. The Governor wished to construct a road, or praya, along the whole sea front of Victoria. The first marine lots all fronted onto Queen's Road and each lot holder had been left to build piers or make other improvements seawards as he chose. Many holders had doubled the size of their lots by unofficial reclamation and were most unwilling to make way for the sea road. Moreover Bowring proposed that the lot holders should contribute towards the cost of the sea wall and piers and should pay additional rent on any reclaimed land which they were allowed to retain. The merchants, led by John Dent, whose company had extensive property holdings in Central, adamantly opposed the scheme and therefore Bowring decided to seek compulsory powers. To his dismay the Legislative Council rejected his ordinance, three of the officials joining the unofficials in opposition. One of the unofficials was Joseph Jardine who had taken over from his brother David in 1856. The praya scheme was shelved indefinitely. The rule had not yet been established that the officials should vote collectively on government legislation so Bowring did not complain against the officials' action on constitutional grounds. He did, however, think that the taipans might have brought pressure to bear on the officials, some of whom earned private fees from the hongs. The Governor's humiliating defeat was also undoubtedly partly a result of the general unpopularity of his schemes.

# 6

# Hong Kong Business and Social Life

ALTHOUGH business was dominated in the 1840s and 1850s by the big hongs, some other merchants did succeed in establishing the basis of substantial enterprises. Some, like W. R. Adamson, followed the well-established pattern of building up an import-export business. Adamson had been sent to China in 1852 by a group of Cheshire silk weavers who wished to find new sources of silk. Adamson branched out into the export of tea and the import of general merchandise. Later his company was joined by G. B. Dodwell who took advantage of the newly developed steamship routes to expand into the freight business to America. He organized the first regular steamship route across the Pacific in 1887. Dodwell, an impressively bearded man of high principles, sang for many years in the choir of St John's Cathedral. The company was reorganized as Dodwell, Carlill and Co. in 1891. A. J. H. Carlill, a former tea-taster, sold his shares to the staff on his retirement.

Less typical was Douglas Lapraik who arrived in the East in 1843, then a young man of twenty-two with little means. In 1845 he was listed as an apprentice to a watchmaker in Hong Kong and in the following year set up his own business. Presumably Lapraik repaired and possibly made ships' chronometers and in this way became involved with sea captains whose property he managed in their absence.

He acquired a shipbuilding yard off Queen's Road, a little to the west of Pedder Street, which he later built on and leased to Lane Crawford in 1859. He was also one of the merchants who bought and fitted out a Chinese junk, the Keying, which left for Britain via the Cape in December 1846. Diverted to the United States by storms, the Keying was a great success in New York where it was said to have been visited by 8000 people a day. After crossing the Atlantic, the Keying tied up at Blackwall where it was visited, amongst many others, by Charles Dickens and by the ageing Austrian Chancellor, Metternich, who had recently been forced to flee from Vienna by revolution, in the company of the Duke of Wellington. The Keying was finally broken up and her timbers used to construct ferry boats on the Mersey. Lapraik claimed in later life that he never made a penny from this venture.

About 1857, together with Captain J. Lamont, Lapraik established Hong Kong's first dry dock at Aberdeen. In 1865 this dock and the nearby Hope Dock were merged with the Hong Kong and Whampoa Dock Co., which had been established in 1863 with Lapraik as secretary and Thomas Sutherland, agent for P. & O., as chairman. This company already owned docks at Whampoa which had been established by John Couper, originally a carpenter with P. & O. During the Second Anglo-Chinese War the docks at Whampoa were damaged and Couper himself was kidnapped and his fate was never known. Couper's son was given $120,000 compensation and he sold his interests to the Hong Kong and Whampoa Dock Co. for $175,000. In 1866 the Company was registered under the Companies Ordinance with a share capital of $750,000 and with James Whittall, a partner in Jardine's, as chairman. About 1860 Lapraik had acquired a steamship which was employed on the coastal trade between Canton, Hong Kong, Swatow, and Amoy. This venture was successful and Lapraik expanded his fleet. At the time of his death in 1869, the fleet totalled seven ships. It was incorporated as the Douglas

Steamship Co. in 1883 by his nephew, John Stewart Lapraik. Another of Lapraik's interests was the Hong Kong Hotel Company which was formed in 1866. Lapraik built for himself a splendid Gothic folly, Douglas Castle, in the countryside at Pokfulam and set an example of civic duty by donating a clock in a tower built at the junction of Pedder Street and Queen's Road in 1865, which in later years became a major traffic obstacle. Lapraik apparently cohabited with a Chinese woman for he drew up a trust deed in her favour. He retired from Hong Kong in 1866, married a lady from the Isle of Wight the following year and died shortly after at the early age of fifty-two.

Two other men who rose from relatively lowly origins to achieve some success were Thomas Lane and Ninian Crawford. The Lane family's connections with the China coast began with Edward Lane who was a butler for the East India Company at Canton. When the colony of Hong Kong was established, another Lane, William, opened a ships' chandlers in Queen's Road and in 1842 bought Lap Tat's Tavern nearby which he renamed the Victoria Hotel. For a time he returned to Canton but in the 1850s began again to operate his hotel, now named the Commercial Hotel. William was one of the partners in the *Keying*. Thomas Lane, who had been employed as a government clerk in 1843 and later became an auctioneer and a shopkeeper, was on the *Keying* between 1846 and 1849. In 1850 he opened a ships' chandlers in Queen's Road with Ninian Crawford, who had earlier been a clerk in a shop, and for a short time was secretary of the Hong Kong Club. William Lane became a partner in 1860 and other members of the Crawford family joined the firm later. In 1859 the store moved to the other side of Queen's Road to the building leased by Lapraik, which was bought from him by Lane Crawford in 1863. Biscuits were an important item in the chandlering business and Lane Crawford took over the Wanchai Steam Bakery and renamed it the Hong Kong and China Bakery. By this time the ships' chandlers was evolving into a department store and subsequently opened branches in Yokohama and Shanghai.

The Lanes and the Crawfords were examples of men from the lower ranks of society with little training or wealth and few influential connections who had gone overseas to make a better living. With determination, energy, and luck, they succeeded, although in the stratified society of Hong Kong they would not have much social contact with the taipans of the big hongs. Another such man was George Duddell who made a living principally by somewhat dubious land speculation and equally shady auctioneering. In 1845 he bought the opium monopoly for one year for $8520 and did well out of it, being paid $1710 a month by a Chinese syndicate for the privilege of operating it. Later he became friendly with Holdforth, Assistant Magistrate and Sheriff, and, reputedly for a price, got from him the right to conduct 'Sheriff's Sales'. Holdforth and Duddell worked together at these sales with Duddell knocking down cheap lots to himself or to Holdforth acting for him. This came to light in 1850 when Duddell knocked down a ship to himself. There were protests and the Chief Justice ordered a re-auction at which the ship fetched $400 more than at the previous occasion. In spite of the flexibility of his ethics, Duddell succeeded in becoming Government Auctioneer in 1857. He also had property interests in Central but was hard hit by the slump of the late 1840s and was obliged to surrender some of his lots. Nonetheless in 1849 he was still listed as the third largest landholder in the colony. Four of his twenty-five lots were said to have been bought by him from the impecunious Auditor-General Shelley at an auction for £1. When Duddell had the gall to apply for a reduction in land rent on these lots, his application was not sympathetically received. With the improvement in business and consequently of land values in the 1850s, Duddell became a man of some substance. He established a bakery in 1857 and signed a contract to supply the armed forces. However his bakery burnt down and he was unsuccessful in his application to the government for compensation. He made his last appearance before the public eye in 1870 when the government bought some land from him to build a hospital. Duddell protested against the scheme, apparently with the aim of securing higher compensation, but, when the government thereupon abandoned the idea of building the hospital, Duddell successfully insisted that it went through with the land purchase. Duddell's land was then added to the Botanical Gardens so that in the words of one historian, he was at least 'an inadvertent benefactor' of the colony. Not long after this he retired to spend his declining years in Brighton.

It was not only Europeans who made money in the developing colony. In 1844 the Colonial Treasurer had written that there was 'not one respectable Chinese inhabitant on the island ... there is, in fact a continual shifting of a Bedouin sort of population, whose migratory, predatory, gambling and dissolute habits utterly unfit them for continuous industry ...'. However by the 1850s the Chinese community was beginning to develop leaders—successful contractors, compradores, and merchants, some civil servants, and Chinese Christians attached to missionary groups.

Typical of this emerging Chinese middle class was the Li family. The founder of its fortunes was Li Sing who came to Hong Kong in 1854 with his brother Li Leong. At first they operated a money-changing business and in 1857 bought a lot in Central and established a trading company there. The interests of the firm were varied and included the purchase of real estate, acting as brokers for interests abroad, seeking coolie labourers, and involvement in gambling and opium monopolies. During the Second Anglo-Chinese War they acted as contractors to the British forces. By the time Li Leong died in 1864, numerous other members of the family had established themselves in Hong Kong. His property was left to a family trust and was later divided into five shares. Li Sing now became head of the family and was one of the most prominent members of the Chinese community until his death in 1900.

Other Chinese became rich by acting as compradores. One example was Kwok Acheong whose family were boat people. He was a provisions contractor to the British forces during the First Anglo-Chinese War and became compradore for the P. & O. Company after they established a branch office in Hong Kong in 1845. When P. & O. disposed of its shipbuilding and engineering department there in 1854, it was bought by Kwok who went on to acquire a fleet of steamships, a bakery, and a trading company. By 1876 he was the third largest ratepayer in Hong Kong and the first among the Chinese. On his death in 1880 an English language newspaper stated that 'he agreed well with and was much respected by foreigners with whom he had constant intercourse and large transactions'. In 1881 the largest Chinese ratepayers were the compradore family established by Ng Acheong who acted for Lapraik. On his death in 1873 Ng Acheong left $260,000.

The foreign merchants of Hong Kong and the treaty ports formed a small and intimate community in these early years. Separated by several months from Europe and America and acutely conscious of their position on the fringe of a teeming and hostile empire, they relied very much on their own resources. A distinctive 'treaty port culture' evolved, assisted by the fact that partners and assistants, as well as consular officials and missionaries, were transferred periodically from port to port. Anchorage, bund, club, church, cemetery, and race-course, a somewhat Mediterranean type of arcaded architecture, derived from Macau, the prevalence of vitriolic personal feuds, a cynical attitude to China and all her works, and a desire at all costs to get rich quick were elements common to all the treaty ports. Newcomers found it difficult to adapt to the humid climate and the other discomforts of life on the China coast. Shortly after his arrival in Hong Kong, Vice-

Consul Henry Sirr was fined $10 for assaulting his land-
lord. He complained that his boarding house was as expensive as a first-class hotel in London and that rain
poured in constantly through the windows.

Initially the hongs maintained the Canton tradition of
collegiate establishments and baronial hospitality. The
Revd James Legge, speaking of his arrival in Hong Kong in
1843, recalled that Gibb, Livingston and Co.'s premises
were 'enclosed within a ring fence . . . where partners and
employees all managed to reside'. This firm had been
founded in Canton in 1836 by two Scotsmen, Thomas Gibb
and William Livingston, who had originally come out with
the East India Company. In common with other foreign
concerns, Gibb, Livingston had its own factory in Canton.
After the exodus to Macau, they had opened an office in
Queen's Road, Hong Kong, in 1841, dealing mainly in the
export of tea and the import of textiles.

However the partners in the larger hongs, like Jardine's,
built themselves houses separate from their business
premises although their assistants still lived together in
messes. Robert Jardine wrote in 1849 that 'the clerks live
over the office and fine rooms they have'. The 'spirit of
exclusiveness' was to become a marked feature of life in
Hong Kong and a correspondent, quoted in the China Mail
in 1876, complained about 'the stiff and pompous government official who is scarcely on speaking terms with any-
body in trade . . . the wealthy merchant who is equally far
removed from his clerks' and the clerks themselves among
whom 'the distinctions real and imaginary are most
absurd. They divide themselves in Seniors and Juniors
and, apart from business, maintain a wide distance
between each other.'

In contrast the life of expatriates in Shanghai retained
much more of the free and easy good fellowship that characterized the early days in Canton. This may have been
because Hong Kong was a Crown Colony with a Governor
and his Lady. Attendance at Government House functions

was an important part of the social ritual in Hong Kong. The hierarchy of government officials and leading taipans created a miniature replica of social life in Britain, the struggle for status being much intensified by the smallness of the expatriate community. The sense of being an isolated island of Western civilization in a vast alien sea was another factor which helped to create the feud-ridden, snobbish social atmosphere that flourished in Hong Kong. Sociologists would maintain that gossip and scandal in these circumstances were the means whereby the European community helped to create and perpetuate its own distinct way of life. Gluckman's Law states that 'the more exclusive a social group is, the more its members indulge in gossip and scandal about one another'. All Europeans in Hong Kong formed an exclusive group but, at the same time, those on the higher rungs of the ladder wished to emphasize that they had no other connection with those beneath them. The taipans despised the clerks and shop-keepers who, in turn, despised the seamen and soldiers. In Canton nearly all the resident Europeans had been at least potential 'officers' but the camaraderie of the officers' mess evaporated because the garrison had been joined by N.C.O.s and privates. As self-made men, the taipans had to demonstrate their officer status by a rigid insistence on their exclusive position within their own small community.

The tendency for the taipans to keep themselves aloof was increased by the establishment in 1846 of the Hong Kong Club from which shopkeepers, Chinese, Indians, women, and other undesirables were rigidly excluded. Admission to the Club was the touchstone of social acceptability. Alfred Weatherhead, a government officer in Hong Kong in the 1850s, wrote somewhat scathingly of it as 'the paradise of the select and temple of colonial gentility' where 'they rejoice greatly in billiards, which game appears to contain the secret of endless amusement, to judge from the unremitting devotion there to displayed by the youthful members of the club'. Albert Smith, who visited Hong Kong in 1858, recorded similar views in his book *To China and Back*.

> The young men in the ... large Houses have a sad, mind-mouldering time of it. Tea-tasting, considered as an occupation, does not call for any great employment of the intellect, and I never saw one of the young clerks with a book in his hand. They loaf about the balconies of their houses, or lie in long bamboo chairs, smoke a great deal, play billiards at the Club, where the click of the ball never ceased from the earliest morning, and glance over the local papers. These journals are mostly filled with the most uninteresting, incomprehensible and infinitesimally unimportant local squabbles. ... [1]

Weatherhead concluded glumly that the principal reason why people remained in such a place was 'the powerful, all-absorbing love of gain', added to which 'life in an Eastern clime has probably engendered habits of indolence, indulgence and exercise of authority' which leave the expatriate unfitted for life in his home country.

The exchange of gossip, 'gup' in local parlance, and the click of billiard balls was stilled for a few minutes one day in 1877 by what might be seen as an individual demonstration of the resentment felt by the lower orders of Europeans against their rich countrymen. A 'mad drunk' army sergeant stormed into the Club with a drawn sword and hacked at several gas lamps and chandeliers. The magistrate, Mr Russell, in his summing up said that the sergeant 'presented his sword to the breasts of two gentlemen and addressed them "you are one of them". Now had it not been for their prompt answers, he might have murdered them.' Sergeant Shannon was ordered to pay $30 amends and was sentenced to three months' imprisonment.

The British merchants, unlike the Dutch and Portuguese traders, were unwilling to adapt their working habits to suit climatic conditions in the East, and they worked the same hours and dressed in the same way as their counterparts in the City of London. Tight-fitting trousers, waistcoats, jackets, and top-hats were *de rigueur* during business hours, although the merchants might relax in Chinese silk pyjamas in the evening. The day began with breakfast, which usually consisted of fish, rice, and fruit washed down with several glasses of claret. After a morning's work, the merchants took an hour off at 1 p.m. for tiffin, a light meal, perhaps eggs or curry, with a glass or two of beer. Work continued between 2 p.m. and 5.30 p.m., later on the days when a mail ship arrived. At 7.30 p.m. taipans and griffins gathered for the main meal of the day which by all accounts was of a very substantial nature and was accompanied by the consumption of large quantities of claret, champagne, and port. Smith noted, 'At 7.30 p.m. to dine with Mr John Dent, whose French cook sent up one of the best dinners I ever sat down to, in London or Paris.'

It was fortunate for the state of their health that the British merchants took with them their love of sport. Indeed, if anything, the cult of sport flourished more vigorously among the British in the East than in the more suitable climate of home. Exercise was considered essential to health and a brisk two-mile walk before breakfast was a universal habit. When the *taotai* at Ningpo tried to restrict closely the areas to which foreigners could go, Consul Thom pointed out that 'All Englishmen from the time of infancy to old age are accustomed to take active exercise without a single exception' and insisted that foreigners should be given access to an area of three miles beyond Ningpo.

One of the principal diversions at Canton in the old days had been rowing and the Canton Regatta Club had been formed in 1837. On one occasion the members rowed the ninety-three miles to Hong Kong. The Club continued and in 1849 John Dent, Chairman of the Club, complained in his report 'against the egress of pullers and others who go out of an evening to enjoy the breeze in the passage' and got in the way of more serious sportsmen. Other Club members tried to get the authorities to remove the Flower Boats

which impeded their sport and also caused other inconveniences since 'the servants spend whole nights there drinking and whoring'. Some of the merchants who moved to
Hong Kong established the Victoria Recreation Club in
1849. Its first rowing shed was on the waterfront at Queen's
Road Central but it later moved to the best beach in Hong
Kong at Causeway Bay where a bathing shed was created.
Some years after, the shed was damaged in a typhoon and
for a time the members had to use a moored boat. When a
leader in the *China Mail* drew attention to the long delay in
replacing the shed, the Governor, Sir Arthur Kennedy, who
was also President of the Club, offered to make the first
contribution towards a fund to build a new shed. The
Victoria Regatta Club was less exclusive than the Hong
Kong Club, for the records show that Indians were admitted as members at an early date.

Since Hong Kong was a place where feuds and factions
flourished, it was not surprising that a group of oarsmen
broke away from the Victoria Club in the 1850s and formed
the Hong Kong Boat Club whose flag was that of the
Victoria Club in reverse colours. It had a matshed at North
Point which was later replaced by a brick rowing shed,
clubhouse, and gym. About 1869 this became the headquarters of the Corinthian Sailing Club which in 1893
moved to Kellet's Island and was reconstituted as the Royal
Hong Kong Yacht Club. Newspapers of the 1870s show that
yacht races, including one for the oddly named 'Shop-
keepers Cup', were regular week-end events although
generally there were not more than half a dozen yachts
participating.

Cricket was another sport which was established on the
China coast in the pre-treaty port days. Early in the nineteenth century Macau had a race-track and cricket ground
adjacent to the Portas do Cerceo. When Happy Valley was
drained in 1846 a cricket ground as well as a race-track was
laid out. The ground was inconveniently distant from the
business area at Central but there was no centrally situated

flat land available. However the army decided that it needed a parade ground near the Victoria Barracks and accordingly levelled a small hill and dumped the soil in the sea. In 1851, when the Hong Kong Cricket Club was formed 'to partake in the lively recreation of cricket', it was granted the seaward portion of the parade ground. One of the stated aims of the Club was to draw members from all levels of expatriate society and when a 'new fangled system of ballot' was introduced the *China Mail* complained that its intention was to keep the cricketers 'somewhat select'. In its early years the Club organized matches among its own members and against service units and, after 1866, against overseas teams, principally from Shanghai and the Straits Settlements. In the match in 1866 against Shanghai, Hong Kong notched up the very respectable score of 430, probably the highest score to be recorded outside England by that date. The total included 43 wides, indicating perhaps that Shanghai bowlers were suffering from the effects of either the sea voyage or an exceptionally heavy dinner.

The taipans, whose origins were chiefly from the ranks of tenant farmers and the lesser squirearchy and whose ultimate aspirations were to retire as country gentlemen, naturally took a keen interest in hunting and horse-racing. The former sport was a frequent cause of trouble with the Chinese authorities as shooting parties sometimes ventured into Chinese territory. In 1843 an American, in search of sport in the countryside near Shanghai, accidentally shot two Chinese boys who were behind a hedge. When the Chinese authorities complained, the British consul, Balfour, took the boys to the consulate and had them treated there. The merchants, feeling that the American, apparently a seaman, had let the side down, clubbed together to give them a purse. Balfour insisted that in future hunters should obtain a consular permit and go with a police escort. Even in those days the anti-blood sport fraternity were active. A report in the *China Mail* that some woodcock had been shot on Hong Kong island prompted a correspondent, using the pseudonym 'Birdett-Coutts',[2] to express the hope that sportsmen 'would allow woodcocks in future to increase in our little island where there is surely room for man and bird'. 'Full Cock' retorted the following day that woodcock were not resident in Hong Kong and that the ones which had been shot must have been migratory. Phineas Ryrie once released some rabbits brought from England on Stonecutters' Island in an attempt to provide some more sport in the Colony.

Horse-racing was well established in Macau and the annual races continued there at least until 1845. The problem in Hong Kong was the lack of flat land and it was not until Happy Valley was drained that there was sufficient land available for a race-track. Happy Valley was first seen as a building site but fever drove the early settlers there away. Snipe shooting continued around a pool in the centre of the course for many years. The first recorded meeting was on 17 and 18 December 1846 and thereafter there was one meeting annually, usually coinciding with Chinese New Year. The letters of William Jardine and his nephews are full of references to horses and horse-racing, both on the China coast and in Dumfriesshire. There were extensive stables in the Jardine premises at East Point and so it was only to be expected that the Jardines participated in the first race meeting. David Jardine wrote to his sister Rachel in 1849, 'We have a nice Race Course here on a place called the Happy Valley, it is here that we generally ride, the place is small but is rather pretty. A good many of the ladies ride which makes it more agreeable and the scene much more lively.'[3]

The following year he injured his leg when his horse, 'Mount Trooper', ran into the railings during a race at Happy Valley. As was the custom in those days, he raced under a stable name, in his case, 'John Peel'. The interest of the Jardines in racing was long-lasting. In 1920 John Johnston wrote to Sir Robert Buchanan Jardine that his son John stood a good chance of winning the Ladies' Purse which had been won by his grandfather, Robert Jardine, in 1852. The horses came from many sources. Some were Arabs imported from England or India while others came from the Philippines and Australia. Their stamina was evidently good for on 6 February 1850 the mare 'Kathleen' won two long-distance races, repeating the feat the following day by winning two more. In the last of the series, she carried 181 lb against 105 lb carried by one of her opponents. The first ponies from Manchuria ran in the Celestial Stakes in 1856, the result of which is recorded as 'won easy—all bolted'. In the 1870s fewer horses were imported and there were many races with only two or three entrants. Consequently Chinese ponies came to dominate racing in the last two decades of the century.

Rickshaws, which were invented by an American Baptist missionary in Japan, did not appear on the streets until the late 1870s and in the earlier years, although sedan chairs were also used, many expatriates used horses or horse-drawn carriages as a means of transport. Smith wrote,

We borrowed a little Croydon basket-carriage and we drove along the Happy Valley, and passed Mr Jardine's at East Point. . . . Granite rocks coming nearly down to the sea, water-rills falling, Chinese graves and fishing stations all the way. Many people out in carriages and some Yankees in light iron four-wheeled trotting gigs; also a string of Mr Jardine's horses, led out for airing by black grooms. . . .[4]

Although Robert Jardine's remarks on Happy Valley indicate that there were some expatriate ladies in Hong Kong and the treaty ports in the early days, in Canton in 1851 there were 317 British or Anglo-Indian resident males and 13 women. The hazards of the journey from Europe to the East were still considerable—between 1850 and 1870 sixteen P. & O. ships were wrecked or disabled in storms—and the South China coast had a bad reputation for ill-health. Besides, few of the merchants contemplated spending a lifetime in the East; their object was to make a fortune and then return home to take a place in regular and respectable society. Significantly, of the five nephews of William Jardine who followed him East, only one married. As Joseph Jardine wrote to his sister, 'a long residence in the East does not certainly improve a man's chance in the matrimonial line'. It was not to be expected that young men in the prime of life would lead a life of celibacy. A glance at the police court records of the time is sufficient to show that there were numerous European prostitutes in Hong Kong, who generally took up residence in the vicinity of Hollywood Road and Lyndhurst Terrace. One aspect of local regulations is indicated by a report in which the mistress of a 'foreign brothel' was fined $100 for admitting a Chinese.

Such establishments, one imagines, were principally patronized by European seamen, soldiers, and artisans. However there were a few which catered for a better class of client. Madame Randall, an actress from Australia, probably has the distinction of setting up the first of these. Her renowned establishment in Lyndhurst Terrace had all the comforts of a middle-class Victorian home. Initially she solved the problem of making the gentlemen of the colony aware of her services by inserting the following advertisement:

HONEY
At Mrs Randall's—a small quantity of good Honey in small jars; also Gin, Brandy, Sherry, Port, Champagne, Claret, Bottled Beer, Porter etc etc
Lyndhurst Terrace,
Victoria, 12th June 1851.

Many of the merchants continued the Macau tradition of settling down with a 'pensioner'. Generally the couples did not actually set up house together but such liaisons often lasted for years and resulted in numerous offspring who were cared for by the mother with financial support from the father. Apparently girls educated in mission schools were much in demand by Europeans seeking Chinese mistresses with some knowledge of the English language who could be expected to bring up any children as Christians. A vice-consul at Ningpo was accused by the Bishop of Victoria in 1853 of having seduced a Chinese girl from Miss Aldersey's Church of England school there and of having taken her with him on his transfer to Foochow where he lodged her in a monastery. A girls' school established by the Bishop's wife in 1859 which later evolved into the Diocesian Girls' School, virtually closed down in 1867 when it was discovered by the church authorities how many of the graduating pupils became the mistresses of Europeans.

There are in Hong Kong today a number of prominent Eurasian families which originated from such liaisons. Margaret Mak Sau Ying, the first wife of Sir Robert Ho Tung, who was known as Lady Mak after he was knighted, was acknowledged as being the daughter of Hector MacLean who was with Jardine's from 1855 until his death in 1894. According to one account Sir Robert, who was born in 1862, was the son of a Belgian merchant named Bosman who later formed a London-based trading company with James Whittall, a former partner in Jardine's. Ho Tung was appointed to the position of Jardine's compradore in 1880 at the age of eighteen. Although Eurasians were not really accepted socially by the Europeans, many prospered. Boys were commonly educated at the Central Government School, later Queen's College, where instruction was in English. Their knowledge of Chinese life and customs, and most preferred to pass as Chinese, together with fluency in both Chinese and English, enabled many to do well in local business or professional circles. Ho Tung made a considerable fortune with Jardine's before he retired in 1900 on grounds of ill-health. He was a well-known philanthropist, was knighted in 1915 and came to be regarded as Hong Kong's 'Grand Old Man'.

Hong Kong and the treaty ports acquired a reputation as

unhealthy places in the first years after the Treaty of Nanking. Three of the British consuls and vice-consuls had died at their posts by 1854. Epidemics of fever visited Hong Kong each summer with a particularly severe epidemic in 1843. The death rate tended to be especially high among servicemen and between June and August of 1843 one regiment stationed at West Point lost over a hundred men. Improved drainage and the end of the first period of intensive building did lead to some improvement after 1845. A Parsee merchant, Hermusjee Rustomjee, offered to contribute $12,000 for a seamen's hospital and a management committee was set up. Rustomjee then went bankrupt but the other merchant firms, headed by Jardine's, gave subscriptions and in 1844 a hospital was opened. Later it was re-established in a new building near Morrison Hill. Joseph and Robert Jardine between them gave $20,000 towards its cost. In 1862 Robert gave a further $25,000 and agreed to maintain the hospital for three years.

The merchants, in common with most of their contemporaries, were practising Christians and no doubt the high mortality rate helped to stimulate their awareness of spiritual values. Most of them supported the Anglican faith but, due to the fact that the construction of an Anglican church was partly the concern of the colonial administration, it was several years before a permanent church was established. Services were held at first in a matshed on Murray parade ground and later in a room at the Law Courts. As was customary, the colonial government was to provide two-thirds of the cost of an Anglican church and the rest was raised by public subscription. However approval of the plans by the home government was delayed on the grounds that they were too costly. It was not until 1847 that the Governor, Sir John Davis, laid the foundation stone. Sir John's coat of arms was placed by the west entrance, much to the annoyance of most of the merchants who cordially disliked him. For many years it was possible to reserve seats and there was a considerable amount of jockeying for the most socially desirable locations.

Looking back over the years it is hard to escape the conclusion that Hong Kong in its early days was not, by and large, a happy place. The taipans and the griffins made the best of it but always with the idea in mind of retirement to England, with its cool climate and ordered society, fox-hunting and shooting parties in the winter, London in 'the season', country house week-ends, Ascot, Henley, Lords, the rustle of newspapers in the club reading room, walks down leafy lanes on crisp autumn mornings, perhaps even the applause of tenant farmers as the Returning Officer announced the results. A few realized these dreams, although even for some of these the dream was ended by premature death. For many the dream receded further into the future and shrank in dimensions to a cosy bungalow at Eastbourne and yarns around the bar at the golf club. Meanwhile there was the boredom and humidity of the East, with its alien ways and teeming masses, the nagging sense of failure, and of futile years wasted to no good purpose. Laurence Oliphant captured this disenchantment in the account of Hong Kong which he wrote in *Narrative of the Earl of Elgin's Mission to China and Japan:*

Often for days together we remained sweltering on board, from lack of energy and sufficient inducement to leave the ship. The charms of the Club or the excitement of a game of billiards failed to tempt us. Hong Kong boasts of only two walks for the valetudinarian—one along the sea-shore to the right, and the other to the left of the settlement: Then there is a scramble to the top of Victoria Peak at the back of it, but this achievement involves an early start, and a probable attack of fever. The monotony of life is varied by this malady alternating with boils or dysentery; so that the proverbial hospitality of the merchants at Hong Kong can only be exercised under very adverse influences. It was not difficult to account for a certain depression of spirits and tone of general irritability, which seemed to pervade the community. A large bachelors' dinner was the extreme limit of gaiety.

It was provoking that a place possessing so many scenic

attractions should have been so entirely devoid of charms. Like a beautiful woman with a bad temper, Hong Kong claimed our admiration while it repelled our advances.[5]

However it is fair to say that some did succumb to the legendary charms of the East, men like Hector MacLean of Jardine's who died in Hong Kong in 1894 after forty years there, having only elected to take one home leave during that period. Some visitors also found it fascinating. Constance Cumming, writing in 1878 from Glenealy, formerly the residence of one of Dent's taipans and in the 1870s in the possession of Gibb, Livingston and Co., exclaimed, a trifle gushingly,

Another week has glided by, and each day convinces me more and more that it would be simply impossible to find more delightful winter-quarters. Morning, noon, evening and night are all beautiful and all pleasant, and there is the delight of continuous fine weather, which is warranted to continue throughout the five winter months. . . . And the human life is equally characteristic. There is a very large, agreeable European society—naval, military and civil—with surroundings of quaint Chinese men and women—the former with their long plaits, the latter with wonderfully dressed glossy hair. Judging from my own experience, I can never again pity any one who is sent to Hong Kong—at least, in winter.[6]

1. Quoted in N. Cameron, *Hong Kong: The Cultured Pearl*, Hong Kong, 1978, 72.

2. Miss Burdett-Coutts was a well-known English philanthropist.

3. Buchanan Jardine Letters.

4. Cameron, op. cit., 72.

5. L. Oliphant, *Narrative of the Earl of Elgin's Mission to China and Japan*, London, 1859, I, 64–5.

6. Quoted in G. R. Sayer, *Hong Kong 1862–1919*, Hong Kong, 1975, 48.

# PART III

# Old and New China Hands

'It requires a great deal of boldness and a great deal of caution to make a great fortune and, when you have got it, it requires ten times as much wit to keep it.'

Emerson

# 7

# The Old China Hands

THE Second Anglo-Chinese War had inevitably disrupted foreign trade but in the early 1860s the prospects looked bright. The disturbances in China, which included the cataclysmic Tai Ping rebellion, helped to swell the Chinese population of Hong Kong, which rose from about 20,000 in 1848 to 122,000 in 1865, with consequent benefits to internal trade and commerce. In spite of the slow increase of legitimate trade with China, the tonnage of ships entering Hong Kong had risen from 190,000 in 1844 to 1,500,000 in 1860, mainly as a result of the colony's pre-eminent position as a distribution centre for opium. The new treaties had opened more ports, and the opening of the Yangtse was of great benefit to Shanghai, while the trade treaties concluded with Japan at this time seemed likely to benefit those merchants already established on the China coast. Finally, the commencement of the Civil War in America gave a great boost to India's cotton exports to Britain and it was believed that a trade could be established in exporting raw cotton from China.

However it was already becoming apparent that major changes in trading patterns were afoot and that, in order to survive, the big hongs would have to adapt themselves to these changes. By this time a well-established class of Chinese compradores, middlemen, and merchants, accustomed to Western trading practices, had grown up and much of local wholesaling and retailing was falling into their hands. In Hong Kong in 1855 there were 2771 Chinese householders liable to pay police rates at or above £10. A Colonial Office official commented that 'This shows a remarkable amount of wealth among the Chinese'. At the same time improvements in communications, especially the development of the steamship and the telegraph, ended the advantages enjoyed in the past by the hongs with their fast clippers bringing advance news of world price changes and their ability to stockpile goods in anticipation of rises in the market. Small merchants could now build up their share of the market, helped by loans from newly established banks. Men like William Keswick of Jardine's decided that their future profits lay in areas outside Chinese competence where considerable capital and expertise would be required. He believed that, as in Japan, the big Western firms would act as suppliers of capital, skills and technology to China in co-operation with progressively-minded Chinese officials. Consequently the hongs began to evolve from merchant houses dealing in commodities into management agencies concerned with shipping, insurance, utilities, engineering, and banking. With regard to the Chinese officials, the policy of Keswick and some other taipans gradually ceased to be to use gunboat diplomacy to browbeat them into opening more of China to trade. Instead they sought to win their acquiescence to the modernization of China and the grant of contracts for this from them, if need be with the lubricant of substantial loans to the right men.

Symptomatic of the new era which was beginning was the departure from China in 1860 of Robert Jardine, the last of William Jardine's nephews to head the Princely Hong. Unlike his brothers, he still had a long life ahead of him. He remained a partner of Jardine and Matheson's until 1882 and also became head of Matheson and Co. He inherited Castle Milk estate from his brother Joseph in 1861 and his brother Andrew's estate at Corrie in 1881 and also made extensive purchases of land on his own behalf. Over the years he established a reputation as a great sportsman. He was M.P. for Ashburton from 1865 to 1868, Dumfries Burghs from 1868 to 1874, and Dumfries County from 1880 to 1890, and was created a baronet in 1885. He married Margaret Seton Buchanan in 1867, daughter of the last chief of the Buchanans. After his death at Castle Milk in 1905, his son Robert William Buchanan Jardine succeeded to the baronetcy. Sir Robert became the head of Jardine's in 1905 and retained a controlling interest in the following year when it became a limited company. He did not, however, take a very active part in the business affairs of the company. Another strand in the web of personal relationships within the hong was spun in 1894, when he married Edith, sister of Mrs James Bell-Irving, whose husband was senior partner in the East from 1896 to 1902.

The management of the firm's affairs in China passed in 1860 to Alexander Perceval, a relation of the wife of James Matheson. He had gone to China in 1846, became a partner in 1852 and retired in 1864. He amassed a large fortune during his eighteen years in the East and with it he repurchased the family estate in Ireland which had been sold by his father. The reins were then taken over by James Whittall, the first of the firm's taipans who was not related in some way to the two founders. In 1874 kinship reasserted itself when William Keswick, son of Margaret Johnstone, a niece of William Jardine, took over. Perceval, Whittall, and Keswick all served on the Legislative Council, the latter two being very active members.

Keswick, who joined Jardine's in China in 1855, aged about twenty-two, started the firm's activities in Japan. In 1858 Whittall chartered Captain Holmes, owner of the sailing ship Troas, to take a cargo of sugar to Nagasaki. Keswick accompanied the cargo. At this time Nagasaki had not been formally opened to foreign trade, although it was due to be in a few months' time, and there was some doubt whether or not the *Troas* would be allowed to enter port. However it was permitted to do so and, having landed the sugar, it took on a cargo of edible seaweed and sailed for Hong Kong, leaving Keswick to begin operations. The *Troas* returned a few months later, again under charter to Jardine's, and was the first British ship to enter Yokohama. There Holmes met up with Keswick and passed over to him a bungalow which, for a time, was to be Jardine's headquarters in Japan. Keswick went to Hong Kong about 1862.

It was to be some time before any change in the attitude of the taipans to China became evident. For some years they continued to press the Foreign Office to seek further concessions from China. However the Foreign Office felt that the concessions already gained from China as a result of the Second Anglo-Chinese War were all that was necessary or desirable in the foreseeable future. It thought that further pressure on the Chinese government might lead to its collapse and that the resulting chaos would disrupt trade and give other foreign powers the opportunity to increase their influence in the area. Britain already had the lion's share of foreign trade with China and only stood to lose from any further alteration of the status quo. Moreover the view within the Foreign Office, that China's self-sufficiency and the poverty of the average person limited the possible expansion of trade, had hardened. There was little sympathy for the demands of those merchants who wanted further concessions from China. *The Times* was following the official line when, in 1870, it declared of the merchants, 'The opening of the country is their cry, "progress" is their motto, war is their object. Trade is slack at present. It is necessary to live and Micawber-like they hope for something to turn up in the general disruption it would infallibly produce.'[1] In fact for more than two decades after 1860 the other powers were preoccupied with their own affairs and had no wish for serious disputes with China or with each other. Consequently after 1860 the Western Powers tacitly agreed to adopt a co-operative and conciliatory policy towards China with the aim of promoting her stability, thus permitting the full development of their trading privileges and easing the way for the modernization of the Celestial Empire. The Chinese government for its part was willing to reciprocate, at least until the mid-1870s when the Conservatives became more influential. China observed her treaty obligations and took a superficial interest in certain aspects of Western technology.

There were by this time quite a number of merchants, known as the Old China Hands, who had served for some years in China before retiring to Britain, where they generally retained an active interest in trade with China. In the late 1860s their chief spokesmen in the House of Commons were Charles Magniac of Matheson and Co. and Colonel W. H. Sykes. Their efforts on behalf of the merchants, however, no longer aroused the same patriotic fervour that had prevailed in Palmerston's day. The hopes of the Old China Hands, that goods imported into China would be exempted from *likin*, or internal duties, and that the treaty rights would be extended beyond the treaty ports, rested on the revision of the Tientsin treaties due in 1868. Accordingly they were dismayed when Sir Rutherford Alcock, the British Minister in Peking, signed a convention in 1869 which would have protected China from having to grant such concessions. Lord Clarendon, the Foreign Secretary in Gladstone's first Liberal ministry, was blamed for adopting a soft line and Hugh Matheson, dean of the Old China Hands, complained to *The Times* that Clarendon had been duped by reactionaries in Peking. In Hong Kong the Chamber of Commerce, chaired by William Keswick, sent a memorial to Clarendon opposing the ratification of the Alcock Convention and insisting that China should be forced to perform all her treaty obligations. The memorial declared that the aim of British diplomacy in

China should be 'the ultimate opening up of the whole of the Empire to commerce and unrestricted intercourse with its people'.

The Alcock Convention might well have put trading relations with China on a sounder footing. In return for increased duties on opium and silk, there was to be a rationalization of the levying of *likin*. In addition there was provision for the appointment of Chinese consuls to any British port. The British officials hoped that a Chinese consul in Hong Kong would be able to 'control the smuggling propensities of his own countrymen in league with foreign merchants', so eliminating a major cause of friction. The merchants did not see it that way and in January 1870 the Old China Hands met in the Lombard Street offices of Matheson and Co. and set up the London Committee of Merchants, with Hugh Matheson in the chair, to press their objections. They managed to rally some influential support and the deputation received by Clarendon in February included thirty-four M.P.s. Clarendon maintained that the concessions in the Alcock Convention would benefit the merchants considerably and that anyway nothing could be gained by force. The Committee kept up the pressure and in the following month Matheson and Magniac had a meeting with E. Hammond, Permanent Under-Secretary of the Board of Trade. By this time the complaints from Sassoons, now the principal opium dealers, about the increase in opium duty had been backed by the Indian government which feared a loss in its revenue. Basic Foreign Office policy remained unchanged but, in face of the concerted opposition, Clarendon decided not to ratify the Convention. The solvency of the British administration in India was probably the clinching factor.

The problem of the revision of the Tientsin treaties still remained. The Foreign Office indicated to the Chinese authorities that although Britain would not press for an immediate revision, eventually it did expect one. No sooner had the Alcock Convention been dropped than the Tientsin Massacre gave the London Committee the opportunity to put pressure on the Foreign Office. By the treaties of 1858 and 1860 Christian missionaries had been permitted to travel in the interior and to buy land and build churches. The officials and the scholar-gentry felt that the missionaries were agents of the West, foisted upon China, who were undermining the traditional way of life. Although most of the missionaries were doubtless well-meaning and worked to improve the lot of the poor, the protection which they afforded to converts against the normal processes of Chinese law caused jealousy and resentment among the other villagers. It was not difficult for the officials to arouse the latent xenophobia of the masses against the missionaries. Nor did the missionaries and their supporters show much Christian humility in their attitude to Chinese tradition and culture.

The French, who occupied Tientsin from 1860 to 1863, behaved with particular arrogance there, going so far as to build a cathedral on the site of the former imperial temple. One reputable historian has stated that 'It is not too much to say that . . . the French nation and the French . . . missionaries were detested'. When an outbreak of disease in the summer of 1870 caused the death of many children at an orphanage in Tientsin run by French sisters, the feelings of the mob were inflamed by rumours that the children had been killed deliberately. The orphanage and the Cathedral were attacked and destroyed and the French consul, a dozen or so priests and nuns and some local Christian converts were killed. The London Committee chose to represent this incident as the beginning of a concerted plan to wipe out foreign influence in China. Alexander Matheson, as its representative, called on the Foreign Office and demanded 'a policy of firmness which should exact the due fulfillment of treaty obligations' as well as large reparations. Britain did join France and America in presenting a joint demand for the punishment of the guilty and the payment of compensation, and backed it up with a naval show of force off Tientsin, but the Foreign Office resisted the merchants' demands that further capital should be made of it.

In the early 1870s British trade with China declined and then stagnated. British exports to China in 1872 totalled only £9 million and between 1877 and 1880 they averaged less than £8 million a year. The Foreign Office increasingly felt obliged to seek an opportunity to sweep aside the procrastinations of the Chinese authorities with regard to the revision of the Tientsin treaties. In 1875 the murder of Augustus Margary, a British consular official, gave the Foreign Office the excuse it needed. The British authorities in India wished to develop trade between Lower Burma, which had been occupied in 1862, and the Chinese provinces of Yunnan, Kweichow, and Szechuan. They were stimulated in their efforts by the French penetration of Indo-China. A British expedition set out from Upper Burma to Yunnan in 1874 to map out a practicable trade route. Margary joined the expedition from Peking, with a passport issued by the Chinese authorities there, to act as an interpreter. Margary left the expedition at Bhamo and went ahead into Yunnan to ensure the route was safe. Here he and his Chinese servants were murdered. Exactly who was responsible is not clear but certainly the provincial authorities had done nothing to ensure Margary's safety, contrary to their instructions from Peking. Sir Thomas Wade, the British Minister at Peking, at once demanded full compensation and the settlement of all other outstanding difficulties between Britain and China.

As a result, the Chefoo Convention was negotiated in 1876. In part it dealt with the redress of the Margary incident but much of it was concerned with the revision of the Tientsin treaties. Four new coastal ports—Ichang, Wuhu, Wenchow, and Pakhoi—were opened for trade together with six ports of call on the Yangtse. This opened up the Yangtse to foreign trade for 570 kilometres beyond Hankow but the British merchants were not satisfied, they wanted no less than the opening of the whole of China. Moreover there was a general objection to the perpetuation of *likin*, albeit in a modified form, while some, although they did not say so openly, no doubt did not favour proposed measures to tighten up on smuggling. The Old China Hands agitated and in 1877 formed another committee, but this time they faced a formidable opponent—the conscience of Victorian England. There had always been a significant body of opinion in Britain which had opposed the opium trade on moral grounds and with the passing of the years this sentiment had grown stronger. By this time Jardine's had got out of the opium trade for sound business reasons but awareness of the growing strength of hostile opinion had played a part. The Anti-Opium Society came out in favour of the ratification of the Chefoo Convention believing that it would help to stamp out the illegal opium trade and to control the legal trade. Significantly, perhaps, Jardine's taipans did not play a very prominent part in the 1877 committee. It is a comment on the state of opinion in Britain that for the last two decades of the nineteenth century, debates on China in Parliament were chiefly concerned with the opium question while the stagnation of trade with China was largely ignored. The dispute between the merchants and the moralists delayed the ratification of the Chefoo Convention until 1885 but most of its provisions were brought into force before this.

The Old China Hands lay low and were politically quiescent during the early 1880s but the return of William Keswick to London in 1886 gave them an energetic and well-connected leader. Keswick took a partnership in Matheson and Co., was High Sheriff of Surrey in 1898 and became M.P. for Epsom in 1899. The Old China Hands met informally at the Thatched House Club and here the idea of establishing the China Association, a permanent body to represent their views, was first broached. The previous

committees had all been temporary *ad hoc* affairs formed
in times of emergency. From the start the China Association was led by the representatives of the big hongs with
vested interests who intended to apply pressure through
friendly contacts with highly placed civil servants and
politicians. It was very much an establishment body which
was going to manipulate the system discreetly through the
old boy network. Prominent members at the formation of
the Association in 1889 were Sir Robert Jardine, Sir
Thomas Wade, Thomas Jackson, Sutherland, Whittall,
MacLean, and Keswick. Sir Alfred Dent was the first
chairman but before long he was pushed upstairs to the
honorary post of president while Keswick took the chair.
Supposedly the aim of the Association was broadly to
counteract the much deplored soft line adopted by the
Foreign Office. Keswick himself observed in 1895, 'I do not
know, indeed, that it would be good for China to be treated
generously; for then the lessons of adversity and of
supreme misfortune might be forgotten.'[2] More specifically, the Association wanted to see Britain's dominating
influence in China maintained in the face of mounting
competition from other Western Powers. As early as 1894
the Association supported pleas from the Hong Kong
Chamber of Commerce that Hong Kong should be
strengthened strategically by the acquisition of territory to
the north. Keswick, who was on good terms with Lord
Salisbury, the Prime Minister, wanted the government to
obtain international acknowledgement that the Yangtse
was within the British sphere of influence. The co-
operative policy of the Powers towards China had been
ended abruptly by the Sino-Japanese War of 1894. China's
humiliating defeat had exposed the sham of the Manchu
dynasty's 'Self Strengthening' Movement and seemed to
foreshadow the overthrow of the government and the
collapse of China into anarchy. In such an eventuality
China might be sliced up between the Powers like a melon
and during the later 1890s the Powers hastened to stake out

their claims. Salisbury had no wish to see China partitioned and hoped that the status quo could be maintained but
he was sympathetic to Keswick's view that, if the worst
happened, then Britain must preserve her interests in
China. After the Germans obtained a lease of Kiaochow in
1897, Salisbury assured the Association that he would take
its views into consideration, and he took the first steps
towards acquiring the lease of the New Territories and of
Wei Hai Wei. He observed resignedly of the latter that 'It
will not be useful and it will be expensive but as a matter of
pure sentiment we shall have to do it'. However he was not
prepared to accept the Association's plea for the 'effective
occupation' of the Yangtse, and the Foreign Office was only
willing to go so far as to agree cautiously that the area was a
British 'sphere of interest' but not a 'sphere of influence'.

Keswick's particular hope was that pressure would be
exerted by the British authorities to get railway concessions for Jardine's. He was convinced that this was the
great new undeveloped field of enterprise which only
Jardine's among the hongs was big enough to handle.
Consequently Keswick was personally far more willing
than most of the other members of the Association to co-
operate with the moderate line adopted by the Foreign
Office. A premature venture into railway construction by
Jardine's between Shanghai and Woosung had offended
Chinese conservatives and ended in failure. After a man
was killed on the line, it was bought by the Chinese authorities who tore up the track and left the rolling stock to rust
on a Formosan beach. In the 1890s the prospects looked
better, for opposition within China to the building of railways had weakened and Salisbury was willing to assist
Keswick's ambitions. The political, economic, and financial ramifications of railway construction in China
were immense. Salisbury realized that the securing of railway concessions was essential in order to keep British
influence in China ahead of the other Western Powers. In
March 1898, at the same time as he requested the lease of

the New Territories, Salisbury persuaded the Chinese authorities to agree to the construction of a railway from
Shanghai to Nanking and an assurance that no exclusive
railway or mining privileges would be granted to France in
Kwangtung or Yunnan.

The financing of railway construction contracts involved the raising of a good deal of capital and in 1898 the
Hongkong and Shanghai Bank and Jardine, Matheson
joined forces 'to form a strong representative and influential syndicate to deal with railway construction'. This
syndicate was called the British and Chinese Corporation
and its principal directors were William Keswick and
Ewan Cameron, the Hongkong Bank's manager in
London. The Bank was concerned, naturally, with the financial side while Jardine's was to act as a contractor,
engaging engineers and supplying the necessary
machinery and rolling stock. German interests backed by
the Deutsche-Asiatische Bank were pressing the Chinese
authorities for concessions and the British government
accordingly recognized the Corporation as its chosen
instrument. The government would help the Corporation
to obtain railway concessions and would then withdraw.
The drawing up of actual contracts was a lengthy proce-
dure—that for the completion of the Tientsin to Newchang
line was signed in 1899, for the Shanghai to Nanking line
in 1903, and for the Kowloon to Canton and Shanghai to
Ningpo lines in 1907. These contracts involved the raising
of capital ranging from £1½ million to over £3 million. The
Corporation also participated with the Germans in the
Tientsin to Pukow line and with an international con-
sortium in the Hu Kuang Railway.

Keswick's policy of co-operating and collaborating with
the Foreign Office had paid off. He had no desire to 'rock
the boat' but within the Association and also in the Chambers of Commerce in Shanghai and Hong Kong there were
vociferous dissidents who wanted to force the government
into establishing a more concrete British sphere of in-

fluence along the Yangtse. Keswick tried to moderate their demands and only unwillingly agreed to an Association resolution in 1899 urging the government to assert a claim to 'prior British rights in the Yangtse valley'. The Foreign Office made it clear that it had no intention of doing so and, when Keswick refused in 1900 to sanction a public campaign, the dissidents broke away and formed the China League to push their views. Those who continued to back Keswick represented the vested interests, men like Ewan Cameron and Sutherland, while the dissidents were those for whom 'the China dream had never matured'.

The China League did not prosper and within the Association the dissidents failed at a meeting in July 1905, by 19 votes to 18, to change the official line. Their bolt was shot. The Boxer Rebellion of 1900 had shown the strength of anti-foreign feeling in China and thereafter the possibility of China being partitioned between the Powers lessened. Few now believed in the China dream. Any profits from the modernization of China would go to the vested interests while the traditional lines of business like opium, tea, silk, and textiles were stagnant or declining. Neither the Association nor the League had a realistic *raison d'être* any longer and, in the final years before the First World War, the efforts of the Old China Hands to influence British policy became weaker than at any time in the previous hundred years.

Meanwhile, in June 1898, the Chinese government had agreed to lease to Britain for 99 years an area to the north of Kowloon, comprising some 355 square miles, known as the New Territories. The British and Chinese Corporation had been given the concession for the Canton–Kowloon railway in the same year and in the following year had agreed to share in an American concession to extend the line to Hankow. However growing nationalism in China had led to some hostility to the grant of railway concessions to foreign companies. The Canton–Hankow concession was withdrawn and in 1905 the Hong Kong government lent the provincial Viceroy the £1,100,000 needed to redeem it. This money was advanced to the colony's government by the Crown Agents. Later it was converted into a loan and increased to £2 million. It was now agreed that the Hong Kong government would build the section running through British-held territory while the remainder would be built by the Corporation's engineers, nominally working under the authority of the Viceroy of Canton. The survey of the British section of the line began in 1905 and the construction of a tunnel under the Kowloon range, one and a half miles long, began the following year. It was hoped that an early start to the British section would allay the hostility of the Cantonese peasants to the foreign juggernaut. Hostility in the New Territories was lessened by the generous consideration given to claims for compensation on the grounds that the local *fung shui* had been disturbed. In some cases walls and culverts were built to protect villages in the vicinity of the line from evil influences. The British section was formally opened in October 1910. The Corporation's engineers began work on the Chinese section in 1907 and the whole line was opened to through traffic in 1911. However the belief of some residents and businessmen that it would be possible to buy a ticket at the Kowloon station for a journey to London was never realized. The other leg of the line, from Canton to Hankow, was not completed for nearly thirty years.

William Keswick died in 1912 and, true to the dynastic traditions which Jardine's taipans seemed to establish wherever they went, his son Henry succeeded to his parliamentary seat at Epsom and held it until 1918. Henry had been born in Shanghai in 1870. After being educated at Eton and Trinity College, Cambridge, he went to China in 1895. He served as Chairman of the Shanghai Municipal Council from 1906 to 1907, and then went to Hong Kong where he became a member of the Chamber of Commerce, the China Association, the Hong Kong Club, the Royal Hong Kong Yacht Club, and a Steward of the Jockey Club.

He was senior partner in the East from 1910 to 1911. During the South African War, he served in the 3rd King's Own Scottish Borderers and commanded the same regiment during the First World War. His country seat was Cowhill Tower, Dumfriesshire.

The pattern of Jardine's taipans continued to run remarkably true to form. Kinship and Scottish origins were not the only requirements for high office but few reached the top without them. The senior partners stayed twenty years or so in the East, played a prominent part in civic affairs of Hong Kong and Shanghai, and then returned to join the ranks of the country gentry. John Bell-Irving, senior partner from 1886 to 1889, and his brother James, senior partner from 1896 to 1902, were the sons of William Jardine's niece, Mary. John inherited the family estates at Milkbank and White Hill, of which he was the seventeenth laird, while James bought Minto House at Hawick and estates at Barnard Castle and Kelso. J. J. Keswick, senior partner from 1889 to 1896, was the brother of William. He retired to an estate at Mabie, Kirkcudbrightshire. In 1884 he married Marion, daughter of Sir Harry Parkes, British minister to Peking, whose sister, Frances, married Charles Dickson, senior partner from 1903 to 1906. Dickson was a great-grand-nephew of William Jardine. He attended Lochmaben Parish School before joining a firm of Edinburgh chartered accountants. He went to the East in 1884, became a partner in 1900, served on the Legislative and Executive Councils and returned to Britain in 1906, buying an estate at Friars' Carse. William Jardine Gresson, senior partner from 1906 to 1910, was a great-grandson of David Jardine. He arrived in Hong Kong in 1889, became a partner in 1901, served on the Legislative and Executive Councils, as well as the Shanghai Municipal Council, and retired in 1910. He bought Stoke House in Worcester, became a J.P. and master of the Croome Hounds and was killed in a hunting accident in 1934. David Langdale, senior partner from 1911 to 1919, was the grandson of Sir William

Jardine, Bart., of Applegarth. After being educated at Fettes, he joined Jardine's in 1890. He became a partner in 1902 and served on the Legislative and Executive Councils. On his retirement, he bought Dalswinton, an estate which had been in his mother's family for 300 years. The web of kinship binding the partners of Jardine and Matheson's throughout the entire nineteenth century, together with the maintenance of acute business acumen, would make a fruitful study for a geneticist.

1. Quoted in Pelcovits, *Old China Hands and the Foreign Office*, 32.
2. ibid., 129.

# 8

# The Sassoons

THE legalization of the opium trade in the peace settlements at the end of the Second Anglo-Chinese War had
been accepted calmly by Jardine's partners. By this time
Chinese-produced opium was beginning to undersell
Indian imports and open sales from established agencies
seemed the only way to compete with locally produced
supplies. Besides, for sound business reasons Jardine's was
diversifying; for social reasons, too, the later generations of
Jardine's taipans wished to distance themselves from the
opium trade. Peddling drugs was hardly a suitable occupation for the lairds of extensive estates in Dumfriesshire.
Nonetheless each year from 1860 to 1872, Jardine's handled
greater amounts of opium, on average about £300,000
annually, but this growth did not keep pace with the
expansion of the market. By 1873 Jardine and Matheson's
had ceased to be an important opium dealer either in India
or China. One of the partners noted in 1871 'The trade has
altogether gone to the dogs . . .', and added that the firm
'now looked to opium only for freight, charges, insurance
and storage'. The trade in locally produced opium was
almost entirely in Chinese hands but Jardine's had been
supplanted as the major importer by the Sassoons, a family
of Indian-based Jews.

The Sassoons had lived in Baghdad for several centuries,

handling financial matters for the Turkish administration. About 1825 David Sassoon left Baghdad, possibly because of persecution, and established himself in Bombay where he began trading, at first mainly in the export of raw cotton to Britain and China. However by the mid-1830s the firm of David Sassoon Sons had begun handling small quantities of opium and in 1845 David's second son, Elias, went to Canton. Sassoon's had no foothold in the coastal trade but Elias was able to make use of the extension of P. & O.'s steamer services to the coastal ports in order to get a larger share of the market. By the 1850s, in association with Jewish-owned Indian agencies, such as E. Gubbay and Co., E. D. I. Ezra and Co. and S. Isaac, Sassoon's had begun manipulating the prices at the sales in Calcutta and Bombay. With the legalization of the trade and the spread of steamships and the telegraph, the advantages which Jardine's and Dent's had enjoyed from possessing clipper fleets disappeared. The key to success now lay in cutting costs at the Indian end of the trade and Jardine's weakness lay in the fact that it had never bought directly in the producing areas, but had relied on its Indian agents to obtain supplies from middlemen. Sassoon's was now employing the methods so successfully adopted by Jardine's and Dent's in the 1830s and 1840s, namely bulk purchases at low prices, regular deliveries, and the advance of credit to Indian and Chinese dealers. In addition Sassoon's used agents to buy unharvested crops directly from the producers. Jardine's long established and efficient shipping, insurance, and broking services enabled it to maintain a position in the trade in the 1860s but by 1871 it only had one large Indian account, Rustomjee Eduljee. Meanwhile in 1867 Dent's had sensationally crashed into bankruptcy and dissolution, taking with it several of its associates. Jardine's made an effort to organize a Parsee buying syndicate to compete with Sassoon's ring but by this time the Jewish agencies controlled 70 per cent of stocks in India and China. This dominating position enabled Sassoon's to undersell the opposition indefinitely. When Eduljee's collapsed in 1872, Jardine's decided to abandon the struggle. The Princely Hong intended to devote its talent and resources to other fields. Previously there had been no real alternative to the opium trade for the large hongs but now the prospective modernization of China promised other and better opportunities.

The Sassoons purchased property near Pedder's Wharf not long after the establishment of the colony. Later they moved to Des Voeux Road where the managing partners lived in the old style over their offices. About the time of the Second Anglo-Chinese War, they bought extensive property in Central District, most of which was sold to Hong Kong Land at the end of the century. Sir Paul Chater, the founder of Hong Kong Land, was a business associate of the Sassoons. David had eight sons and several of them, notably Reuben David, Solomon David, Arthur, and Frederick, took turns to direct affairs in Hong Kong while the others supervised the family's extensive concerns in India and Shanghai. After David's death, Elias formed his own company, E. D. Sassoon and Co., with offices near those of David Sassoon Sons. The brothers lived unostentatiously and, judging by their subsequent way of life in Britain, this was probably not by inclination but as a result of social prejudice against them in the higher reaches of Hong Kong society. Frederick was elected to the Legislative Council by the J.P.s in 1884 when it was enlarged but he never seems to have joined the Hong Kong Club, the members of which were notorious for their propensity to blackball applicants on the least excuse. They did, however, play an active part in the affairs of the Jewish community which was small and closely knit by ties of marriage. An acrimonious dispute occurred within this community over the building of a synagogue in 1897. Another prominent Jewish businessman, E. R. Belilios, who arrived in Hong Kong in 1862 and initially established himself as an exchange broker, agreed to buy a site for the synagogue on behalf of the Jewish community. However when the synagogue trustees tried to take possession, Belilios claimed that he had only acquired half of it for the synagogue. A costly court case followed with the Sassoons acting on behalf of the community. Belilios was eventually awarded the decision. However Elias's son, Sir Jacob Elias, subsequently put up the money to build the synagogue on another site. It was named after his mother, Leah Gubbay.

The sons of David Sassoon might not have been in the first rank of Hong Kong society but they made up for it when they went to England. The remote hills of Dumfriesshire and the backbenches in the House of Commons were not for them; instead, they mixed in the very highest society, holding their own in the circle of financiers and *demi-monde* which surrounded the Prince of Wales, later Edward VII. Arthur and Reuben became close confidants of the Prince. Daisy, Princess of Pless, in her memoirs scathingly described Arthur, who frequently went racing with Edward, as 'the Jew page boy . . . who gets up after each course to make bets for the King and the others while they were at lunch'. Daisy might sneer, but when Edward had the choice of visiting the Duke of Richmond at Gordon Castle or staying with 'dear Arthur' at Tulchan Lodge in Speyside, he preferred the latter, even at the cost of putting up with his host's insistence on observing the Jewish Day of Atonement. In all Edward made six visits of a week at a time to Tulchan Lodge and its grouse moor. This was at some cost to Arthur who had to accommodate Edward's equerries, valet, secretary, and numerous servants, not to mention converting a room into a private telegraph office and providing a supply of the Prince's favourite aubergines, ginger biscuits, bath salts, and cigars.

The social rise of the Sassoons was one of the most remarkable in the nineteenth century. David Sassoon spoke no English and lived as an oriental merchant, yet his sons were to be leaders in the King of England's entourage. The Sassoons had early shown where their allegiance lay. Arthur was sent to England for part of his education in 1855 and the following year Albert, who was to be knighted in 1872, named his son Edward Albert, this being long before he met the Prince of Wales personally. Sassoon David Sassoon set up a cotton manufacturing and trading firm in England in 1858 and lived on a 200-acre estate at Ashley Park, Surrey. The Prince of Wales was entertained by the Sassoons when he visited India in the 1870s; not long after the Sassoons presented the city of Bombay with a large equestrian statue of him.

Reuben and Arthur settled in England in 1867, the latter having just finished six years of managing affairs in Hong Kong. Both quickly established themselves socially. Arthur's wife, Eugenie, was a member of a rich Italian-Jewish family and she became one of London's leading hostesses. When her sister married Leopold de Rothschild in 1881, Arthur provided the wedding breakfast and the Prince of Wales attended the service in the synagogue. Reuben went so far as deliberately to cultivate his physical resemblance to the Prince. His house in Belgrave Square had its stables on the roof, the horses and carriages being conveyed there by lift. The Sassoons also had out-of-town houses in Brighton, which Labouchere described as 'a sea coast town, three miles long and three yards broad with a Sassoon at each end and one in the middle'. Edward frequently attended Reuben's annual ten-day party for the Brighton races which was 'packed from morning to night with entertainment and delightfully amusing people'.[1]

When Albert took up residence in England in 1873, those who disapproved of the arrival of more *nouveaux riches* from the East circulated a scurrilous poem beginning

Sir Albert Abdullah Sassoon
That Indian auriferous coon.

However Albert could afford to ignore such petty backbiting. In 1873 he was the first Jew to become a freeman of the City of London and in 1880 he gave a ball at which the Prince of Wales was the guest of honour. He was later raised to the baronetcy, largely as a result of his efforts to entertain the Shah of Persia on his visits to England in 1873 and 1889. The Shah spoke little English, spat cherry stones on the carpet at Windsor, and most of his retinue were considered by Edward to be 'scallawags'. However Albert strove manfully to amuse the Shah, speaking to him in Persian, giving a dinner in his honour with several hundred guests at the Empire Theatre, and even having him to stay at his Brighton house for the week-end. His son, Edward Albert, married Aline, daughter of Baron Gustave de Rothschild of Paris in 1887 and the Prince, who admired her beauty and brilliance, named one of his yachts after her. The Sassoons might have difficulty in becoming members of the Hong Kong Club but they were favoured guests at Balmoral and Sandringham. However, while the Princely Hong still flourishes in Hong Kong and the Jardine and Matheson families still own estates in Scotland, the Sassoons no longer play any part in Hong Kong business life and Tulchan Lodge and Ashley Park have long since passed into other hands.

By the end of the century, the Sassoons were beginning to dispose of their interests in Hong Kong. This was largely because it was becoming clear that without strict regulation the opium trade would not survive for much longer. David Sassoon and Co., which became a limited company in 1901, now concentrated on the family's trading and manufacturing interests in Bombay and Shanghai. E. D. Sassoon and Co. continued to play a prominent part in the business life of the colony, mainly in the field of finance and banking. After the formation in England of the Society for the Suppression of the Opium Trade in 1874, there had been continuous pressure against the trade both in and out of Parliament. Even in Hong Kong support for the trade had become muted and qualified. As early as March 1876 a leader in the *China Mail* had deplored the hope that opium consumption might rise, '. . . recognizing as we do the fact that opium, like spirits, does work an undoubted amount of harm. . . .' In 1895, the British government declared that it would control the trade in the future, although no date was specified. Reformers in China also grew increasingly vocal and in 1906 an imperial decree was issued declaring that the trade would be abolished in ten years' time. Three years later the Hong Kong government forbade the export of opium to any country which prohibited its import. By 1913 consumption in the colony, which was still permitted, had dropped to 540 chests, while only 120 chests were exported. In the same year the government of India, which had long since ceased to be dependent on revenue from opium sales, forbade the export of the drug. Shortly before it did so, the two Sassoon firms, by this time well out of the trade, sent a memorial to the Indian government in favour of the ending of opium exports.

The Chairman of David Sassoon and Co. from 1901 until his death in 1912 was Sir Edward Albert Sassoon, who, from 1899, was also Conservative M.P. for Hythe, a seat previously held by Baron Mayer de Rothschild. His wife Aline was one of London's leading hostesses. As well as a house in Brighton, they had a country house at Sandgate in Sir Edward's constituency, another near Barnet, a shooting box in Scotland, and a magnificent mansion in Park Lane, once owned by the millionaire Barry Barnato, which covered 13,000 square feet of floor space. In addition there were two sumptuous but rarely visited residences in Bombay and Poona and Aline's Rothschild Hôtel in Paris. Although Sir Edward was an assiduous M.P., he did not take more than a dutiful interest in the family business and gradually gave up active participation in Jewish affairs. He died worth a little over £1 million but gave nothing in his will to charity as a protest against death duties. However, after earnestly advising his children to avoid 'all extravagance and gambling', he expressed the hope that they would 'devote some part of their time and money to objects of benevolence'.

1. Cecil Roth in *The Sassoon Dynasty*, London, 1941, relates that included in the auction of Reuben's effects after his death was a choice collection of cigars amongst which were 1,200 Villar y Villar, 800 La Rosa Aromatica, and 700 Flor de Cuba, an indication perhaps of Edward's tastes rather than those of Reuben.

# 9

# Banking

UNTIL the 1840s banking facilities were provided by the big hongs, principally Jardine's, Dent's and Russell's. However after the establishment of the treaty port system, a number of joint-stock banks, mainly with headquarters in India and London, commenced business. One of these was the Chartered Bank of India, Australia and China, now the oldest established bank in Hong Kong, which was granted a Royal Charter in 1853 and opened a branch in Des Voeux Road in 1859. The principal promoter of the Chartered Bank was James Wilson, an M.P. and founder of *The Economist*. Wilson was an archetype of the successful businessman of the early nineteenth century. Born in Hawick in 1805, he was the third son in a family of fifteen of a prosperous wool merchant. At the age of fifteen, James was apprenticed to a hat-maker and showed such an aptitude for business that his father bought the hat-maker's for him and an elder brother. In 1824 the business moved to London and twenty years later James retired as a man of substance. Meanwhile, after years of private study, he had established a reputation as an economist and, on the strength of this, entered Parliament in 1847 as a Whig. Within six months he was offered a government post and from 1848 to 1852 he was Joint Secretary to the Board of Control. Wilson was convinced that the expansion of steamship services would lead to a great growth in Britain's trade with Australia and the East, in which field, following the slump of 1847, banking facilities had actually declined.

The new banks mainly concerned themselves with exchange operations and there was a feeling among the merchants in Hong Kong that a local bank would be more attentive to their needs especially with regard to the expansion of trade. When it was learnt in 1864 that the promoters of the Bombay-based Bank of China were only going to offer 5000 of the 30,000 shares in Hong Kong and the treaty ports, there was a reaction. A number of merchants, led by the Dent partners and Thomas Sutherland, superintendent of the P. & O., decided to form their own bank. The Governor, Sir Hercules Robinson, gave his support, hoping that the new bank would assist the government to raise funds for public works. Sutherland, who was later chairman of the P. & O., and a director of the Suez Canal Company, described at a dinner in 1909 the almost casual way in which the enterprise began:

... without the assistance and without the cooperation of any person at that moment, I wrote the prospectus with my own hand. . . . I happened to be in the beginning of the year 1864, a passenger on a small P. and O. steamer that was then making the voyage from Hong Kong to Swatow, Amoy and Foochow. . . . There were on board that ship a number of copies of Blackwood's magazine which contained articles on the subject of banking and I absorbed these articles: they fascinated me. I have never had a banking account in my life. I had only an account with a compradore which was generally overdrawn; but it appeared to one that, if a suitable opportunity occurred, one of the very simplest things in the world would be to start a bank in China more or less founded upon Scottish principles.

When he heard the news of the formation of the Bank of China

... that very night I wrote the prospectus in question as it stands now in the archives of the Hong Kong and Shanghai Bank. The capital was only five million dollars, a highly modest sum when we think of the position of the Bank today. I took the prospectus next day to my friend Mr Pollard, who was at that time the most eminent counsel in Hong Kong, and I said to him 'You may make a business of this'.[1]

The bank opened for business in 1864 and was incorporated by ordinance in Hong Kong in 1866, adopting the name of the Hongkong and Shanghai Banking Corporation. It was given the name 'Wayfoong', meaning 'Abundance of Remittances', by the Chinese and this first appeared on the bank's notes in 1881. All the major merchant houses supported it except Jardine's, who had a major share of the existing exchange business and whose rivalry with Dent's was still active. Among the members of the provisional committee were Thomas Sutherland, Douglas Lapraik, R. Chomley of Dent and Co., A. F. Heard of Augustine Heard and Co., Woldemar Nissen of Siemssen and Co., Henry Lemann of Gilman and Co., Arthur Sassoon of David Sassoon Sons, and several Parsee merchants. Heard's was an American firm founded by Augustin Heard who had left Russell's in 1836, while Siemssen's was a German firm established in Canton in 1846. Gilman's had been founded in Canton in 1840 to deal in tea, silk, and Manchester goods by Richard Gilman, formerly a tea taster with Dent's, and his brother Ellis. The latter returned to England in 1845 and his partnership there provided the bank's first office in London. The new bank was, in effect, a merger of the banking interests of the old established agency houses and its success was largely due to its intimate local connections. No other locally established bank was able to develop more than limited business with the Chinese market. The bank was also fortunate in its first manager in Hong Kong, Victor Kresser, who had earlier established a branch of the Comptoire d'Escompte de Paris in the East. Sir Thomas Jackson, who became Chief Manager in 1876, wrote of him that he was

. . . a marvellously clever man, of immense energy and it would
have been impossible to find anyone better able to start a venture
of this kind. He was full of zeal and threw himself heart and
soul into the work, established agencies all over the East and
everything went fairly prosperously for the balance of the year
1865.[2]

However the following year was disastrous for business in
the East. Over-trading and a slump caused numerous merchant houses, many of which were under-capitalized, to go
bankrupt. The crash of Overend and Gurney with debts of
over £5 million brought down several credit houses and
spread waves of panic along the China coast. Of the dozen
foreign banks in Hong Kong at the beginning of 1866, only
six remained at the end of the year. The Hongkong and
Shanghai Bank weathered the storm in spite of the collapse
of Dent's, one of its major backers. Dent's was in a vulner-
able position. Like Jardine's, it had lost ground in the
opium trade. In an attempt to diversify it had bought two
large steamers, the Fusiyama of 1215 tons and the Hirado
of 1294 tons, to ply the newly opened Yangtse, but this
venture had not proved profitable. In 1865 a partner in
Russell's noted 'Dent and Co are by no means in a sound or
safe condition . . . they owe a great deal of money and have
immense sums locked up in real estate, steamers and other
unproductive properties'. In November 1866 another
partner wrote, 'Dent's are winding up their business and
Heard's are in a very bad way'. Heard's had approached
Jardine's on their behalf and that of Dent's for some aid or
co-operation but this was not forthcoming. Pao-shun
Hong—the Precious and Compliant Company—was no
more. Incidentally the collapse of Dent's severely curtailed
the activities of the Morrison Education Society, which
provided education in Hong Kong for Chinese children,
and which relied heavily on Dent's for funds. Some blamed
the rashness of John Dent, the principal partner in Hong
Kong, for the collapse of the company. He had certainly
lived in some style. In the 1850s he had paid £10,000 for a

racehorse in order to try and win the Hong Kong Cup from Robert Jardine. His nephew, Alfred, who was in Hong Kong with the firm, wrote 'It was a bitter moment when we had to haul down the old house flag'. However subsequently Alfred and his brother Edward organized a new partnership in London but it had few dealings with the China trade. In 1870 the brothers helped to found the British North Borneo Company which administered British North Borneo for over seventy years and Alfred was later knighted. He was the first chairman of the China Association.

The years that followed the crisis of 1866 were not easy ones for the Hong Kong merchants or for the Hongkong and Shanghai Bank. A drop in demand for Chinese tea and silk, over-trading caused by the opening of the Suez Canal, a drop in the value of silver, which was the main medium of exchange in the East, combined to bring about a slump in 1873. Influenced perhaps by the nature of its shareholders, the bank became involved in a number of unsuccessful ventures. In 1870 Kresser resigned after the failure of the China Sugar Refinery and his successor, James Greig, resigned when Heard's, which was in debt to the bank, collapsed in 1875. There were also some scandals, one of which involved W. H. Vacher, the bank's London agent, formerly of Gilman's, who in 1873 lost £81,000 speculating in South American railways. He owed the bank personally £19,000 but managed to repay about £16,000. Confidence in the reliability of the Hong Kong merchant houses was not increased when it leaked out about the same time that A. F. Chambers, an employee of Jardine's, had embezzled a large sum from his company. In 1874 the bank reported a loss and the following year passed up its dividend. However the worst was now over for the bank. It had had successes to balance the losses, notably in Japan where a branch had been opened at Yokohama in 1866. Most of Japan's foreign trade for the next two decades was financed by the Hong Kong and the Chartered Banks. The appointment of Thomas Jackson in 1876 brought firmness and stability to the management. He remained as chief manager until 1902. In 1877 he persuaded William Keswick to become a director and from this time on the bank and Jardine's were to co-operate closely, especially in railway developments in China. Keswick became chairman of the bank in 1880.

1. M. Collis, *Wayfoong*, London, 1965, 21−4.
2. ibid., 24.

# 10

# Taikoo

In spite of the hopes of the merchants after the Second Anglo-Chinese War that China would start to modernize herself as rapidly as Japan was doing, by 1880 there was still not a single mile of railway nor a single machine-driven spindle in China. In the first two decades after 1860 the main technological development in the China trade and almost the only significant one, apart from the introduction of the telegraph, was the replacement of the sailing ship by the steamship. It was in this field that cut-throat competition, reminiscent of the old opium smuggling days, developed between the leading companies, the three most important of which had forty-two steamships plying the coast and rivers of China in 1880.

The earliest local steamship company was the small Hong Kong and Canton Steam Packet Company which was established in 1849 and expired five years later. The old established hongs, with their superb fleets of clippers, were hesitant; the early steam engines were not very efficient and even on short trips between the treaty ports a lot of space had to be set aside for fuel. It took the British-based P. & O. line to show, in the early 1850s, that a good profit could be made by using steamships on the coastal run, and also to prove that the virtual monopoly which the older hongs held over the opium trade could be broken. In the same year, 1855, the three biggest hongs, Russell's, Dent's, and Jardine's, decided that they could no longer ignore these noisy, dirty interlopers, aesthetically bearing no comparison with the elegant clippers, but having definite advantages in the variable and sometimes tempestuous weather of the South China coast. These three, together with the P. & O., were the major rivals in the late 1850s and early 1860s, although some smaller companies were able to carve themselves a niche by specializing in routes neglected by the bigger concerns. For example, of the six steamships which regularly visited Foochow in the mid-1860s, three were owned by Douglas Lapraik.

The opening of the Yangtse to foreign shipping after the Second Anglo-Chinese War gave a great boost to steamships. The interior was in a disturbed state and it was safer to carry goods into the interior by water than by land. Steamships had a distinct advantage over sail in the navigation of riverine routes. Russell's, the American hong, had established a strong position in the carrying trade during the clipper era. The fact that the Americans had considerable experience in designing steamships for domestic routes, such as the Mississippi, gave Russell's the edge when it came to ordering suitable vessels. The principal partners in Russell's at this time were Warren Delano, Junior, grandfather of F. D. Roosevelt, and an old China hand from the Canton days, Paul Sieman Forbes, who had left China in 1853 but who still had a stake of about $300,000 in the hong, and Edward Cunningham, chief partner in Shanghai. The first two were not very enthusiastic about venturing too much on this novel enterprise, in spite of the fact that Forbes had invested heavily in railway stocks in the U.S., and it was Cunningham who took the initiative. He was kept short of funds by his partners and so raised the capital for the Shanghai Steam Navigation Company (the S.S.N. Company) from the public, mainly in Shanghai. Until the formation of the Hongkong and Shanghai Bank it was the largest public joint-stock company in China. Most of the money came from Chinese compradores and merchants or from small British and Parsee firms who were offered the use of the S.S.N. Company's godowns, thus enabling them to avoid renting space from Dent's or Jardine's.

The S.S.N. Company made a good profit on the Yangtse in 1863 and this encouraged Dent's to go into competition with its two large steamers, the *Fusiyama* and the *Hirado*. There was a bitter rate-war throughout 1864 but the S.S.N. Company was short of capital, so rather than fight it out to the bitter end, Cunningham came to an agreement on the rates with Dent's. By this time the latter was being pushed to the edge of bankruptcy by the slump of the mid-1860s. Desperately it sought to organize a joint service with Augustine Heard's, which also had two ships, but neither had sufficient capital to invest. An approach was made to Jardine's without success and, shortly after, Dent's crashed. Dent's Yangtse steamers and Shanghai godowns were mortgaged to Jardine's but as Jardine's had concentrated on the coastal routes, it sold Dent's interests to the S.S.N. Company which, in return, agreed not to challenge Jardine's south of Shanghai. On the strength of its new acquisitions, the S.S.N. Company issued more shares and got a loan from the Hong Kong branch of the Comptoire d' Escompte de Paris. With ample capital in hand and virtually no competition on the Yangtse, by 1872 the S.S.N. Company was able to build up a fleet of nineteen ships, totalling about 28,000 tons, and its assets to over $1 million.

After the agreement with the S.S.N. Company, Jardine's concentrated on developing coastal routes north and south of Shanghai. Francis Bulkeley Johnson, senior partner in Shanghai and later in charge in Hong Kong,[1] believed that it was necessary to follow Russell's example and build up a fleet of at least four steamships on the potentially lucrative Shanghai−Tientsin run. When Keswick and Whittall proved reluctant to invest the necessary capital, he encouraged Chinese merchants to invest in ships which then operated under Jardine's agency. By 1870 Jardine's had four ships on the Tientsin route and was able to negotiate a route agreement with the S.S.N. Company from a position of strength. Keswick was sufficiently encouraged by this progress to favour Johnson's suggestion that they launch a joint-stock company, but Whittall was opposed to the idea. At this point it looked as if Russell's and Jardine's between them would take a major share of the rapidly developing steamship trade. However they were to be challenged by a new arrival on the scene, John Samuel Swire, a forceful North Country man whose acumen, ruthlessness, and single-minded devotion to business emulated that of Dr William Jardine himself. J. S. Swire was the driving force behind Butterfield and Swire's, which today, together with Jardine and Matheson's, ranks as Hong Kong's leading hong. In spite of the fact that he only spent a short time on the China coast he must be regarded as one of Hong Kong's principal taipans.

J. S. Swire was a forthright and energetic businessman who drove himself relentlessly and ruled his staff with a rod of iron. Although quickly aroused to impatience and anger by the incompetence of others, nonetheless he recognized and carefully analysed his own mistakes and took pains to ensure that they were not repeated. Business was his prime interest; he did not venture into politics and discouraged members of his staff from involving themselves in the civic affairs of the ports in which they were based. Such leisure time as he had was mainly devoted to riding to the hounds, for he was a keen horseman, although his firm did not participate in racing in Shanghai and Hong Kong. He was quick to recognize and exploit any new commercial opening but in his business methods he was somewhat conservative, preferring a regular trade with small profits and quick turnover, to speculation or attempts to take advantage of possible price rises by stockpiling. His standards of business and personal morality were high and he disapproved of his employees drinking or gambling. This however did not prevent him from establishing an agency for Guinness in Australia. He was inclined to be dictatorial and prided himself on his bluntness, writing, 'I always endeavour to avoid hurting any man's feelings but I write, as I speak, to the point'. At the same time, he could be generous. When a Liverpool business associate faced ruin after the failure of the White Star Line, he wrote to him 'I am sorry to hear of your misfortune. I have lying at my bankers £20,000. You can make any use of it you please.' He first made his mark in the China trade in collaboration with Alfred Holt, the Liverpool shipowner, and Frank Forbes of Russell's wrote prophetically,

> I was much struck with the man. I fancy he is a person who lives by and for business alone . . . he has had the shrewdness to link his fortunes to an able specialist like Holt, and emboldened by the past, he probably sees nothing in the future which he may not attempt. He will be a tremendous success or as 'damnable a fizzle' as Abe Lincoln's hatchet. [2]

The Swires were a family of small Yorkshire landowners and businessmen. J. S. Swire's father, John, was born in Halifax in 1793 and at the age of nineteen went to Liverpool to work for his cousin, a general merchant. Liverpool was a place of great opportunity in those days and in 1816 John went into business on his own account, importing goods from the West Indies and the U.S.A. He married Maria Roose, daughter of a shipowner and merchant, in 1822 and, after the birth of his two sons, John Samuel in 1825 and William in 1830, he renamed his firm John Swire and Sons. The family firm enjoyed not more than modest prosperity. On John's death in 1847, he left his sons £1000 each to continue the business. The brothers tried widening the variety of goods which the firm imported and bought small shares in ships but the profits did not rise significantly. In 1854 John Samuel decided to go to Australia, without any definite plans, but he spoke of 'returning unsuccessfully in two years or else not before ten years'. Apparently he tried his luck in the gold fields and at sheep farming for a time without any great success, before setting up an agency in Melbourne to handle exports from the family firm in England, which was being kept going by William. Meantime William had married the daughter of an insurance broker, in spite of opposition from her father, who thought poorly of William's financial prospects. It is not clear how long John Samuel did stay in Australia but he was back in England by 1859 when he married Helen Fairrie, daughter of a sugar refiner. Helen gave birth to a son, John Samuel, junior, in 1861. After her death the following year, John Samuel went to live with William and his wife. Many years later, in 1881, he remarried and had another son, George, in 1883.

John Samuel's visit to Australia was to bear richer fruit than was at first apparent. He had become convinced that there was a great future for both Western business and shipping in Australia and the East. When trade with U.S.A. slackened in the early 1860s because of the Civil War, Swire's began to export cotton and woollen goods to China and to import tea and silk. Some of the cotton goods were supplied by a mill-owner, Richard Butterfield, and in 1866 he and the two Swire brothers formed a partnership. Swire's had also begun bottling Guinness for export to Australia and were interested in establishing a stake in a shipping company in order to transport the bulky cases of stout more cheaply. Accordingly, when Philip and Alfred Holt formed the Ocean Steam Ship Company in Liverpool in 1865, with the intention of serving Eastern routes, the Swires were among the initial subscribers, taking up £1570 worth of shares. The Holt and Swire brothers were undoubtedly already well acquainted and had formed a mutual respect for each other's abilities. Later when William bought a yacht, the *Menai*, all four used to go sailing together.

Alfred Holt, who was born in 1829, was trained as a

railway engineer but by the time his apprenticeship had finished in 1851, the railway boom was over. As a result he began his career in the more promising field of steamship design, from there graduating, with his brother, into the management of steamships. By 1864 the brothers had accumulated about £20,000 between them and had inherited £9000 from their father, as well as owning an office block, India House, in Liverpool. The success of P. & O. in pioneering steamship links with the East had encouraged other British shipping companies to follow suit. By 1863 the Ben Line, the Shire Line, Brocklebank's, and the British India Steam Navigation Company had all established routes. The Holts had no knowledge of the China trade, although it is not unreasonable in the light of subsequent events to think that they may already have talked with J. S. Swire on the prospects. However they did have a belief in the future of steamships and in particular believed that the new compound tandem engine would overcome the problem of high fuel consumption. The Holts laid down three ships with these engines for a total cost of £156,000 and in April 1866, the *Agamemnon* set sail for China on the first voyage of the Ocean Steam Ship Company. The advantages of Holt's ships over the clippers were obvious; a clipper could carry about 1000 tons from China to England in 120 days or more, whereas the *Agamemnon* could carry 3000 tons in 77 days. However the cost of running steamships was higher and so consequently were their rates. The key to success lay in getting a good agent in China who would ensure that the ships had cargoes for the homeward trip.

It can hardly have been a coincidence that J. S. Swire went to Shanghai in 1866. He arrived on 28 November and within a day or two had bought out his former agent there, Preston Bruell, acquired the premises of Fletcher and Company, moved in Preston Bruell's furniture, installed a staff and chosen a Chinese sobriquet, Taikoo, or Great and Ancient, for his firm. On 4 December, the *North China Daily News* announced the establishment of the firm of Butterfield and Swire and on 1 January business began. William Jardine could hardly have done better. Initially there were three expatriate staff. R. N. Newby dealt with Yorkshire goods, William Lang dealt with Manchester goods and was later senior partner in the East until his retirement in 1888, and James Scott, a bank-clerk aged 21 who had gone to Shanghai with a letter from Alfred Holt, was engaged as a book-keeper. He succeeded Lang as senior partner in the East. Another early appointment was Edwin MacIntosh, who joined John Swire and Sons in 1869, went to China the following year and was to be manager in Hong Kong from 1879 to 1895. In Shanghai Swire's used the Chun family as compradores and in Hong Kong the Moks. Butterfield's direct connection with the firm ended in 1868, probably as a result of a personality clash with the imperious John Swire, who wrote succinctly, 'Mr B. retired from our firm at my suggestion—he was grasping and bothered me.'

Within a few weeks of opening in Shanghai, Swire pulled off a minor coup. Holt's *Achilles* was about to sail without a cargo because of a prejudice against shipping tea by steamship. Swire discovered a clipper loaded with raw cotton which had been detained due to the bankruptcy of the owners. He arranged to transfer the cargo to the *Achilles* and, in the process, confirmed the grant of Holt's agency in Shanghai to Butterfield and Swire. It was a bold move on the part of Holt's to engage a new and untried agency. Kinship played an important part in the affairs of firms like Jardine's and Sassoon's. Mutual respect and friendship and a common background were other bases for business trust and co-operation. By 1876 Swire's stake in the Ocean Steam Ship Company had risen to £20,000 and John Swire and Sons acted as Holt's agents and distributors in Britain. In return Holt's invested in Swire's China Navigation Company (C.N. Company), formed in 1872, which acted as a feeder for its ships. The establishment of branches in Yokohama, Foochow, and Hong Kong by Swire's was mainly to foster its agency for Holt's. J. S.

Swire wrote in 1869, 'We think that Holt's line is only in its infancy, and that Hong Kong is far the most important station in the East for the future of the steam trade.'

J. S. Swire's spell on the China coast had led him to believe that there was room for another major shipping company in China's riverine and coastal trade. The C.N. Company was formed initially to compete for the Yangtse business. Butterfield and Swire's was to act as its manager. The entire capital of $360,000 was raised in Britain, the principal shareholders being John and William Swire, the Holt brothers, and a number of businessmen engaged in the China trade, who were encouraged to back this new venture partly because the returns on the old established export-import trade were declining. Swire realized that he would need at least four ships to go into competition with the established companies and that at first he would have to be prepared to absorb losses. However he was confident that he could succeed and his reputation for shrewdness attracted the necessary funds. His competitors were impressed. One of the partners in Russell's commented apprehensively that Swire's seemed to be backed by a 'practically unlimited supply of British pride and capital'.

The only way that Swire's could break into the pre-existing network of agreements was by a frontal assault. The agreement between Russell's and Jardine's, that the former should have the Yangtse and the latter the coastal routes south of Shanghai, still held good, although Russell's had an agreement with the small Union Steam Navigation Company allowing it to operate on the Yangtse. Russell's and Jardine's shared the Shanghai to Tientsin route and the Hong Kong, Canton and Macau Steamboat Company had a monopoly of the Canton river. Another new element was the formation in 1873 of the China Merchants' Steam Navigation Company (the C.M.S.N. Company) with backing from the Chinese government.

Swire wasted no time. In 1873 he bought out the Union Company and began a bitter rate-war with Russell's S.S.N.

Company. At first the going was hard and Swire noted at the end of the first year that 'the differences in earning 'twixt the C.N. Company and the S.S.N. Company is most disgusting'. In order to strengthen his position he laid down two new ships, the *Foochow* and the *Swatow*. As he was short of capital these were partly financed by the Butterfield family and by James Scott, already a partner in Butterfield and Swire's. They operated at first as the Coast Boats Ownery but were amalgamated with the C.N. Company in 1883.

Another of his tactics was to woo the Chinese merchants and it was partly for this reason that he lured H. B. Endicott, Augustine Heard's Chinese-speaking shipping manager, into the service of Swire's, where he remained until his death in 1894. The old established hongs, for too long used to having things their own way, were disgusted at these unorthodox methods. Frank Forbes of Russell's wrote in 1873,

> Butterfield's have given a big chin-chin dinner to all the freight brokers, at which the foreign clerks assisted. Respectable Chinese laugh, as they ought to do, at this. It is an undignified style of action.
>
> On my return I found the Swire lot blustering away among the Chinamen, giving dinners to all the freight brokers large and small (at which the foreign clerks hobnobbed with every unwashed devil in the place) and announcing that their steamers were to go full at any price and etc.[3]

Russell's had reason to be alarmed for, like Heard's, they were in financial difficulties. Problems caused by the changing pattern of trade on the China coast were exacerbated by a slump in America. In 1874 Paul Forbes, the principal shareholder, went bankrupt as a result of the failure of his New York, London and Pacific Steamship Company. In the same year Russell's capitulated and came to a pooling agreement with the C.N. Company on the Yangtse. This proved a temporary expedient. In 1876 the

S.S.N. Company was sold to the China Merchants' Company and this virtually marked the extinction of Russell's in the China trade. Within a few years it had been taken over by Shewan, Tomes and Co. Like Dent's, the American hong had failed to move with the times and, as is the nature of things, had been forced to give way to a younger and more vigorous competitor.

These years were also difficult for Swire's. Throughout the 1870s the export of textiles to China became increasingly unprofitable and Swire's lost £97,000 in this field from 1868 to 1880. J. S. Swire persisted with them partly to provide an outward cargo for Holt's but he noted as early as 1874 that 'nothing but loss is apparent'. By 1890 Swire's had ceased to export textiles. It was a sign of the times that this was now partly compensated for by the acquisition of an agency to export locomotives from Fowler's of Leeds in 1887. Tea exports were also declining in face of competition from India, although they remained very marginally profitable. Swire's gave up the export of tea to Britain in 1893. Exports to Australia, which filled up empty space, continued until 1900. These problems were accentuated by a shortage of capital. The resources of Swire's were gravely strained when William retired because of ill-health in 1876. His share in Butterfield and Swire was now worth £136,000, probably rather less than his brother's, but not all of his capital was withdrawn at once. His place was taken by the partners in the East. In 1888 the main shareholders, with more or less equal holdings, were J. S. Swire, his son J. S. Swire, junior, Scott, MacIntosh, and F. R. Gamwell, the London manager. J. S. Swire remained optimistic through the difficulties of the 1870s. In 1875 he wrote, 'We are very hard up (for loose cash)—but very snug, and scarce any China house is in so safe a position. We shall come out second to none and a great future will be before us—but safety is our first consideration.'[4]

Safety meant cutting down on all unnecessary expenditure. Swire kept a close eye on the smallest details. When Lang requested permission to buy more furniture for his quarters in 1873, Swire wrote sarcastically, 'if you had half a dozen wives and each prolific, you could not require more'. Another expedient was running down the unprofitable activities—'we have too many white elephants'—and increasing commission work and shipping. After his success on the Yangtse, Swire decided to expand into the coastal trade. His tactics would be the same as before—a sudden vigorous attack which would dishearten the rivals and force them to concede a pooling or rate-fixing system. However to expand into the coastal trade would mean challenging the Princely Hong itself.

At first Swire's avoided a direct challenge. Instead, the *Inchang* was sent to break the Hong Kong, Canton and Macau Steamship Company's monopoly of the Canton route. Swire had heard that this company was thinking of changing from its existing agent, Heard's, and he hoped to persuade it to switch to Butterfield and Swire. However Jardine's had an interest in the Canton Company and William Keswick, a doughty fighter, was on the board. The agency did not go to Swire's and when the *Inchang* began rate-cutting, the Canton Company did likewise. Swire was annoyed and blamed Keswick for encouraging the Canton Company to hold out. However, in spite of the low rates, the *Inchang* managed to avoid operating at a loss by acting as a feeder ship for Holt's.

Another rate-war broke out on the Yangtse, this time on the initiative of the China Merchants' Company. Here again Swire believed that Keswick had a hand in the matter, especially as there was a rumour that Jardine's might put some capital into the China Merchants' Company. Swire fought back by invading the Shanghai to Ningpo route and also complained to the British government that the Chinese government was subsidizing the China Merchants' Company by giving it rice cargoes at very high rates, but the British government refused to intervene. Swire, as usual, favoured coming to terms and in 1877 he came East for this purpose and succeeded in making an agreement with the China Merchants' Company by which the C.N. Company was to have 45 per cent of the Yangtse and 50 per cent of the Ningpo trade. Jardine's now declared that they considered the 1867 agreement with Russell's, by which it had kept out of the Yangtse, had lapsed, to the surprise of Swire who had deliberately avoided challenging Jardine's on the Tientsin route. When he heard that Jardine's was building two ships for the Yangtse, he decided on all-out war, resolving to spread the fight to other fields, such as sugar refining. Shortly after, he finally reached an agreement with the Canton Company, whereby the C.N. Company was to have three-eighths of the trade. Swire was exultant, writing, 'What a fool K.[eswick] has made of the Boat Co. . . . K. simply wrecked them to serve his own ends of having a fight with us in which he has lost.'

The next logical step was an agreement with Jardine's and in 1879 Swire suggested a quadruple pool with the China Merchants' Company and Siemssen's but Jardine's, although polite, was not willing to compromise. Swire wrote of Francis Johnson of Jardine's that he was 'particularly courteous in manner, very friendly, but of course I am aware that he hates me like poison'. Jardine's began to consolidate its shipping interests into the Indo-China Steam Navigation Company in order to strengthen its position and Swire in turn began to prepare the amalgamation of the C.N. Company and the Coast Boats Ownery. By 1882 there were twenty ships in the two Swire's companies showing an average profit of 20 per cent a year. Swire observed confidently that 'Jardine, Matheson and Co. now see that they must take us into account', and indeed in that year Jardine's and the China Merchants' Company, like Russell's and the Canton Company before them, decided to come to terms. In future the China Merchants' Company was to have 42 per cent of the Yangtse trade, the C.N. Company 38 per cent, and Jardine's 20 per cent, while the C.N. Company got 28 per cent of the Shanghai–Tientsin route, Jardine's 28 per cent, and the China Merchants' Company 44 per cent. Swire regarded the agreement as a victory, writing 'we are strong enough now to be respected—even if we are not beloved'.

It was certainly true that Swire's ruthless and thrusting competitiveness had not endeared him to the other merchants; moreover the C.N. Company had a reputation for being a demanding employer. Its European officers were paid less than the general rate but were compensated for this with a quarterly good service bonus. In 1891, after arms were found on board the S.S. Sung Kiang by the Shanghai customs, the officers were informed in Hong Kong that they would not receive the bonus. The second officer refused to sail and, after prosecution, was sent to jail for seven days. This caused a furore in Hong Kong and gave an opportunity for the airing of some deeply felt resentment. A letter signed 'Gauntlet' in the Hong Kong Telegraph asked,

Shall Butterfield and Swire, the everlasting Bugbears of Eastern commerce, the nigger-drivers, the sweaters, the Jews . . . shall they go on paying starvation wages, promising a 'bonus' like a cooperative grocery, and then sneaking out of it, and deliberately breaking their promise and defrauding a poor man of what he earned, on a frivolous pretext?[5]

Unpopular or not, the C.N. Company continued to do well in the years after the 1882 agreement. Between 1883 and 1889, the earnings of the C.N. Company were estimated to be three-and-a-half times higher than those of the Indo-China Company, which failed to attract its agreed share of business. Accordingly, when the agreement came up for renewal in 1889, Swire felt he was in a position to take a strong line. He stated the share which he wanted for the C.N. Company, leaving the Indo-China Company and the China Merchants' Company to divide the rest. The others would not accept this and so the agreement lapsed. Jardine's and the China Merchants' were soon quarrelling with each other and in 1890 Swire wrote, 'J. M. and Company want us to help them pull the chestnuts out of the fire and to take their side against the China Merchants' Company. The position is very laughable. . . .' Finally a new agreement was drawn up in 1893 which lasted into the next century. Swire told MacIntosh, 'You have now got the upper hand—keep it.' In 1899 the C.N. Company had 29 ships totalling over 35,000 tons against the Indo-China Company's 22 ships totalling about 24,000 tons. The C.N. Company's profit in 1900 was £306,000 against £158,000 in 1889.

Jardine's acted as agents for the China Sugar Refining Company and Swire's rivalry with the Princely Hong spurred him on to enter a field of which he presumably had acquired some knowledge from his first marriage to the owner of a sugar refinery. A careful study convinced him that there was room in Hong Kong for two refineries and in 1881 he floated shares worth £198,000 in the Taikoo Sugar Refinery, for which Butterfield and Swire were to act as agents. Many of the shares were taken up by John Swire and Sons, Holt's, the Butterfield family, and other British business associates of Swire. The construction of the refinery proved to be a protracted affair and Swire suspiciously noted that the contractors 'may have been "got at" by someone who is interested'. Operations began in 1884 and, in spite of the availability of cheap supplies of raw sugar from the Philippines and the Dutch East Indies, trading conditions were at first difficult. No dividend was paid in the first year and in the second only one of 5 per cent. However Taikoo's plant was more modern than that of the China Sugar Refinery and in 1887 Taikoo made a profit of $450,000 on a capital of £198,000 against the China Company's $199,000 on a capital of £430,000. Much of Taikoo's sugar was carried by the C.N. Company but in 1890 Taikoo built two ships of its own.

The expansion of the refinery, which for a time was the largest in the world under one roof, and the need to build reservoirs as a precaution against droughts, required a large amount of working capital. Swire was reluctant to borrow money from the Hongkong and Shanghai Bank because of its connections with Jardine's, and so John Swire and Sons met the liabilities from its reserves as they arose. This imposed a severe strain on the parent company which by 1900 had lent £700,000 to the refinery. Nonetheless the refinery was a profitable concern and the accumulated profit over the first fifteen years topped £1 million. The land acquired for the refinery at Quarry Bay was too extensive for its needs and the Hong Kong managers suggested establishing a dockyard there, initially to service the C.N. Company's ships. Swire turned the proposal down, not wishing to challenge Jardine's in yet another field and one in which he had no expertise. However in 1900, two years after his death, work began on this scheme and in 1909 the Taikoo Dockyard and Engineering Company opened for business.

In 1900 a dispute broke out between Belilios, the principal shareholder in the China Sugar Refinery, and Jardine's, the agents. Belilios wanted a reduction in the agents' commission but Henry Keswick refused. To strengthen his position, Belilios got his Chinese and Indian friends to buy up shares, raising the price from $112 to $133 and threatened to give the agency to Shewan Tomes and Co. Keswick thereupon earmarked land on which to build Jardine's own refinery. This would be to Taikoo's disadvantage and Herbert Smith, Butterfield and Swire's Hong Kong manager, tried to arbitrate. Meanwhile Keswick played Belilios at his own game. He got his associates to buy shares in the refinery and when the price rose above $145, some of Belilios's friends sold out with the result that he lost control and was obliged to drop his original demand. Keswick did not proceed with his threat to build another refinery, to Smith's relief, but the latter noted that the affair had been 'rather an unclean business'. Swire died in 1898, rich in business prestige and honour. His willingness to challenge established companies on their own ground and his expectation that his employees would devote themselves single-mindedly to the good of the business had not made him popular but he was widely respected for his integrity and acumen. His personal fortune at the time of his death was not immense, about £220,000, but he had already passed many of his assets to his two sons. The principal partners after 1900 were J. H. Scott, John Swire, junior, and E. MacIntosh, who died in 1904. G. W. Swire, J. S. Swire, senior's son by his second marriage, became a partner in 1905, and C. C. Scott, son of J. H. Scott, in 1910.

J. H. Scott, who became the taipan after 1900, followed very much in the steps of J. S. Swire, senior. He disapproved strongly of what he regarded as loose living and wrote sternly to an offender, 'You are ruining your chances as regards advancement in our firm—"American women and Nips!" We will not tolerate these vices, they lead a man into trouble, destroy his efficiency and he sets a bad example to others.'[6] When E. F. Mackay asked for permission to stand for the Shanghai Municipal Council in 1911, Scott replied to him, quoting J. S. Swire,

'If managers have spare time during business hours, they should use it in trying to devise ways of improving the business of their employers.' However, as we are frequently told that our staff have to work hard and continuously to keep things up to date, we cannot bring ourselves to believe that a man in Mackay's responsible position can spare the time required for the duties of a Municipal Councillor.[7]

Swire's had evolved from a very different tradition to that of the original hongs of the Canton days and Scott intended that the house style should be maintained.

1. He ceased to be a partner in 1886 and died at Cannes the following year. His son Charles became a Brigadier-General, one of his daughters married a baronet's son and the other the son of Lord Annaly.

2. S. Marriner and F. Hyde, *The Senior, John Samuel Swire 1825—1898*, Liverpool, 1967, 2.

3. Liu Kwang-ching, *Anglo-American Steamship Rivalry in China 1862—1874*, Harvard, 1962.

4. Marriner and Hyde, op. cit., 29.

5. Quoted in C. Drage, *Taikoo*, London, 1970, 289—90.

6. ibid., 99.

7. ibid., 177.

25. Sir William Robinson with members of the Legislative Council about 1897 (*Hong Kong Museum of Art*)

26. Lane, Crawford's original ships' chandlers in Des Voeux Road
(Lane, Crawford Ltd.)

27. The Hong Kong cricket team, 1891 (*Hong Kong Cricket Club*)

28. Lane, Crawford's expatriate staff Christmas dinner, early 1900s
(*Lane, Crawford Ltd.*)

29. Lane, Crawford's expatriate staff outing, early 1900s (*Lane, Crawford Ltd.*)

30. Sir F. H. May, Governor of Hong Kong, 1912-17, at the opening of a dispensary (*Hongkong and Shanghai Banking Corporation*)

31. J. H. Ruttonjee and his family. The small boy on the right is Dhun Ruttonjee, later a member of the Legislative Council. (*H. Ruttonjee and Sons Ltd.*)

32. Sir Paul Chater (*Hongkong Land Co. Ltd.*)

33. The outside of Marble Hall, Chater's palatial house in Mid-Levels
(*Public Record Office, London, and Dr P. Wesley-Smith*)

34. Marble Hall: the entrance hall (*Public Record Office, London, and Dr P. Wesley-Smith*)

35. William Keswick (*Jardine, Matheson and Co. Ltd.*)

36. Sir Robert Buchanan–Jardine (*Jardine, Matheson and Co. Ltd.*)

37. View from the Peak looking east, early 1900s

38. The new Hong Kong Club built in 1898

39. Wyndham Street, the heart of Hong Kong's business district, early 1900s

40. The Golf Course, Deep Water Bay, built between 1891 and 1894

41. The Queen presenting the Queen Elizabeth Cup at Happy Valley in 1975, while the Jockey Club Stewards look on (*Royal Hong Kong Jockey Club*)

42. The waterfront in Hong Kong's Central District, 1989. Jardine House (left) is home to the Jardine group, while Exchange Square (centre and right) houses the Stock Exchange and many financial companies (*Hong Kong Tourist Association*)

# PART IV
# Hong Kong—the Old Order Changeth

'Nothing will improve your lot
If you yourselves do not'.

Brecht

# 11

# Civic Affairs

AFTER the Second Anglo-Chinese War the merchants played a more important part in civic affairs. The activities of the colonial administration were expanding and consequently were of more significance to the business houses. Trade with China did not develop to the expected extent but, as the population of Hong Kong rose, there were increasing opportunities to make a profit in the colony itself. At the same time there was a growing number of taipans who spent most of their working lives on the China coast. Indeed many of the new generation of taipans who emerged in the closing years of the century were Asians or Eurasians to whom Hong Kong was as much a home as anywhere. They were content to live and die in Hong Kong, with no thought of returning to England and using their wealth to acquire social status there.

Merchant opinion obtained another forum besides the Legislative Council when the Chamber of Commerce was founded in 1861 with Alexander Perceval of Jardine's as its first chairman. The Chamber protested vigorously in 1865 when the Governor, Sir Richard MacDonnell, introduced a Stamp Ordinance whereby all official documents, including bank notes, were to pay stamp duties. MacDonnell was unmoved, maintaining that additional revenue was needed in order to improve the water supply necessary to make Hong Kong 'a healthy place of residence'. The Chamber protested in vain to the Secretary of State and a Reform Association was formed to agitate for more unofficial representation on the Legislative Council but by 1869 MacDonnell reported that it had 'died out through sheer inanition'. The Chamber was not merely obstructive, however. In 1874, now chaired by James Whittall of Jardine's, it suggested that lighthouses should be erected on the approaches to the colony. As a result three lighthouses were built and dues of one per cent per ton were charged on shipping entering the harbour. When Sir Arthur Kennedy became Governor in 1872 he was instructed by the Colonial Office to permit the Legislative Council to debate any question it wished. Consequently the unofficials had more opportunity to voice their opinions on the day-to-day affairs of the colony. In 1874 they criticized the Superintendent of Police for confining the police to their barracks during a severe typhoon and tried to cut his salary. In the same year they tried to reduce the vote to the fire brigade because of dissatisfaction with its organization.

Both Kennedy and MacDonnell were generally respected and liked by the merchants. Sir John Pope Hennessy, who became Governor in 1877, was not. He was a volatile and idealistic Irishman who succeeded in arousing controversy in each of the six colonies in which he served as Governor. He left Hong Kong more hated by the expatriate business community than any Governor since Sir John Davis. From 1866 onwards the Colonial Office's instructions to the Governor had stressed that equal treatment must be given to all Hong Kong's inhabitants regardless of race, but in practice this had been given little more than lip-service. The colonial officials generally had accepted the merchants' view that Hong Kong was, first and foremost, a place where British merchants could trade and live in peace and security. The Chinese population was, of course, vital to the colony's existence but if the Chinese chose to come and live and work in a Crown Colony, they

must put up with the inconveniences necessary to preserve the well-being of the expatriates, just as the merchants in earlier days had put up with the inconveniences
of life in Canton under the Eight Regulations. This idea was
not a surprising one, perhaps even an inevitable one, in the
1840s. However, to an impartial outsider, it was clearly
untenable by 1877 when there were about 130,000 Chinese
in the colony, a proportion of whom were prosperous
and well educated, and less than 10,000 non-Chinese.
Hennessy's appreciation of this won him the support of the
vocal section of the Chinese population during his administration and has earned him posthumous praise since. No
one today would take exception to his statement to the
Legislative Council in 1881 that the duty of a Governor 'is
to avoid the encouragement of any body or of any class, but
to simply hold the balance evenly between all men' but, at
that time, it signified a positive change in official policy
and not one to the liking of the merchants who felt in no
uncertain terms that it was the Governor's duty to encourage them. It was unfortunate that Hennessy's well-
intentioned perceptiveness of the need for change was
combined with a gift for exciting bitter personal hostility
and distrust.

In order to control the lawlessness that was prevalent in
the colony's early days, a body of harsh penal law had been
built up by which common criminals, in the circumstances
almost all Chinese, were liable to public flogging, branding, and deportation. In Britain such harsh deterrents had
given way to more humane treatment and Hennessy was
only acting in accord with the enlightened opinion of the
time when he proposed to abolish these penalties. To the
British merchants in Hong Kong, these proposals were
woolly-minded folly and pro-Chinese to boot. As it
happened, there was an exceptional amount of violent
crime in 1878, culminating in September in an attack on a
shop in Winglok Street by an armed gang of over fifty
Chinese, who sealed off the street, shot it out with the

police, and fled in a steam launch. The spokesmen of the merchants, William Keswick and H. B. Gibb, both unofficial members of the Legislative Council, called a meeting at the City Hall to protest against the Governor's lenient attitude. However Chinese opinion supported Hennessy and something of a contretemps occurred when 300 Chinese, led by Ng Choy, the first Chinese barrister in Hong Kong and a 'crony' of the Governor's, turned up at the meeting. The Europeans left the City Hall and held their meeting at the nearby cricket ground instead. There they passed a resolution stating that the breakdown of law and order was a result of the Governor's 'undue leniency towards the criminal classes' and requested the Secretary of State to set up a commission to inquire into the administration of criminal law in the colony. Three weeks later an address signed by 2000 Chinese was sent to London expressing support for the Governor's views and actions. The Colonial Office refused to appoint a commission and in 1879 the Colonial Secretary, Lord Kimberley, approved nearly all of Hennessy's proposals for the reform of the criminal laws. All laws directed specifically against Chinese offenders were repealed, public flogging was ended, and flogging itself was restricted to cases where it was permitted in Britain. The partial remission of sentences in return for voluntary branding and deportation was also ended. The Colonial Office however was not entirely happy with the way in which Hennessy went about things. One official commented that 'The Governor made some changes in the criminal law of Hong Kong about flogging and branding, which were good in themselves but which he carried out with a singular want of tact and judgement.'

The hostility between the Governor and the merchants was not lessened when Hennessy showed scant sympathy for pleas that he should take some action against the Chinese customs stations which had been set up in 1867 on the approaches to the harbour. These stations were claimed by the Chinese merchants, who tended to monopolize local trade, to interfere with and dislocate legitimate trade while the Chamber of Commerce complained that the presence of the stations was contrary to Hong Kong's status as a free port. Hennessy made it plain that he thought the real cause of their complaints was the fact that the stations acted as a check on salt smuggling and the evasion of opium duties. He told the Legislative Council in 1878 that, unless the merchants gave up such practices, they could not hope for the removal of the customs stations, nor should they look to him for any help. Hennessy's attitude was in marked contrast to that of MacDonnell whose forthright support of the merchants' complaints had drawn disapproval from the Colonial Office where it was noted that the Governor seemed to question the right of the Chinese government 'to exercise its own jurisdiction over its own subjects in its own waters in a manner which it considers conducive to its own interests'. The problem of the so-called 'blockade' was not settled until 1886 when an Anglo-Chinese commission agreed on various measures which greatly reduced the smuggling of opium from the colony to China.

Hennessy had the opportunity to make clear that in future the administration would pay greater heed to local Chinese opinion when Hugh Gibb went on leave in 1880. The Governor, without consulting the Colonial Office, promptly appointed Ng Choy to fill the temporary vacancy on the Legislative Council. A memorial from prominent Chinese residents had been sent to London the previous year expressing the wish that representatives of the Chinese community should be given a share in the management of the colony's affairs. There was no open opposition from the expatriate unofficials but, probably as a result of the opinion which they had already formed of Hennessy, there was a feeling that this was 'an attempt to create an anti-English party feeling in Hong Kong'. The Colonial Secretary, Sir Michael Hicks Beach, refused the Governor's request that Ng Choy should be given a permanent seat on the Legislative Council but this may have been due to misgivings about Hennessy's manner of implementing his policy. This is borne out by the fact that the Colonial Office now decided that Hennessy's successor should be instructed to appoint a Chinese member of the Legislative Council. In 1881 Hennessy nominated Belilios to the Legislative Council but, although he was a Jew of Indian origin, this was not a very controversial move as Belilios was on the board of several European-owned companies and was, in fact, at that time chairman of the Hongkong and Shanghai Bank.

More heat was generated when the Governor opposed racial discrimination in the use of the City Hall library and museum, which was restricted to Europeans on Sundays and at certain hours during the week. The funds for the building of the City Hall had been largely raised by donations from the merchant houses, with the largest amount being given by Jardine's, although the government contributed an annual subvention. Keswick was on the management committee of the City Hall and took an active part in its affairs. In fact Keswick wished to encourage Chinese use of the City Hall's facilities. At a meeting in the Museum in 1876, Keswick and the Curator agreed to ask prominent Chinese to contribute towards an extension to the Museum which would help 'in making the museum a place of amusement and instruction to the Chinese'. At this meeting it was noted that in the previous week 14,000 Chinese as opposed to 300 Europeans had visited the library and museum. Keswick's phraseology sounds a shade patronizing to modern ears but it might be noted in passing that a few years earlier Jardine's had subsidized Dr James Legge's famous translation of the Chinese classics. At any rate Keswick was furious with the Governor's interference in the running of the City Hall but, when the Colonial Office backed Hennessy's threat to withdraw the government subvention if the rule was not cancelled, the management committee had to give way. Insult was added to injury when the Governor stopped the sale of alcohol at

City Hall functions on the ground that a licence had not been obtained, although the practice had gone on for years. The Colonial Secretary noted, a trifle wearily, of Hennessy's reports on these incidents that 'a little tact might usefully have replaced these impassioned harangues'.

The mutual animosity between Keswick and Hennessy came to the surface when the King of Hawaii, who was on a world trip, visited Hong Kong in 1881. Keswick was the Hawaiian Consul-General and when the King's ship arrived he personally went to invite the King to stay at his house. Hennessy heard of this and, while Keswick was still on board, the Governor's twelve-oared official barge arrived with 'an invitation from the Governor . . . in the name of the Queen, to be his guest'. The King, much to Keswick's annoyance, decided that the Queen's wishes took precedence over those of the Princely Hong. Hennessy, as usual, wrote at length to the Colonial Office on this petty incident which Lord Kimberley dismissed as 'a miserable squabble'. A day or two later Paul Chater, a leading businessman, gave a lunch party for the King at his luxurious bungalow in Kowloon, at which the composition of the guests showed that on such occasions there was no racial discrimination. An American member of the King's party noted that there were present 'English free traders, American protectionists, large-framed and clever-looking Chinamen, Frenchmen in exile from the Parisian Jerusalem and Japanese getting into Western ways'. Hennessy was also present and, in what was no doubt intended as jest, referred in his speech to 'trifling incidents . . . in past years, such as the killing of Captain Cook by his Majesty's predecessor'.

It was with relief and with no demonstrations of appreciation that the expatriate community greeted the departure in 1882 of Hennessy to the governorship of Mauritius where he soon stirred up more controversy. Sir George Bowen, who succeeded him in Hong Kong, had to spend most of his short period of administration, from 1883 to

1885, in sorting out the administrative muddles left behind by Hennessy, who had found routine work boring. Nonetheless, in spite of his failings, the temperamental Irishman had set the colony on a new course necessary for its future survival. Demands for a municipal council had revived during Hennessy's governorship but Bowen did not favour them. Apart from any other consideration there were now 83 British ratepayers, against 647 Chinese and 98 other nationalities and therefore it was unlikely that many British representatives would be elected. Bowen observed to the Colonial Office that as Chinese views on 'water supply, sanitation, police, harbour regulations . . . differed widely from those of Europe', this would cause considerable difficulties. He favoured the further expansion of the Legislative Council to make it more representative and his suggestion was accepted by the Colonial Office. The number of unofficials was increased to five, of whom the Chamber of Commerce and the J.P.s were to nominate one each, while the Governor was to nominate the other three, of whom one was to be Chinese. The official members were increased to six. Bowen introduced two other important constitutional reforms. Municipal rates were now placed within the jurisdiction of the Legislative Council and it was accepted that the official majority would not be used to steam-roller a united unofficial opposition especially in financial matters.

The unofficials came to regard themselves as 'the lawfully constituted guardians of the public purse' and subjected the financial affairs of the colony to close scrutiny. In 1890, led by T. H. Whitehead, manager of the Chartered Bank, they objected strongly to the doubling of the colony's financial contribution to the garrison, an issue which still periodically arouses passions in Hong Kong. As a gesture of protest, they opposed the raising of the salaries of government officials, in spite of having earlier agreed to it, and were only defeated by the combined votes of the officials. The Governor, Sir William Des Voeux, always displayed a keen interest in his own emoluments and he found this gesture and a letter subsequently written to him by the unofficials 'highly objectionable'. He was slightly mollified when J. J. Keswick later apologized personally and withdrew his name from the letter.

1891 was the colony's fiftieth anniversary. The Queen's congratulations and wishes for its continued prosperity were sent to the Governor by telegram. In its jubilee year, the colony did seem to have attained stability and the future seemed reasonably bright. A Frenchman, J. Chailley-Bert, wrote with admiration untypical of his nation,

There life rolls by, varied, swift, happy, useful. After three or four years one goes to recuperate in Old England. After fifteen or twenty years one retires there. One is looked up to by reason of this hard-earned wealth; and thereafter, attentive and indulgent, one follows and encourages the efforts of those who, in their turn, strive and strain to conduct on so high a plane, with such faith and indomitable energy, the destinies of the Anglo-Saxon race.[1]

To some extent both the stability and the prosperity were illusory or, at any rate, were built upon shifting sands. The arrival of the new Governor, Sir William Robinson, at the end of 1891 marked the beginning of a series of misfortunes. In 1892 the dollar dropped 20 per cent in value against the pound and in the following year dropped a further 16 per cent. By December 1894 it needed ten dollars to buy one pound against six in 1891. Since the government's revenue was in silver but much of its expenditure was in sterling, projected public works, such as improved water and sewerage schemes, were threatened and it was necessary to raise a loan of £200,000 from the home government to cover the proposed expenditure. In 1892 the P. & O. *Bokhara* sank off the South China coast taking with it many Hong Kong residents including all but two of the colony's cricket team returning from Shanghai. In 1894 Hong Kong was struck by two exceptionally severe typhoons and, even worse, by an outbreak of bubonic plague, hitherto unknown in the colony. As the deaths mounted, mainly in the poor Chinese quarter of Tai Ping Shan, large numbers of Chinese left the city. Official figures admitted to a temporary exodus of 80,000, or nearly half the population. As a desperate remedy, the government pulled down about a tenth of the buildings in Victoria. Robinson reported to the Colonial Office that 'so far as trade and commerce are concerned, the plague has assumed the importance of an unexampled calamity'. The epidemic had died down by the end of the year but recurred in 1896 and thereafter annually for some years. Even the colony's income from opium was threatened for there was growing agitation in Parliament for the systematic reduction of the trade.

In this time of stress, demands for constitutional reform once again became a popular topic in the smoking-room of the Hong Kong Club. A number of expatriate residents led by Whitehead, Jackson, and Chater established a Reform Association which demanded, amongst other things, un-official control over legislation and finance. The unofficials on the Legislative Council decided to pursue a policy of persistent opposition and, following the precedent estab-lished in Des Voeux's time, voted in 1892 in support of a motion to reduce the salaries of civil servants to the level of 1890. When the measure was defeated by the officials, Whitehead complained that this was unconstitutional since the officials were interested parties voting on measures which would directly affect them. Prompted by the Colonial Office, Robinson agreed to set up a Retrench-ment Committee with an unofficial majority to consider economies in the government service. This committee reported in September 1894 in favour of the abolition or amalgamation of a number of posts and the reduc-tion of staff in many departments, economies which had in fact been earlier suggested by the Governor.

In 1894 a petition signed by many ratepayers which

demanded that representatives of British nationality should be freely elected to the Legislative Council and that the elected members should be in the majority was sent to the Secretary of State. Robinson commented to the Colonial Office that he thought the agitation had been caused by the increased military contribution in 1890 and that if it was cut the agitation would die away, but Lord Ripon took the matter more seriously. In the course of a long despatch to the Governor he stated his belief that Hong Kong had prospered because it had been under colonial administration and that in future the Crown Colony government must be maintained, which meant in practice that the official majority in the Legislative Council must remain. Besides he thought that the existing system would safeguard the interests of the general public better than a small and unrepresentative elected oligarchy. However he was prepared to consider certain minor reforms such as increasing the number of both officials and unofficials on the Legislative Council and permitting unofficials to attend the Executive Council from time to time. He also expressed the hope that the Sanitary Board might develop into a municipal council. This body had been created by Bowen and, after modifications, comprised four official members, six others, of whom four were to be Chinese, appointed by the Governor and two elected by those on the jury list. However Lord Ripon concluded that no changes could be considered until the Sino-Japanese War ended and normality returned to China.

Agitation continued in Hong Kong and Whitehead went to London to press the views of the reformers. Robinson reported, with a touch of asperity, that he could not discover 'any real desire among the inhabitants of the colony for any change in its constitution' which, as far as the Chinese inhabitants were concerned, was almost certainly true. In the Sanitary Board elections of 1894 only 25 out of 500 eligible cast their votes. This apathy to civic affairs among the general public still regularly manifests itself in the low turnout for elections to the Urban Council, which replaced the Sanitary Board in 1935. There had been official complaints about the inefficiency of the Sanitary Board and its 'long, wordy, windy, desultory, rambling discussions . . . ending in nothing being done'. At the end of 1895 Robinson proposed that the membership be amended to three *ex officio* and two elected members. However he yielded to opposition by agreeing to hold a plebiscite on the question of whether or not there should be an elected majority. Of the 331 residents who voted not one was Chinese and more than 90 per cent favoured an unofficial majority. Somewhat illogically Robinson nonetheless urged the Colonial Office to agree to his original plan. The Secretary of State, Joseph Chamberlain, did not approve of the Governor's meddling, noting that 'it is inconsistent with Crown Colony government to seek the guidance of a plebiscite'. Robinson was curtly instructed to drop his proposals and leave matters as they were.

In July 1896 reforms on the lines of Ripon's proposals were implemented. J. J. Bell-Irving and C. P. Chater became the first unofficial members of the Executive Council. The Colonial Office had wanted one of the two to be Chinese but Robinson had objected that no Chinese could be really independent. The Legislative Council was increased by one official and two unofficials, one of whom was a Chinese, Wei Yuk. As a result of these changes, and possibly of improved trade, the reformers' demands once again died away. If they had been originally stimulated by the increased military contribution, their object was not obtained. In 1896, noting that government revenue was rising, the Secretary of State substituted a percentage charge of $17\frac{1}{2}$ per cent of gross receipts in place of the previous fixed charge.

The principal event in the governorship of Sir Henry Blake (1898–1903) was the leasing of the New Territories. This had been advocated for some years by merchant opinion in Hong Kong led by Chater. A principal motive was the fear that a hostile power, not necessarily China, in control of the Kowloon hills could use modern artillery to dominate the harbour and the city of Victoria, although there was also a hope that the extension of the colony's borders northwards might offer commercial opportunities. The more active also waxed enthusiastic over the possible extension of sporting and recreational facilities. In September 1895 the Chamber of Commerce and the unofficial members of the Legislative Council made representations to the Colonial Office urging the acquisition by the colony of more territory. The Governor supported these representations with a telegram, drawing the comment from the Foreign Office that 'Sir William Robinson seems a somewhat impulsive gentleman'. Opinion in the Colonial Office was equally unenthusiastic and one official inquired, 'Can he so far have lost his head that he wants to annex Canton?' However the Sino-Japanese War of 1894—5 had shattered the co-operative policy between the Powers and led to 'the scramble for concessions'. The representations from Hong Kong were backed by the China Association as well as military opinion and Salisbury reluctantly concluded that he would have to seek the lease of the New Territories.

The grant of the lease in June 1898 was greeted in Hong Kong with jubilation. Local opinion in the New Territories was hostile to the take-over which was not actually effected until April 1899. To some extent this hostility was the result of misapprehensions with regard to the consequences of the British take-over. Matters were not helped by a syndicate of Hong Kong Chinese businessmen, including Ho Kai, an unofficial member of the Legislative Council, which bought land at rock bottom prices by spreading a rumour that the British would seize all the land. Blake threatened to restore this land to its original owners but legal complications prevented him from doing so. Chater invested in a small iron mine and Jardine's made a search for coal but it was not long before it was concluded that the New Territories offered few viable commercial opportunities and for many years it remained a largely agricultural backwater.

In the remaining years before the outbreak of the First World War, there was little agitation for further alterations to the constitution of the Legislative Council. However the annual outbreaks of plague stimulated demands that the Sanitary Board should become in effect a municipal council. The connection between the plague and rats was widely suspected but in 1900 a commission of inquiry into this connection was told by the Medical Officer of Health that it was 'more probable that rats caught plague from man rather than that men were infected through rats'. In 1901 the epidemic was especially severe and the Chamber of Commerce demanded the reform of the Sanitary Board and that a commission of inquiry be sent out from England. The Governor, Sir Henry Blake, agreed to reconstitute the Board with four officials and six unofficials but its powers were only advisory and the Medical Officer of Health continued to be directly responsible for all sanitary matters. After further complaints, the Board was made directly responsible to the government in 1907 but the prospect of it developing into a municipal body was still remote. Meanwhile in response to the complaints of the Chamber of Commerce, two specialists, Professor W. J. Simpson and Osbert Chadwick, had been sent out in 1902 to consider health matters. As a result of their report, the Public Health and Buildings Ordinance, which sought to set up machinery to enforce rules of hygenic living, was passed in 1903. The link between malaria and the mosquito was now realized and Simpson also recommended the treating and rebuilding of nullahs. However it was not until after the First World War that plague and malaria, the twin curses of Hong Kong, were finally brought under control.

The years around the turn of the century were a time when public benefactors made considerable contributions to the health and education of the colony. Although some

significant donations were made by European businessmen, the Asians and Eurasians, influenced no doubt to
some extent by the desire to win honour and recognition in
Hong Kong, were well to the fore. Ho Kai, son of the Revd
Ho Fuk Tong, who had made a small fortune by judicious
property investments, was one of the first Chinese to be
educated in England. He returned to the colony with
degrees in law and medicine and an English wife named
Alice. She died after a short time and in 1887 Ho Kai
endowed the Alice Maternity Hospital and the Ho Min
Ling Hospital. These hospitals, like the Nethersole Hospital, endowed by W. H. Davis in memory of his mother,
were run by the London Missionary Society and were later
amalgamated into the present Alice Ho Min Ling Nethersole Hospital. Ho Kai was the first permanent Chinese
member of the Legislative Council and was eventually
knighted. The Matilda Hospital, which was erected by
Granville Sharp, a broker, as a memorial to his wife, was
opened in 1907.

In 1902 a committee, which included Ho Kai, was set up
to report on local education. One of its recommendations
was that Queen's College, hitherto a mixed school for boys
of all nationalities, should cease to cater for Europeans, for
whom a separate school should be provided. Queen's
College had numbered among its pupils many of the Eurasian offspring of European businessmen. One of these was
Robert Ho Tung who had just offered to build a school in
Kowloon in which instruction was to be in English. He had
evidently intended the new school to be the Kowloon
equivalent of Queen's College, for he only reluctantly
agreed to the government's suggestion that it should be the
proposed European school, commenting that this was 'so
much opposed to the spirit which prompted my offer of the
school'. E. R. Belilios had also presented the government with a reformatory school. Strangely there were no
prospective inmates and so it became a girls' school
using English as the language of instruction.

For many years Queen's College had been Hong Kong's most advanced educational institution, except for the small College of Medicine which had been founded in 1887. The medical college was incorporated in 1907 and a Chinese businessman, Ng Li Hing, gave $50,000 towards a new building for it. This development prompted no less a person than the Governor, Sir Frederick Lugard, to propose that Hong Kong should establish its own university. He and others of like mind believed that a university in Hong Kong, dissociated from Christian teaching, would have a unique opportunity to assist China in the acquisition of modern technical and scientific knowledge. A few also thought that it might assist Britain to acquire some knowledge of the philosophy of the East. Lugard's appeal for funds did not, at first, attract much support; many Chinese were still suspicious of Western learning, while most European businessmen felt that a university was an unnecessary luxury. However a start was made when a wealthy Parsee, H. N. Mody, offered $150,000 for the building and $30,000 as an endowment. Mody had come to Hong Kong in 1858 at the age of nineteen with a firm of Indian bankers and opium dealers. He established his own opium business but, after Sassoon's came to dominate this trade, he turned to exchange brokerage and dealing in shares. He became the director of so many companies that he was known as the Napoleon of the Rialto. He was closely associated with Paul Chater in the development of Central District in the 1890s. His generosity to the university and to charity earned him a knighthood.

Others were inspired to follow Mody's example. J. H. Scott persuaded Swire's to give £40,000 to endow a chair of engineering. In 1921 Swire's gave a further $100,000 towards engineering studies. Ng Li Hing gave the anatomy building in addition to the new medical college, and a Straits Chinese, Cheung Pat Sze, helped the arts faculty. Over $1,250,000 had been promised by the time the foundation stone was laid in March 1910. Ho

Tung later endowed a chair of surgery.

The small Parsee community was notable for its contributions to charity. Hormusjee Ruttonjee arrived in Hong Kong from Bombay in 1884 to join a kinsman who had been there since 1862. At first he was employed as an assistant in a Parsee business house but later set up on his own, dealing in provisions, wines, and spirits. He was assisted by his son, J. H. Ruttonjee, who in the course of his long life contributed over $2 million to the war against tuberculosis, being largely responsible for the building of the Ruttonjee Sanatorium, the Grantham Hospital, and a convalescent home. J. H. Ruttonjee expanded his business interests, developing property in Kowloon, having an interest in the Kowloon and Palace Hotels, and, after the First World War, establishing a successful brewery.

1.  Quoted in Sayer, Hong Kong 1862–1919, 71.

# 12

# Business and Social Affairs

AT the time of the establishment of the Hongkong and Shanghai Bank, silver, in the form of Mexican and Spanish dollars or fifty-ounce ingots, was still the principal medium of exchange in the East. An advance under a bill of exchange was paid to a Chinese merchant in silver and this was repaid in London in sterling within six months. Until 1873 the value of silver remained fairly stable but then it began to fluctuate downwards due to the discovery of silver in Nevada and to the sale of silver stocks by Germany, Holland, and Sweden, after they went on to the gold standard. Dealing in bills of exchange became a gamble and a few men with exceptional financial flair managed to make their fortunes in this way. One of these was Paul Catchik Chater who came to Hong Kong in 1864, aged eighteen, as a clerk in the Bank of Hindustan and who was to be described later by the *Sunday Times* as 'one of the most powerful and . . . the most beneficent figures in the Empire'.

Chater was born in Calcutta, his family being of Christian Armenian origin. His maternal grandfather, Agah Catchik Arnkiel, was a prominent merchant who had close connections with the British administration, and although both his parents died while he was young, he had a good education. After serving for three years in the Bank of

Hindustan, he started his own broking business with some backing from the Sassoons. He made sufficient in this to go into real estate, buying a site in 1870 which he later leased to the Victoria Club. Over the next ten years in association with several other Asian businessmen, such as the Sassoons, E. R. Belilios, H. N. Mody and Hormusjee Ruttonjee, he acquired and developed several sites in Central District.

Chater was a remarkably active and versatile businessman and played a major part in establishing several of Hong Kong's most important companies. In the 1870s there were few listings on the Hong Kong Stock Exchange. Important additions in the 1880s with which Chater was closely connected were the Hong Kong Rope Manufactury (1883), Hong Kong Wharf and Godown (1886), Hong Kong Electric Company (1889), and the Hong Kong Land Investment and Agency Company (1889).

He was far-sighted enough to realize the potentialities of real estate outside the central business area and in the 1880s two of the areas of which he pioneered the development were Kennedy Town and Kowloon. Kennedy Town, named after the Governor, Sir Arthur Kennedy (1872–7), on the north-west coast of Hong Kong island, began to have some commercial importance after the opening of the Suez Canal and the spread of the telegraph made it necessary for merchants to maintain stocks of goods, stored in large godowns in Eastern District, in order to take advantage of price fluctuations. Instead, incoming goods were now unloaded at more convenient wharves on the western approaches to the harbour. Chater was associated with the reclamation of twenty-six acres in Kennedy Town and a street in the area, Catchik Street, commemorates his involvement.

The Kowloon peninsula had developed only slowly after its acquisition by Britain at the end of the Second Anglo-Chinese War. A military base was established there, but for some years it was chiefly regarded as a quiet place to spend the week-end. Chater was sufficiently interested in

Kowloon to take the unusual step, in those days, of having a bungalow there, in addition to 'Marble Hall', his palatial residence on the island. He later put up most of the money and gave part of the land beside his bungalow to assist the construction of St Andrew's Church. Chater realized that the undeveloped shoreline could be used for wharves and godowns to relieve the pressure on Hong Kong island. Backed once more by the Sassoons, he built the first public godown in Kowloon in 1871. At this time there were no alongside berths on either side of the harbour and the unloading of cargo into lighters often took a week or more. Chater believed that it would be possible to build such berths on the western edge of the Kowloon peninsula. With that attention to detail which distinguishes the great from the mediocre, he personally went out in a sampan with a plumb-line in order to test the depth of the water offshore. Apparently he had sufficient influence in government circles to ensure that he was the only one to get permission to build wharves in Kowloon. In 1884 he formed the Hong Kong and Kowloon Wharf and Godown Company and two years later he arranged a merger with Jardine's wharves and godowns on Hong Kong island. From that time the chairmanship of the board was held by the managing director of Jardine's.

The early days of the new company were not without difficulties. The lighter coolies, who were well organized into their own 'hongs', naturally objected to the development of onshore berths. They made difficulties and combined to raise wages. The management circumvented them by building its own fleet of lighters and by importing workers from Swatow. This workforce expanded to 1500 men but unfortunately the Swatow workers generally returned home for the summer months, partly to escape the annual outbreak of plague in the coiony's slums. In order to encourage them to stay permanently, the Company decided to provide quarters for all of them. This policy paid off in 1895 when the Swatow labourers remained at their jobs during the general strike of that year. While the expansion of the commercial and residential areas on Hong Kong island led to the rapid disappearance of godowns there, the Wharf and Godown Company bought up more land in Kowloon. The development of the Kowloon—Canton railway gave the company a further boost and in 1906 it increased its paid up capital from $1 million to $3 million in order to finance further expansion. The following year the chairman reported that Hong Kong harboured annually the largest aggregate of registered tonnage of any port in the world.

The most notable real estate development with which Chater was associated was the so-called Praya Reclamation in Central District, on which now stand the Supreme Court, the Hong Kong Club, Mandarin Hotel, Prince's Building, St George's Building, Union House, Alexandra House, and the P. & O. Building. Most of the commercial buildings are owned by Hong Kong Land, the company Chater formed in association with Jardine's. Proposals to reclaim this area had been mooted for years, one of which was Bowring's abortive scheme. Apart from difficulties with the marine lot holders, the main obstacle to any government proposals was that the government did not have the money to undertake such an ambitious scheme. In 1887 Chater came up with a solution; an area amounting to 57 acres would be reclaimed by the marine lot holders at their own expense but under government control. The owners would get the new land adjoining their existing lots at $200 per quarter acre. His proposal was very advantageous to the lot holders since the cost was estimated at about $2 million and the profit at nearly $6 million, of which the government would only get $1 million. The Governor, Sir William Des Voeux, argued that the premium to the government should be increased, but in a rather half-hearted way, so that when Chater went to London to argue his case at the Colonial Office, his scheme was finally accepted with only slight modifications.

To take advantage of the land investment opportunities offered by the Praya Reclamation Scheme, work on which began in 1890, Chater formed Hong Kong Land. Chater was on good terms with John Bell-Irving, who succeeded William Keswick as senior partner of Jardine's in the East when the latter returned to Britain in 1886. They shared a common interest in horse-racing, were both members of the Legislative Council—Chater had become a member when Frederick Sassoon retired in 1887—and had been associated in the merger of their respective wharf and godown interests. Accordingly Chater co-operated with Jardine's in setting up Hong Kong Land and when the new company was incorporated Chater and J. J. Keswick, who had just taken over from Bell-Irving, were permanent joint managing directors.

The early days of Hong Kong Land were not without difficulties. The first issue of shares provided a working capital of $1¼ million. Practically all the original share-holders were European, and a group of local Chinese businessmen decided to set up a rival real estate company. To counter this, the board made a further issue of 25,000 $50 shares, fully paid and with a premium of $50, thus doubling the company's working capital and establishing a reserve fund of £1¼ million. Half the shares were offered to existing shareholders, some of whom borrowed heavily to take up their allocation, and half to Chinese investors. However, since the reclamation scheme had only just begun, a major problem was to find profitable investments. In the first year of operations property costing $800,000 was bought and mortgage loans amounting to $1.3 million were made. At the first Annual General Meeting in 1890 a dividend of 7 per cent was declared on the working capital, with no return to the shareholders on the reserve fund. Angry shareholders complained that Chater had exaggerated the prospects and that the $50 premium had not been justified. However Keswick, who was known as James the Bloody-Polite, calmed the meeting by explaining that it took time to 'invest judiciously' in property. Keswick, a large man, whose formidable black-bearded appearance was belied by the suavest of manners, reputedly gained his nickname after an occasion when he very gently, with many amiable and lengthy expressions of esteem and regret, gave an employee of Jardine's the sack. As the man backed through the door of Keswick's office, he was heard to exclaim in tones of genuine gratitude, 'Thank you so very much, Mr Keswick. Thank you very much indeed.'

The mid-1890s were a time of economic depression in the East, aggravated in Hong Kong by the bubonic plague epidemic of 1894 which caused a partial exodus of the Chinese population. The shareholders reconciled themselves to slow growth. Robert Shewan told the 1896 Annual General Meeting, 'This is not a speculative stock; it is a stock eminently for the cautious and careful investor who above all things seeks safety for his investments.' Nonetheless the company paid an 8 per cent dividend throughout most of the 1890s, rising to 10 per cent in 1898 and 12 per cent in 1899. By this time the reclamation scheme in Central was beginning to bear fruit. The first building owned by the company to be completed was the New Oriental building, on the present site of the Furama Hotel, in 1898. Between 1904 and 1905 King's, York, Alexandra, Royal, and St George's Buildings, all in the typical Italianate arcaded style of the period, were finished. Meanwhile Sir Paul, who had been knighted in 1902, had begun buying up property in Eastern District in anticipation of another project, the Praya East Reclamation Scheme. He was somewhat premature, for work on it did not begin until 1921, at which time Sir Paul's foresight finally paid off.

The establishment of the Hong Kong Electric Company was closely involved with the Praya Reclamation Scheme and involved several of the same principals. The prime initiator in the formation of the company was Bendysche Layton, a partner in Gibb, Livingston and Co., which already acted as agent for the Shanghai Gas Company. In

1888 Layton interested Henry Dalrymple, chairman of the Hongkong and Shanghai Bank, in the idea of setting up an electric company. Another interested party was Lorenz Poesnecker, a director of the Hongkong and Shanghai Bank, and partner in the German firm of Arnhold, Karberg and Co., agents for the Allgemeine Electricitats Gesellschaft, a major manufacturer of electrical machinery. To attract local investors to support such a scheme would need big names—and who was bigger in Hong Kong than Jardine's and Chater? Both Chater and Bell-Irving were members of the Legislative Council and at this time Layton was elected to the Council by the Chamber of Commerce to fill a temporary vacancy. Layton's first meeting was that at which Chater stated he would go to London to put the case for the Praya Reclamation Scheme. After the meeting Layton, Bell-Irving and Chater got together, doubtless at the Hong Kong Club, and agreed to co-operate in setting up the Hong Kong Electric Company. Before his departure, Chater advised Layton that an old centrally situated cemetery in Wanchai, due to come up for sale, would be the ideal site for a power station. It was intended that the company would eventually light the reclaimed area and in those days electricity could not be transmitted for long distances. The lot was duly bought and when Chater returned from England with approval for his scheme, the promoters had already obtained a government contract to light most of Central District. The company was incorporated in January 1889 and among the directors were Chater, Bell-Irving, Dalrymple, and Poesnecker, with Layton as chairman.

The company's prospectus confidently declared that

The advantages of the Electric Light are so well recognized that little need be said on the subject. It is, however, peculiarly adapted for use here on account of its being almost entirely free from heat and unaffected by wind, and also on account of its almost perfect freedom from danger by fire. The Directors have no doubt that light can be supplied at rates which will compare favourably with the price paid for Gas in the Colony, while for quality, power and convenience, the light will be much superior to any other kind of lighting. . . .[1]

Some, of course, were sceptical but, as intended, the electric lights in Central District came on for the first time at 6 p.m. on 1 December 1890. The *Hong Kong Telegraph* declared enthusiastically the same night in its last edition, which had been held back for the occasion, 'The light is beautifully bright and as steady as that reflected by old "sol" himself'. However, after two nights, the lights failed. The *Daily Press* commented in magisterial tones, 'The electric light was far from a success last night. After a good deal of jumping it went out altogether on the Caine Road at 9.30 p.m., while the lamps on the lower levels gave a diminished and fickle light. It is to be hoped that the new illuminant will prove steadier and more reliable in future.'[2] It was found that the failure had been caused by the fact that some of the lamp hoods were touching the lamps, allowing the current to escape. The hoods were removed for adjustment but on the night of 8 December, unusually for the time of year, there was a local rainstorm over Central and all the lights went out. The *Daily Press* became sarcastic. 'The gas was turned on as of old in the thoroughfares turned over to the Electric Company. It is to be hoped that the occurrence of a rain or thunderstorm is not always to cause a suspension of the light.' However after two more days the hoods were restored and the lights came on again. There was not to be another breakdown for twenty-six years.

The provision of fuel for the Electric Company gave Chater another opportunity to provide a service at considerable profit to himself. In 1892, in association with Mody, he founded the Société Français des Charbonnages du Tonkin to develop coal mines at Hongay in Vietnam, thereby undercutting the price of coal from more traditional sources. This has been described as 'one of the only truly successful commercial undertakings in the entire history of French Indo-China', and a grateful French government rewarded Chater with the Légion d'Honneur. Chater, in spite of his wealth, power, and prestige, was not immune to the vanity that afflicts lesser mortals. In 1908, after he had put on the market Victoria Lodge, a residential property in Mid-Levels, he was approached by M. Liebert, the French Consul-General. When Sir Paul learnt that the French government was interested in buying the property, he obligingly reduced the price from $80,000 to $65,000, making it plain that in return he expected to be awarded a higher rank in the Légion d'Honneur. The deal was arranged and the French government obtained the lease of Victoria Lodge, which is still the home of the French Consul, for 999 years.

In common with some other Anglo-Asians, Chater showed, to the phlegmatic English, an almost indecent enthusiasm for all things British, in particular the Crown, and an equally enthusiastic generosity to his adopted homeland in the form of charitable donations. He was chairman of the Jubilee Committee of 1897 which decided to mark the occasion by erecting a hospital and a nurses' institute and by building a road around the island, the cost to be borne by public subscriptions augmented by a government grant. As well as largely financing the building of St Andrew's Church, he gave $250,000 to Hong Kong University, $250,000 to St John's Cathedral, and $100,000 to the Union Church, Kowloon. In his will he bequeathed Marble Hall and its contents, which included the Chater Collection of China coast paintings, to the people of Hong Kong, after the death of his wife. Incidentally Sir Paul, who died at 5 a.m. on 26 May 1926, caused considerable confusion by leaving instructions that he was to be buried within twelve hours. The stock exchange opened only to declare that it was closed for the day. After much frantic telephoning, a funeral service was held at the Cathedral at 11 a.m. and the body was duly interred by 5 p.m.

Sir Paul's estate totalled $4,900,000, his main shareholdings being of about $250,000 each in the Hongkong and

Shanghai Bank, the Star Ferry, the Hong Kong and Kowloon Wharf and Godown Company, Hong Kong Electric and Hong Kong Tramways, $166,000 in Hong Kong Land and $151,000 in Hong Kong and Shanghai Hotels. In a codicil in his will, Sir Paul nominated to succeed him as permanent managing director of Hong Kong Land, firstly, Sir Victor Sassoon, provided that he paid $800,000 into Chater's estate, or if he refused, Sir Robert Ho Tung, provided that he observed the same condition. In the event of them both refusing, he nominated his nephew, John Theophilius Bagram. Sassoon and Ho Tung did decline and in July 1927 the codicil was the subject of a case between Bagram and Hong Kong Land heard in chambers. The Acting Chief Justice ruled that the codicil was void since one of the terms of the original agreement giving Chater the right to nominate his successor was that the appointee should be the senior representative of a firm carrying on business in Hong Kong. The executor had asked Bagram to accept the office in September 1926, at which time he held no such position. However when he accepted, in January 1927, he had become the senior representative of the Hong Kong Finance and Investment Company. He admitted at the hearing that the company had not carried on any business, had a subscribed capital of $1000 and in fact had been formed to qualify him for the appointment. Justice Wood noted that this was 'at its best . . . merely a titular qualification'. Bagram did not stand to benefit financially himself since Sir Paul had added the provision that any benefit which he might receive as a result of his appointment was to go to the residue of Chater's estate.[3]

Chater served on the Legislative Council for nearly twenty years and he and J. J. Bell-Irving became the first unofficial members of the Executive Council in 1896. He was a prominent Freemason, an art collector, and undoubtedly Hong Kong's keenest racegoer. After attending his first race meeting in 1865, he never missed another for sixty years, a record which would be difficult to beat. In 1872 he set up a stable with Mody, Chater racing under the name 'Mr Paul', later 'Sir Paul', and Mody as 'Mr Buxey'. In 1884 they won 17 out of 26 races, which says much for their trainer, Mr Curreem, who was never known to get astride a horse. Although the Jockey Club did not admit Chinese members until 1926, there was no bar against other Asians, a piece of liberality that probably dated back to racing in eighteenth-century India and later Macau. Racing gave Parsee and Jewish businessmen, who would have found entry to the Hong Kong Club difficult, an opportunity to meet the European taipans socially on equal terms and to acquire some standing in the expatriate community. Other leading Asian owners were Dorabjee Naorojee, David Elias Sassoon, son of Elias David, who was a prominent local rider for some years, winning his first race, the Ladies' Purse, in 1887, Sir Victor and Hector Sassoon and E. S. Kadoorie. Chater was Chairman of the Jockey Club from 1892 to 1926 and, it might be added, was also a member of the Hong Kong Club.

Sir Paul's marriage was childless, not altogether surprisingly, since it did not take place until 1910 by which time he was sixty-four. Christine, Lady Chater, was an attractive Scandinavian brunette aged about thirty-one at the time of her marriage, which took place several years after she began living with Sir Paul. She had originally come to Hong Kong to marry someone else but, as was not uncommon in those days, by the time she arrived either she or her intended had changed their mind. Some ladies in this predicament found themselves in the position of choosing between an ignominious return home or finding some means of making a living in Hong Kong. The choices were few and not surprisingly some became members of the demi-monde. In spite of the increase in the number of European wives living in Hong Kong, it was still not uncommon for expatriate businessmen, whether married or not, to have a mistress. The area around Happy Valley was a popular place to house a mistress since the proximity of the race and golf courses gave straying husbands an excuse for being in the vicinity.

Ellis Kadoorie had arrived in the colony from Baghdad in 1883 at the age of eighteen. Initially he had been employed by Sassoons and it was perhaps the Anglophilic attitude of his employers that led him to do business under the name of Kelly for a few years. He soon struck out on his own as a broker and merchant and was joined by his younger brother, Elly. The brothers prospered. One of Ellis's interests was the hotel business. By 1906 he had accumulated 20,000 shares in the Hong Kong Hotel Company. Other prominent shareholders were Chater and Ho Tung. In 1914 Ellis was invited to join the board. The origins of the Hong Kong Hotel Company went back to the mid-years of the nineteenth century. One of the most prominent Parsee businessmen in the Canton days had been Dadabhoy Rustanjee, son of the wealthy shipowner Rustanjee Cowasjee. In 1841 'Daddy Boy', as he was generally known, had purchased Marine Lot 5 in the first auction of land in Hong Kong. This prime site on Queen's Road, then the waterfront, was sold seven years later to Dent's. When Dent's was obliged to sell off its assets in 1866, the building was bought by the newly formed Hong Kong Hotel Company and became the colony's first major hotel. Hitherto visitors, who did not stay on board ship, had lodged with acquaintances or had put up at one of several somewhat sleazy guest-houses. Some enterprising businessmen realized that improved communications would increase the flow of visitors. The age of tourism was beginning. After the Hong Kong Hotel was rebuilt in 1892, it claimed to be 'The most commodious and best appointed hotel in the Far East'. An advertisement in the *Hong Kong Telegraph* of that year proudly declared that

The Table d'Hôte, at separate tables is supplied with every delicacy, the cuisine being under experienced supervision. The

Bedrooms, with adjoining bathrooms, are lofty and well venti-
lated, open onto spacious verandahs, are lighted by gas and fitted
throughout with electric communications. The Reading, Writing
and Smoking Rooms, Ladies Drawing Rooms, the New Bar and
public billiard rooms (with 6 English and American tables) are
fitted with every convenience. A handsomely appointed grill
room where chops, steaks etc are served at any hour adjoins the
hotel and is under the same management. The wines and spirits
are selected by an expert and the best brands only are supplied.
Hydraulic ascending-rooms of the latest and most approved type
convey passengers and baggage from the Entrance Hall to each of
the five floors above.

The monthly rates for a room without board began at $45.
Oddly, the hotel's telegraphic address was 'Kremlin'.

Both Kadoorie brothers held the view that 'wealth is a
sacred trust to be administered for the good of society'.
Ellis alone gave over $500,000 to charitable causes before
the outbreak of the First World War. Schools and hospitals
were established in Iraq, China, and Hong Kong. The objects of Kadoorie benefactions in Hong Kong were certainly
varied, extending from scholarships for underprivileged
Indian children to a hostel for single, expatriate ladies.
Ellis also took a keen interest in the turf and dispensed
lavish hospitality in his private stand at Happy Valley.
During the First World War he organized a campaign to
raise funds to buy aircraft for the Royal Flying Corps and
was duly rewarded with a knighthood in 1917. His brother,
who succeeded him on the board of the Hong Kong and
Shanghai Hotel Company, was knighted in 1926.

Another Asian businessman with both hotel and racing
interests was Dorabjee Naorojee, who arrived in Hong
Kong in 1852. He became a partner in Duddell and Co.,
provisioners, established a bakery, built godowns, and
acquired the Victoria Hotel. When industry began to develop in Kowloon, he decided to start a ferry service between Hong Kong and Kowloon beginning with a steam
launch. Later, in 1898 the newly formed 'Star' Ferry Com-

pany bought the Kowloon Ferry Company from him. Naorojee also owned the Kowloon Hotel. In spite of the establishment of a regular ferry service, expatriates were slow to settle in Kowloon. However the establishment of the Hong Kong and Whampoa Dock Company and of the Wharf and Godown Company did lead to gradual development, sufficient for the government to decide in 1902 to establish a school there for British children. The construction of waterworks began in the same year and many minor British and Portuguese government officials who had hitherto lived in the vicinity of Central District moved into the more salubrious surroundings of Kowloon. These developments encouraged the formation of the China Light and Power Company in 1901, with share capital of $300,000, for the purpose of building and operating an electric power station in Kowloon. The moving spirit behind the company was Robert Shewan of Shewan, Tomes and Co., who became the company's first chairman and remained so for over thirty years.

While the construction of the Kowloon power station proceeded, the company acquired the Canton Electric Supply Undertaking, hardly a major concern since it only supplied about 700 candle-power lamps and a fire pump. Shewan expressed the hope that this business would expand but the first year of operation showed a loss of $7000, attributed to the 'state of utter neglect and confusion' at the Canton power station. In 1904, after new machinery had been installed, a profit of $48,000 was made. However thereafter profits were affected by the growing hostility in China to foreign-owned concerns. About 1909 the Canton power station was sold to a Chinese company for $1.3 million.

Meanwhile the supply of power in Kowloon had begun in 1903. Although Shewan declared that 'profitable business is bound to come in time', in the first year the monthly revenue was $1200 against expenditure of $1900. Progress was slow for by 1910 the company was still only showing a profit of $2661 against paid-up capital of $300,000. In nine years there had only been two distributions to shareholders. There were demands for the company's liquidation but Shewan beat these off by revealing that a contract had been won to supply the newly completed Kowloon–Canton railway. Once again his optimism proved premature. By 1914 no further dividend had been paid and profits had only reached $25,000. However the industrialization of Kowloon was now gathering pace and by 1918 the old power station was unable to meet the growing demand. It was decided to reconstitute the company with a share capital of $1 million. Prominent shareholders were Ho Tung and the Kadoories. The first year of operation showed a profit of $115,000 and an 8 per cent dividend was paid.

Shewan Tomes continued to act as managers for some years. However by 1932 the principal shareholders, led by the Kadoories, felt that the time had come for the company to control its own affairs. Robert Shewan offered to retire if he was paid $1 million compensation. This proposal was rejected but it was agreed to put the matter to arbitration. The result was not to the shareholders' liking for the court awarded Shewan Tomes $2 million. This sum, described at the Annual Meeting in 1933 as 'a very severe blow', was paid off in instalments, the final one being made in 1950. A balance of $1 has been shown in the company's accounts ever since.

Social life in Hong Kong changed significantly after the opening of the Suez Canal in 1869. The journey from England to Hong Kong was considerably shortened and steamships by this time were much more reliable. Wives and families could now travel out in safety and comfort to a well-established colony which had largely lost its early reputation for lawlessness and ill-health. Hong Kong left its raffish days behind and, as far as expatriates were concerned, rapidly assumed a respectable, somewhat philistinic way of life. As far as can be ascertained, of the first eleven partners in Jardine and Matheson, eight died unmarried, two married after they had retired and only one, Alexander Matheson, married while still serving in the East, whereas all of the next eleven partners married, five of them while in the East. Another factor encouraging the adoption of family life was that, with the end of the halcyon days by the mid-1860s, few businessmen could entertain hopes that they would return home rich men after only half a dozen years.

Life for the family man was not cheap. The most modest middle-class household was expected to have at least a cook, two chair coolies, an amah, a houseboy, and a house coolie whose wages would come to the equivalent of £120 a year, a fairly high sum by English standards. Rents, too, were more than double those in London. However the pay of griffins was at least 20 per cent higher than they could expect in London and rose faster.

In 1867 the Governor, Sir Richard MacDonnell, bought a disused military sanatorium on the Peak, where the temperature was 14°F less than that in Central District in the summer, and converted it into a summer residence called Mountain Lodge. After a police station was established on the Peak in 1869, other Europeans began to follow the Governor's example. When the colony was visited in 1881 by the young sons of the Prince of Wales, Albert and George, they noted in their journal, which was written for them by their tutor,

> Looking eastward along the ridge from Victoria Peak to Mount Gough we were much surprised to find what a number of merchants' houses—we can count more than 50, each with its lawn-tennis court and racket court—have been built up there, on what a short time ago was a barren hill top with nothing but scrub and heather. There are admirable roads, and telephone and telegraphic communication with the town below, and they are talking of making a wire tramway up and down.[4]

Among the merchants' houses was, of course, one belonging to Jardine's, 'The Mount'. At the end of the century a

visitor wrote that 'a man's exact position on the social scale
is not infrequently determined by the altitude of his house'.

The idea for a 'wire tramway' had originated in the brain
of yet another Scotsman, Alexander Finlay Smith, late of
the Highland Railway. He interested Phineas Ryrie in his
scheme, having demonstrated to him that, even if only
forty families lived on the Peak, their annual expenditure
on the tramway would be over $45,000. Furthermore Smith
intended to cater for those who wished to escape to Hong
Kong's 'hill station' for a few weeks in the summer by
building a hotel next to the Peak terminus of the tramway.
A detailed plan was drawn up and submitted to the Legislative Council in 1881. The plan for a High Level tramway
was approved in the Tramway Bill, in which there was also
provision for a Low Level tram system. This latter system
was to be built by the Hong Kong and China Tramway
Company. An attempt was made by this company to amal-
gamate the two schemes but the proposed merger fell
through. In spite of the fact that the Hong Kong Tramway
Company was chaired by Keswick and backed by such
eminent figures as Chater and Frederick Sassoon, the
public did not subscribe the necessary half million dollars.
The Low Level tramway system was not built for another
twenty years. Meanwhile Smith and Ryrie had succeeded
in raising their more modest requirement of $125,000.
Work began in 1883 and was completed by 1888. The track
was 4500 feet in length and is still the steepest funicular
railway in the world using a steel rope as the only means of
haulage.

The Governor, Sir William Des Voeux, and his wife formally opened the tramway and then took the inaugural
trip. A special seat indicated by a brass plaque was thereafter reserved for Des Voeux and subsequent Governors
who commuted between Mountain Lodge and Government House in the summer. The China Mail observed of the
inaugural trip that the passengers 'were agreeably surprised by the pleasantness of the journey' and added that 'it

is better to ride up the Peak . . . than to be jostled by coolies'. No doubt the coolies were also relieved. After the opening of the tramway, the Peak became a popular but exclusive residential area for the wealthy. The European Reservation Ordinance reserved the Peak for European-type buildings. Special permission from the Governor was needed to live on the Peak. Sir Robert Ho Tung, who bought a group of three bungalows there in 1906, was the first Eurasian to be given such permission.

In 1905 the Peak Tramway became a limited company. One of its principal shareholders was C. C. Moxon, a partner of Elly Kadoorie. A Sunday treat for Elly's sons, Lawrence and Horace, later to be Chairman of the Board, was to be taken for a ride on the tramway. In 1922 the Hong Kong Hotel Company bought the Peak Hotel from C. Findlay Smith for over $600,000. The hotel was less successful in its later years and was not replaced when it finally burnt down in 1938.

The growing tendency among expatriates to marry and raise a family while in the East led some of the privileged few on the Peak to keep a few cows to supply their household needs. The luxury of having a private dairy herd was not for the majority. In order to serve their needs a Mr J. Kennedy imported cows and milkmaids from England and established a dairy on Garden Road in 1880. The venture soon collapsed and there is no record of what happened to either the cows or the milkmaids. However Patrick Manson, a Scottish physician, later to be knighted for his work in hygiene and tropical medicine, decided to make another attempt. He enlisted the support of Chater and in 1886 the Dairy Farm Company was formed with capital of $25,000, increased three years later to $100,000. The company's prospectus declared,

The price of good milk in Hong Kong at present ranges from twenty to twenty-five cents per bottle of twenty-four ounces. These prices, unless in the case of the rich, are simply prohibitive.

A principal object of the proposed Dairy Company will be to reduce the price so as to bring milk within the reach of the poor, say to ten cents or less per large bottle. A second object will be to secure its purity and remove it from the category of typhoid fever and other disease causes; and a third object to place the concern on a sound financial basis and make it a source of profit to the shareholders.

A herd of 80 cows was purchased and kept on 300 acres at Pokfulam. The company did well and in 1895 paid a dividend of 10 per cent on a gross profit of $18,000. Unfortunately in the following year almost the entire herd was wiped out by rinderpest. The company went into liquidation but was immediately reconstructed. A new herd was bought and measures taken to prevent further serious outbreaks proved effective. The company established a head office on Wyndham Street and in 1904 opened a retail shop there for the sale of meat and general provisions.

Racing remained the main relaxation of the taipans. A correspondent of *The Times* noted in 1858 that race week was 'the single holiday of the merchants. They spend weighty sums on importing horses from all parts and training them for the contest.' In the 1880s John Bell-Irving was a particular enthusiast, leading in his winners with marked zest and, according to Sir William Des Voeux, looking 'more like an English squire than a merchant'. A leading rider of the time was the Scottish businessman, John MacGregor, who raced as 'Mr Risk'. He maintained a large stable in Shanghai and from 1880 made annual visits to Hong Kong. MacGregor and his partner, Jack Caldbeck, another rider, catered to the expatriates' need to help to maintain the stiff upper lip with a regular intake of whisky sodas and gin tonics. In 1864 MacGregor, a former sailor with no knowledge of the wine trade, bought up the small Shanghai trading firm of George Smith and Co. and became a wine and spirits importer, bringing Caldbeck in with him. Business boomed and before long there were branches all along the China coast. In 1882 a London office was set up under the name MacGregor, Caldbeck and Co. and following this the business expanded to other popular watering holes like Singapore and Penang. After Caldbeck's death in 1908, the business was run by the MacGregor family who continued to control it until 1967.

Patronage of the race-meetings by the Governors continued from the early days. It was the custom for the Governor to lunch with Jardine's on the first day of the meeting and, after the collapse of Dent's, with Russell's on the second. Des Voeux noted that 'good food and abundant champagne produced much hilarity', adding as an afterthought, 'but nothing in the least disagreeable'. To some, at least, the refreshments and the accompanying socializing were the *raison d'être* of the whole proceedings. One observer commented that 'nobody so far forgets himself as to show more than a languid interest in the proceedings'.

Not all the taipans approved, however. Butterfield and Swire, founded by hard-headed Yorkshire businessmen, was a relative newcomer among the hongs and had taken Dent's place as Jardine's chief rivals. The indulgent ways of the Princely Hong were not for them. In 1900 all its expatriate staff were sharply informed that 'the Firm do not approve of their Employees being interested in Race Ponies and that to so interest themselves, in future, will certainly prejudice their chance of promotion'.

For about forty years racing at Happy Valley was controlled by a Race Committee, not always in the most professional way, for a correspondent of the *China Mail* in 1865 gave a critical account of that year's meeting, observing of the starters that 'a more complete acquaintance with their business and stricter attention to it when that acquaintance has been acquired would be of immense value to all concerned'. He concluded that 'the tiffins laid down in the tents adjoining the different stables were the most pleasing feature that came under my notice'. In 1884 a meeting was called to put racing in Hong Kong 'on a more stable footing'. The thirty-four people who attended agreed to set up a Jockey Club and to take over the assets of the former Race Fund standing at $10,889. The following year the newly formed Club went into debt because the track was ruined by flooding. The remedy included draining the pond in the middle of the course, which ended the snipe shooting there but enabled a 9-hole golf course to be established. Race courses had been made in some of the other treaty ports and the merchants began to send their horses to the May and Autumn meetings at Shanghai. Horses from Shanghai and Amoy also came to Hong Kong and enjoyed a good deal of success. In 1868 the Governor, Sir Richard MacDonnell, referring to Mr Rennie, the chairman of the committee set up to organize the building of the City Hall, said 'all were so grateful for his exertions that it must add to their regret that he had not been more fortunate during the last week at the races. Like Hong Kong residents in general, Mr Rennie had to endure the spectacle of all the good prizes going north to Shanghai.'

The formation of the Hong Kong Golf Club in 1888 illustrated the fact that the comment of a correspondent of The Times in 1858 that 'means of amusement are not numerous in Hong Kong' was no longer true. Moving spirits behind the formation of the Club were Sir Gershom Stewart and several officers of the Argyle and Sutherland Highlanders. The clubhouse was initially a 'dark and cavernous place' under the racecourse grandstand. The Club enjoyed august patronage. The Governor, Sir William Des Voeux, was a keen player and another Governor, Sir William Robertson, on behalf of the Club, applied for the title 'Royal' on the occasion of the Queen's Diamond Jubilee. Between 1891 and 1894 several members went to Deep Water Bay to picnic and during this period they constructed a 6-hole course. They subsequently made this over to the club and it was extended to 9 holes. A clubhouse was built there in 1898. At this time access to the Deep Water Bay course was chiefly by sea.

Most of the houses on the Peak had tennis courts and

croquet lawns where the expanding female population could fill in some of their time. The Hong Kong Club did not admit women but the wives of the taipans were catered for by the Peak Club which was formed in 1893 by Sir Thomas Jackson and some other Peak residents. It had facilities for tennis, croquet, and cards, as well as a bar, and dances there became a regular week-end event. In 1888 the Polo Club, which had lapsed for many years, was revived. The first chairman was John Bell-Irving. At the inaugural meeting he expressed the fear that the sport might lack supporters as 'not many here knew much about polo', which brought forth the reply from a Captain Fletcher that 'all you have got to do is sit on your pony and hit the ball'.

In 1869 the opening of the City Hall, which comprised a library, museum, assembly hall, ballroom, supper room, and theatre, had given scope to social activities. Dancing now became the chief amusement in the winter, the season opening with the St Andrew's Ball and ending with the Volunteers' Ball. The first St Andrew's Ball was held in 1877 and the St Andrew's Society, which received much support from the predominantly Scottish employees of Jardine's, was formed in 1881. The first president was Phineas Ryrie, chairman of the Chamber of Commerce, member of the Legislative Council, and partner in the firm of Turner and Co.

The City Hall theatre gave the Amateur Dramatic Corps, formed in 1844, its first permanent home. Previously it had used either the upper storey of a godown in Wanchai, which was reputedly very malodorous from having been used to store dried fish, or a matshed on Queen's Road which was erected each year in the cool season. There was also an amateur theatrical group organized by army officers which used an army hall. Civilians were admitted to its performances but there was a fuss in 1859 when some Parsee merchants were refused tickets. This was a probable cause of it amalgamating with the Amateur Dramatic Corps shortly after. In the early days the theatre was considered rather raffish, and all the women's parts were played by men until Mrs Philip Barnard broke the ice by appearing in 'School for Scandal' in 1879. The men used stage names until the 1870s, apparently because the taipans objected to their employees' names appearing in the programmes. The opening performance at the City Hall theatre, put on by the Amateur Dramatic Corps in collaboration with the German Club, was attended by the Duke of Edinburgh and thereafter the theatre became more respectable. The wheel turned full circle and by the end of the century producers for the Amateur Dramatic Corps had to submit the names of their casts to the committee for scrutiny to ensure that all the players were accepted in polite society. A most popular amateur actor in the 1870s was Mr Beart, Secretary of the Hong Kong Club. In 1881 his impersonation of the Governor, Sir John Pope Hennessy, brought the house down. It was said that his performance was only bettered by that of the Lieutenant-Governor, General Donovan, who managed to keep a straight face throughout the evening. In 1900 Colonel Newnham Davis in his book on the amateur theatre described the Amateur Dramatic Club as 'the best organised . . . I have found in the uttermost parts of the earth'.

The passing of the collegiate bachelor way of life in the messes of the hongs, the increases in the number of expatriate wives with ample time to devote to the finer points of the local pecking order, and the movement of the rich to the seclusion of the Peak, all helped to intensify the tendency of the expatriate community to divide itself into mutually exclusive cliques. A visitor commented,

Among Englishmen who have never visited the outlying portions of the Empire, the idea prevails that social distinctions are forgotten in the presence of the stern realities of life in the Colonies and that 'all sorts and conditions of men' are united in the bonds of brotherhood by a common feeling of expatriation. But though this idea may not be without justification in the backwoods of Canada, the bush of Australia and the veldt of South Africa, it is certainly a travesty of the conditions obtaining in our

Crown Colonies. Nowhere, perhaps, is it more completely repudiated than in Hong Kong, where society is cast into innumerable divisions and subdivisions.... In this little community are produced all the characteristics of suburban life in England, intensified by peculiar local circumstances.[5]

Racial exclusiveness in social life was, of course, the general rule in colonial territories in the nineteenth century but even in those class-conscious days Hong Kong also had a reputation for snobbery. This was not because the predominantly British expatriates came from the top drawer in their own country, indeed the strict insistence on the finer points of class distinction probably stemmed from the fact that they did not. Entrants to the British civil service did not regard Far Eastern Cadetships very highly. The Foreign Office and the Indian Civil Service were considered to be much more prestigious and among the Far East Cadets, Ceylon was the first choice. The scions of noble houses who entered the army sought postings in India, where a Viceroy graced the scene. Even the unmarried girls who set out from England on the 'Fishing Fleet' to find husbands in the colonies regarded Hong Kong as the last port of call, both literally and metaphorically.

Apart from rather better prospects of making money, to many it seemed that Hong Kong had little to distinguish it from dozens of small British possessions scattered around the globe. Major Henry Knollys, in his book *English Life in China*, published in 1885, wrote approvingly of the taipans

... whose energy and ability have so largely contributed to raise the colony to its present condition of prosperity. Pleasing in manner, of enlarged ideas, and the essence of liberality, their presence is a credit to Hong Kong—would be an honour to any community in the world.

However he was distinctly scathing about the rest of Hong Kong's expatriate society.

Then we have a small sprinkling of able administrators from the mother country, a large proportion of Anglo-Chinese officials whose views scarcely range beyond the town of Victoria, and a number of clerks whose thoughts are engrossed with dollars, and who are seeking their fortunes, which probably will be ultimately largely swallowed up in drink, play and rowdyism.[6]

Fortunately, for gentlemen with similar views to those of Major Knollys, there were the army officers of the garrison who comprised 'by far the greater proportion of the educated and gentlemanlike stratum'. The major ungallantly added that there were few ladies in Hong Kong 'with whom an English gentleman would care to exchange two words of conversation'.

The major was, perhaps, taking an excessively jaundiced view. Then, as now, Hong Kong seemed an exotic and fascinating place to Western travellers and was an essential stopping point on any visit to the East. The dinner tables of the taipans were enlivened by a constant succession of visiting dignitaries who, on the whole, sound more interesting than the company presidents and American senators who today spend a few days among the fleshpots of Hong Kong before setting off on trips to Canton or Shanghai. Sir William Des Voeux noted in his memoirs that during 1889 he entertained

... their Royal Highnesses Prince and Princess Henri de Bourbon. . . . the Grand Duke Alexander Michaelowitch of Russia, the Archduke Leopold of Austria, and admirals, commodores and captains of the navies of the United States of America, Russia, Germany, France, Austria, China and Japan. . . . and various peers and members of the House of Commons.[7]

These visitors must have brought with them fashions and gossip from the salons of London, Paris, and Vienna, and a desire not to appear provincial in their eyes no doubt helps to explain the ostentatious display of wealth which accompanied any society function in Hong Kong. Sir William commented, disapprovingly, that such occasions '. . . savoured more of fashion and expenditure than any I had seen in other colonies . . .'. Judging by his frequent complaints to the Colonial Office with regard to such matters as his salary, pension, entertainment allowance and so on, Sir William was very cautious with his own money, and he added, with a touch of complacency, that 'The income of the moment is treated as if permanent, and luxurious living is frequently followed by extreme indigence'.

In spite of the snobbery and insistence on petty social distinctions, there was, by the end of the century, a freer atmosphere. The author of *A Handbook to Hong Kong* published in 1893 contrasted the old days with the new era,

. . . the road to Shaukiwan was the Rotten Row of the Colony in those stupid days when everyone thought himself bound to keep a carriage whether he could afford it or not and the sole amusement was solemnly driving along this weary road every afternoon! Those were stupid times, may they never return. There was no croquet, there was no lawn tennis. The man who walked on the level was a pauper. There was no real pleasure, nothing but a heavy and pompous extravagance, with no return for the large sums fooled away, an outstanding ignorance of all the surroundings, the Chinese, their language and their ways, or even of the very place itself, and a great deal of insolence. . . [8]

Sir Henry May, Governor from 1912 to 1919, was a typical English sportsman and gave enthusiastic support to the expansion of recreational facilities. He stocked the reservoirs with fish and took the opportunity offered by the acquisition of the New Territories to indulge his interest in game shooting. Birds provided most of the sport but there were also numerous wild pigs, and a tiger was shot in the New Territories as late as 1915. The development of a new golf course at Fanling in the New Territories owed much to May's assistance. By Christmas 1911 18 holes were being played there. Tiffin and drink were sent by train to a matshed above the 9th green. The number of cricketers had expanded sufficiently for an eight-team league to be established in 1903. Some termed it 'second class cricket' although the *Hong Kong Weekly Press* took the trouble to explain that this term did not 'imply social distinction'. May, his private secretary, Ponsonby Fane, and the Colonial Secretary, Claude Severn, were all keen cricketers. Fane was a somewhat eccentric character who batted and kept wicket without pads and apparently never took a bath. May was also Commodore of the Royal Hong Kong Yacht Club from 1896 to 1904. His autocratic ways aroused resentment and, as a result, some disgruntled members broke away and formed the Corinthian Yacht Club in 1904. This survived until 1921.

The advent of the motor car only slowly affected social life. As late as 1912 there were less than ten miles of carriageway on the island outside the town and it was not until 1915 that Deep Water Bay was accessible to cars. Prior to the First World War, the only access to the New Territories was provided by the railway and a rough road which stopped at Tai Po. Consequently few if any foreigners established houses there. The ownership of small launches proliferated, however, and week-end picnics in remote bays were very much in fashion.

For those expatriates with some wealth and social position, the final years before the outbreak of the First World War were perhaps the most pleasant they were to experience. G. R. Sayer has described the off-duty hours of a typical griffin at this time:

At five p.m. (at any rate when the north-east monsoon is blowing) the Englishman strolls to the Cricket Club where the immortal 'Tadpole' has rigged up cricket nets. For tennis he must take a chair to the Ladies' Recreation Club on the middle levels and for polo a rickshaw to East Point. Happy Valley still provides the main centre for golf . . . for the yachtsman there is the Corinthian and the Royal Hong Kong. . . . At the Club . . . he has the choice of bridge, and even auction bridge, or bowls, and in the billiard room, five or six tables are in regular demand each evening. Into this menu has to be fitted a minimum of military drill, for volunteering is fashionable, all the most eligible young men are members, mounted or otherwise, of Hong Kong's Mounted Troop, raised and commanded by a leading member of the princely hong.[9]

Three hundred of Hong Kong's most prominent residents greeted the first day of 1914 at the annual fancy dress ball at the Kingsclere Hotel. In Hong Kong success was all and no one hesitated to indulge in an ostentatious display of wealth. The *South China Morning Post* noted that 'many of the costumes were both costly and magnificent' and declared the ball to have been 'a brilliant success'. Those with lower social aspirations attended balls given at the Taikoo Dock and the Hong Kong and Whampoa Company's Dock in Kowloon.

Expatriates from Canton and the smaller settlements and concessions visiting Hong Kong during the holiday season now had the choice of a dozen or so hotels. The Hong Kong Hotel offered 'large, airy rooms, electric lighting, lifts and fans . . . bedrooms with European bath and lavatory attached. Perfect sanitation'. The King Edward Hotel promised convenience— 'trams pass entrance'—the Grand offered 'a first class stringed Orchestra [which] renders selections during Tiffin and Dinner', while the Craigieburn had facilities for tennis players. At the lower end of the scale, the Victoria House had breakfast at 75 cents and dinner at a dollar.

Compared with Shanghai, Hong Kong was a sedate, orderly and rather dull place, pervaded by a general air of colonial complacency and provincial petty-mindedness. In February the Sincere Company was prosecuted for selling indecent pictures. In spite of the manager's claim that the pictures were works of art, indeed were reproductions of pictures hanging in the art galleries of Europe, a fine of $100 was imposed. The magistrate strongly criticized businessmen 'who stoop to seek a profit in exciting base passions and desires'. He was warmly applauded by the *South China Morning Post* which declared that 'the canker which has been eating into the healthy morality of a model colony has received a death blow'. Such expressions of righteous indignation inspired other guardians of public morality. Before long a correspondent was complaining of 'bathers who totally disregarded the common laws of decency by dressing and undressing on board steam launches in the full view of ladies and children'.

Hong Kong was a good place for the family man. Life on the Peak was relatively healthy and the physical as well as the moral well-being of the young was assured of close attention. Dr Cantlie advised anxious parents that, as a rough guide, a child should wear one pound of clothes for every stone of weight. Healthy sports-loving bachelors were also well catered for. There were weekly cricket and football fixtures during the season. The Royal Hong Kong Yacht Club and the Corinthian Yacht Club offered a choice of regattas. The latter advised members intending to take part in its championship races that boats were to be sailed by Europeans only, no Chinese crewmen being allowed. The golf club at Fanling had proved a great success and was extolled by the *South China Morning Post*, which seemed to go in for extreme views, as 'a resort unexcelled east of Suez'. In June plans were announced to build a hotel at Fanling station where golf widows and their children could spend the week-end.

In the draw for new subscription horses in January, Ellis Kadoorie, D'Almada, Sir Paul Chater, and 'John Peel', the name used by Jardine's stable, were reported to have done well. Thereafter, until the annual race week at the end of February, the newspapers carried lengthy daily reports on the progress of the entrants. Jardine's main entry for the Derby, 'President', which did eventually win, was handled personally by Mr Gresson. Early in February a large contingent of riders arrived from Shanghai, one of whom was J. Bell-Irving, who rode many of Jardine's entries. In the event, the meeting was dominated by the horses of Chater, who had eleven winners, 'John Peel', with nine winners, and Kadoorie, with four. Kadoorie's 'Fijian Chief' won the Jockey Club Stakes and one report stated that 'the repeated applause which greeted the owner as he led last year's champion in clearly showed that the victory was a most popular one'. No other owner had more than one winner, except 'Mr Medico', whose horse 'Aldwych' won three races. Bell-Irving failed to boot home a winner and had to be satisfied with one third place. Nonetheless he apparently had his share of lordly graces for one correspondent to the newspapers declared,

I'd love to become a swell jockey
Like Irving and Lindsay and Co.
My word I'd be awfully cocky
When coming home first on 'What Ho'

Trade with China in 1914 was slow and businessmen complained that the godowns were full of unsold goods. In spite of the restrictions on opium sales, there was 'still a brisk demand and a ready market for the drug'. About 5000 chests were estimated to be held in Hong Kong and early in the year, the price jumped from $400 to $600 a chest. Local business concerns continued to report improved profits although Jardine's closed its large cotton mill in Causeway Bay, which had proved uneconomic. The stock exchange listed around fifty-five companies. The majority have since disappeared but among the familiar names were the Hong-kong and Shanghai Bank, Kowloon Wharf, Hong Kong and Whampoa Docks, Hong Kong Hotels, Hong Kong Land, Dairy Farm, the Green Island Cement Company, Hong Kong Electric, Hong Kong Trams, the South China Morning Post, the Peak Tram, and Watson's.

It would not be true to say that events in Europe went unnoticed, for throughout the early months of 1914, the papers were full of war scares, international crises, and the arms build-up. One prophetic correspondent wrote in February that 'the destruction of the Powers seems imminent if the madness for increased armaments is not immediately cured'. The assassination of Franz Ferdinand merited two columns in the *South China Morning Post* on 1 July, and it continued to be extensively reported for several days. Thereafter there was a lull for three weeks or so until the presentation of the Austrian ultimatum to Serbia at the end of July. Tension rose. The Governor, Sir Henry May, advised the boys of the Central British School on 1 August to join the Cadet Corps: 'I should suggest to the boys who do belong to it that they should see to it that those who do not, quickly join. . . . There is no more important duty than that English boys should learn to defend themselves, their kindred and their country.' The *South China Morning Post* remained hopeful that Britain would keep out of the looming conflict and would continue to 'pursue in peace her policy of colonizing and building up the outlying Dominions'. Two days later, on 3 August, the leader writer was more pessimistic, expressing a devout hope that Britain would be able to maintain its position of 'calm aloofness'. Crisis or no, business had to be carried on and the edition of 5 August carried advertisements from several German companies, including Norddeutscher Lloyd of Bremen which cautiously recommended readers to book early for its sailings to Europe. On 6 August the announcement of Britain's entry into the war was made. The *South China Morning Post* struck a note of defiant patriotism: 'Hong Kong-Ready', it declared, adding that if the enemy should dare to approach Hong Kong he would find the colony 'in the mood to accord him the warmest of receptions—and this is neither bluff nor bluster'.

In Hong Kong, thoughts of how to make a profit from the direct international crisis are never far from the surface. On 7 August the *South China Morning Post*'s leader writer struck a distinctly optimistic note, the fruit no doubt of a lengthy session at the Hong Kong Club the previous evening,

Leading businessmen regard the present deadlock with some little satisfaction. Provided that it is not unduly protracted, they

consider it a splendid medium for reducing the huge accumula-
tion of stocks at Shanghai and Hong Kong which have glutted the
market for many months . . . the renewal of normal business some
six or eight months hence, with empty godowns, is an event that
the merchants can anticipate with only the keenest pleasure. . . .
Some firms in Shanghai go so far as to state that not only do they
anticipate a brisk trade but a state of prosperity such has not been
witnessed for many years. It has been said that the war will be
short, sharp and severe. The consensus of opinion is that it will
not last more than six months. In that case, as far as trade is
concerned . . . there is not much to be alarmed about.

In the same edition Caldbeck's announced a special sale of
its stocks of Pilsner Beer.

1. A. Coates, *A Mountain of Light*, Hong Kong, 1977, 19—20.

2. ibid., 34.

3. Bagram remained in Hong Kong and died after being interned by
the Japanese during the Second World War.

4. Quoted in C. Crisswell and T. Briggs, *The Vanishing City*, Hong
Kong, 1978, II, 10.

5. A. Wright, *Twentieth Century Impressions of Hong Kong,
Shanghai and other Treaty Ports of China*, London, 1908.

6. Henry Knollys, *English Life in China*, London, 1885, 30—1.

7. Sir W. Des Voeux, *My Colonial Service*, London, 1903, 230.

8. M. Greenberg, *A Handbook to Hong Kong*, Hong Kong, 1893.

9. Sayer, op. cit., 109.

# Epilogue

'The more things change, the more they remain the same.'
Alphonse Karr

THE outbreak of the First World War was initially
viewed with mixed feelings in Hong Kong. The expatriate businessmen had formed a close-knit community
and personal friendships seemed more important than
distant events in Europe. The marauding German
cruiser *Emden* had been a frequent visitor to Hong
Kong and her band had repaid the generous hospitality shown to the ship's crew by giving concerts in
the City Hall. According to one contemporary account,
the Hong Kong expatriate community followed the
exploits of the *Emden* with a certain proprietary pride.
*Schadenfreude* rather than indignation was the emotion experienced by the stalwarts of the Hong Kong
Club when the news came that the *Emden*, disguised
with a false funnel as a Russian warship, had sailed
into Penang harbour to sink a merchant ship there
before the eyes of members of the Penang Club.
Meanwhile, business boomed and, although the cost
of imports increased, the rise in the value of silver in
relation to gold trebled or quadrupled the assets of
many local entrepreneurs. As the war dragged on and
the casualty lists lengthened, a more sombre attitude

prevailed and the anti-German sentiments current at home became more widespread. Sizeable voluntary contributions were made to the war effort and the government organized a loan of $5 million which was given to the Imperial government as a gift. In 1917 a war rate of 7 per cent was introduced and the proceeds, about $1 million a year, were also given to the home government. In the same year the British Chamber of Commerce unsuccessfully urged the Hong Kong government to exclude German merchants from the colony for ten years after the end of the war.

The immediate aftermath of the war included the dislocation of world trade and a shortage of commodities. The fourfold rise in the price of rice, together with growing nationalism in China, contributed to labour unrest which culminated in the general strike of 1925. Although it was not apparent to many at the time, the war had brought an end to that freebooting era of Victorian economic individualism, already on the wane by the end of the nineteenth century, during which Hong Kong and its taipans had flourished. The heyday of British commercial and industrial supremacy, which Hong Kong had been created to serve, was over. With the eclipse of Germany and Russia, Japan became Britain's major rival in the East and the world economic crash of 1929 was to spur her on to military adventures in China which, in 1941, led her to launch a direct attack on the European and American presence in the East. Equally significant was the gradual emergence of a new China. The establishment in 1928 of the National Government of the Republic of China, controlled by the Kuomintang, was followed by strident demands for the acceptance of China's equality by the other powers, together with the ending of foreign concessions and the abrogation of unequal treaties.

However, Hong Kong has shown a remarkable ability to adapt itself to the rapidly changing political and economic circumstances of the twentieth century. Today, having survived occupation by the Japanese in the Second World War, the establishment of the People's Republic of China, and the decline and fall of the British Empire, Hong Kong is one of the few remaining bastions of free-wheeling and free-trading capitalism of a type to warm the heart of Adam Smith. With a population of 5.8 million, this minute British Crown Colony, sometimes described as a pimple on China's backside, manages to export more annually than India's population of 820 million. The living standards of Hong Kong's workers are substantially better than those of their counterparts in the People's Republic of China and are probably equal to those in the southern half of the European Community. Although wages are lower than those in Western countries and Japan, low taxation, subsidized housing, and cheap public transport combine to boost spending power. These are facts which make all but the most blinkered of Chinese chauvinists regard the British hand-over of sovereignty to China in 1997 with trepidation.

In the decades since the outbreak of the First World War, Hong Kong has changed as much as England in the two and a half centuries since the Industrial Revolution began. In 1914 the population of Hong Kong was around half a million; since then it has increased more than eleven times, roughly the same proportionate rise as that of England's population since 1700. Hong Kong's public revenue has increased from $8.5 million in 1913 to over $60,000 million in 1989. Today, the streets of Hong Kong carry the heaviest density of traffic per mile in the world; then, cars were a rarity and rickshaws, ox-drawn carts, and chair coolies provided the main hazards to pedestrians crossing from one banyan-shaded side of the street to the other. After scarcely a mile Kowloon's main artery, Nathan Road, then known as Nathan's Folly, ran through paddy fields and buffalo wallows. The New Territories was an almost totally undeveloped rural backwater still roamed by bandits and tigers, although both of these were admittedly much reduced in number. Perhaps the greatest change has taken place among the Chinese population of Hong Kong. In 1914 few Chinese wore Western dress, spoke English, or indeed had any more than the most superficial contact with or knowledge of Western ways. None ventured to provoke the water devils by swimming and not more than a handful played any Western sport. None was admitted to membership of the Hong Kong Club, the Jockey Club, or the Golf Club. Only the most emancipated of middle-class Chinese women were bold enough to walk the streets and none of these would risk their delicate complexions by exposing them directly to the sun.

The degree of change in different fields has varied greatly. If the founders of the colony were to return today, they would be overwhelmed by the pace of life in modern Hong Kong: the vast crowds of people and unending lines of traffic pressing their way along the canyons between high-rise buildings, the screaming jets, the constant cacophony of construction work that has swept away all but a very few nineteenth-century buildings. Yet politically Hong Kong is an anachronism, a Crown Colony frozen in the attitudes of the nineteenth century. The Union Jack still flies over Government House and the administration is presided over by the Governor-in-Council. After nearly one hundred and fifty years of 'semi-Victorian plumed-hat colonialism with no election nonsense', the first elections for one third of the members of the Legislative Council are scheduled to take place in 1991. However, this is not being done as a preliminary step towards full democratic government, which is generally perceived as being an unrealistic aspiration once China resumes sovereignty over Hong Kong. The representative element in the administration is seen rather as a check on possible attempts by over-zealous party cadres to curb Hong Kong's 'freedoms' which do not include the right to elect top administrators but, as one Chinese businessman put it, 'freedom to express one's opinion, freedom to come and go as one pleases, freedom to create wealth in a favourable tax environment, so long as one is willing to work hard.'

In the nineteenth century there was a popular saying that Hong Kong was ruled by Jardine's, the Jockey Club, the Hongkong and Shanghai Bank and the Governor, in that order of importance. Today, it is the views on Hong Kong of China's officials that are the subject of intense scrutiny by government officials but, even in the aftermath of the massacre in Tiananmen Square, the tenor of these views has been, in the words of Xu Jiatun, China's representative in Hong Kong in the 1980s, that 'we unequivocally and unmistakably declare our intention to maintain the capitalist system in Hong Kong.' In 1978 Professor Harris described Hong Kong's politics as 'administered capitalism in the service of China' and the Legislative Councillors as 'classic spokesmen for the employers' lobby' and it is still true today that one of the government's main concerns is to preserve 'the freedom to create wealth.' The maximum rate of salaries tax is 15.5 per cent, profits tax for corporations amounts to not more than 17 per cent, the maximum estate duty is 18 per cent, and there are no capital gains or transfer taxes. There are probably more Rolls-Royces per head in Hong Kong than anywhere outside the Arabian Gulf. Ocean-going yachts by the score lie off the moorings of the Royal Hong Kong Yacht Club and the Hebe Haven Marina. The cost of land in Hong Kong's business district is the highest in the world and rents for residential apartments equal those of Tokyo and New York.

Hong Kong's businessmen are gamblers. In 1989 bets on horse-racing totalled $4.5 billion, which was more than China received in foreign loans and investments. Between 1950 and 1990 the number of people employed in factories increased fourfold and production increased by as much as sixty times. With over four hundred financial institutions, Hong Kong can credibly claim to be, together with New York and London, one of the world's leading financial centres. Hong Kong is too valuable an asset for China to waste and, envious though they may be of Hong Kong's lifestyle, there cannot be too many Chinese officials whose thoughts go no further than Field Marshal Blücher's observation on seeing London, 'What a city to plunder.' The superiority of the capitalist system in producing large quantities of goods capable of competing in world markets seems incontrovertible and, in spite of the gloom cast by the crushing of the reform movement in China in 1989, most businessmen feel that the odds are in favour of Hong Kong continuing to prosper in the twenty-first century. A lot of smart money is said to be waiting on the sidelines for the inevitable slump in the stock-market before 1997 to snap up cheap shares and make a handsome profit in the years to come.

The Hong Kong Club is still flourishing although, to the dismay of conservationists, the Victorian clubhouse was demolished in 1981. The golf course at Happy Valley has gone but new applicants for membership of the Royal Hong Kong Golf Club at Deep Water Bay and Fanling may spend years on the waiting lists. Racing still takes place at Happy Valley, and at the new course at Sha Tin, under the auspices of the Royal Hong Kong Jockey Club. The jockeys are now professionals, but entertainment in the taipans' boxes continues to be lavish. Racing is now big business: eighty million dollars can be bet on a single race. In the smoking rooms of the Hong Kong Club, the owners' enclosure at Happy Valley, and the locker room at Fanling, there are now many affluent members of Hong Kong's sophisticated and Westernized Chinese business class. Among the crowds in the football stadiums, on the beaches, in the arrival and departure halls at Kai Tak Airport, or hiking in the New Territories, a European face is the exception.

Judged simply by numbers, the majority of what passes for an upper class in Hong Kong are now Chinese. Many are relatively recent arrivals. Large numbers of capitalists from Shanghai and Canton fled to the colony before the Communist take-over of China in 1949, a few crossing the border in Rolls-Royces or Cadillacs so laden down with gold bars that the springs were near breaking-point. As well as gold, they brought with them the business acumen that has helped to transform Hong Kong from what was basically an entrepôt into one of the main manufacturing centres in Asia. Some Chinese businessmen are notable for their devotion to public service and their massive donations to charity have been rewarded with the ultimate accolade of the British colonial system, a knighthood. Men like Sir Y.K. Pao of the World Wide Shipping Agency, Sir Run Run Shaw of Shaw Brothers Films, and Sir S.Y. Chung, Chairman of the two Polytechnics and the Provisional Health Authority, are very rich and very influential.

A few of the old established Eurasian families continue to flourish, notably the numerous descendants of Sir Robert Ho Tung and his brothers. Of these the most successful is perhaps Stanley Ho, the managing director of Sociedade de Turismo e Diversões de Macao, which is the principal gambling casino and hotel operator in Macau. Parsee financiers have virtually ceased to play a distinctive part in Hong Kong business affairs, their role having been taken over by the banks, of which there are more different companies than practically anywhere else in the world. There are still some successful Indian businessmen. Doyen among them is Hari Harilela, who began as a contractor to the British army and is now a multimillionaire. In recent years he has expanded into Hong Kong's booming hotel industry. The Kadoories remain prominent among Hong Kong's Jewish community. Lawrence and his brother Horace were both educated at Clifton College, England, and are now joint partners of Sir Elly Kadoorie and Sons. Horace is chairman of Hong Kong and Shanghai Hotels and the Peak Tramways Company, while among Lawrence's chairmanships are Sir Elly Kadoorie Successors Ltd., China Light and Power, Kadoorie Estates, and Hong Kong Carpet Manufacturers. In 1981 Lawrence became Hong Kong's first peer, partly as a reward, it is rumoured, for a huge order that China Light placed in Britain for a new power station. Lawrence's son, Michael, who could be described as a member of Hong Kong's jet set, is heir to the Kadoorie empire. Educated at La Rosey, Switzerland, he lists among his clubs Annabel's and Les Ambassadeurs, London, the Vintage Sports Car Club, and Hong Kong Aero Club.

A surprising number of the older business houses still survive, although many have in reality been taken over by conglomerates. However, a roll call of the names of Hong Kong's nineteenth-century taipans reveals the remorseless way in which Time condemns all but the fortunate few to oblivion. Where are the Magniacs, Dents, Russells, Dodwells, MacGregors, and Ryries today? Even to the better-educated younger generation in Hong Kong names like Chater, Shewan, Belilios, and Mody mean little or nothing. *Kelly's*

*Handbook of the Titled, Landed and Official Classes*
and *Who's Who* reveal no Dicksons, Bell-Irvings,[1]
Whittalls, Percevals, or even Sassoons.

Yet a study of eight leading executives in five of the
major expatriate-dominated hongs, Jardine's, Swire's,
the Hongkong and Shanghai Banking Corporation,
Hongkong Land, and the Inchcape Group reveals an
interesting pattern.[2] All the executives are British and
kinship continués to be a significant career factor. Six
attended Eton College and either Oxford or Cambridge
universities. Several did military service in a good
regiment in the British army — as officers, naturally.
Almost without exception those who are resident in
Hong Kong belong to the Jockey Club, the Hong Kong
Club, and the Shek O Club. The ambitious young men
of the nineteenth century who flocked to the China
coast from Europe, America, the Middle East, and
India in search of the wealth that would buy them
position and power have been succeeded by the
scions of the establishment. The true heirs of William
Jardine and James Matheson are to be found today
among the ranks of the rising Chinese businessmen.

The survival of the class system in Britain, with its
trappings of title and privilege, owes much to the
willingness of the upper class to open its ranks to the
*nouveaux riches*. It would be hard to find two families
more typical of the popular image of the landed gentry
than the Jardines and Mathesons today. The estate at
Lochalsh bought by Alexander Matheson passed eventually to the fifth baronet, the late General Sir Torquhil
Matheson, KCB, CMG. He was educated at Eton,
served in the Boer War, and commanded the Coldstream Guards and later the Guards Division in the
First World War. He was frequently mentioned in dis-
patches and was awarded the Croix de Guerre with
Palmes and the Russian Order of St Stanislaus. From
1920 to 1924 he commanded the Waziristan Field

Force and ended his military career as general in charge of West India. After his retirement he became a county councillor in Ross and Cromarty and, during the Second World War, raised and commanded a Home Guard company there. The sixth baronet, Major Sir Torquhil Alexander Matheson, KCB, CMG, was also a professional soldier, serving in the Coldstream Guards during the Second World War. He married Serena, daughter of Lieutenant Colonel Sir Michael Peto, the second baronet, and now lives at Standerwick Court, Frome. The estate at Castle Milk, bought by Andrew Jardine in 1854, which passed to his brother Robert, is now the seat of the fourth baronet, Major Sir Rupert Buchanan Jardine, MC. He was educated at Harrow, served with the Guards during the Second World War, and was awarded the Military Cross in 1944 and the Bronze Lion of the Netherlands. He retired in 1949, married Fiona, daughter of Sir Archibald Edmonstone, the sixth baronet, the following year, and became joint master of the Dumfriesshire Foxhounds and a Justice of the Peace.

The Mathesons have long since ceased to play a part in the affairs of Jardine, Matheson but the Jardines retained their control until relatively recently. After the death of Sir Robert Buchanan Jardine in 1927, he was succeeded as chairman by his son, Sir John, the third baronet, who resided at Castle Milk, was Master of the Dumfriesshire Hounds for many years, a Justice of the Peace, and a member of the Royal Company of Archers. Sir John owned much property in Shanghai and Hong Kong as well as having a 75 per cent share of Jardine, Matheson. However, he lost his Shanghai assets after the Second World War and, by 1961, when Jardine, Matheson went public, he had sold all his shares in the company as well as his property in Hong Kong. He later retired to the south of France leaving his estates in Scotland to the management of his son, who had preferred a career as a professional soldier to that of entering business.

Most of the Jardine family's shares were bought by the Keswicks, whose fortune, estimated at over $160 million, ranked eightieth in a recent survey of Britain's richest people. After the death of Henry Keswick in 1928, the estate at Cowhill Tower passed to his oldest son, David. His second son, John, joined Jardine, Matheson in 1929 and was chairman of the associated company, Matheson and Co., from 1966 to 1972, a position also held by his younger brother William. Both brothers were knighted in 1972. Sir William's son, Henry, was the managing director in Hong Kong for some years and is now chairman of Matheson and Co. In 1985 he married the daughter of the seventeenth Baron Lovat and is the proprietor of *The Spectator*. Another fourth-generation Keswick, Simon, joined Jardine, Matheson in 1964. Henry's successor in Hong Kong made some unwise investments and in 1979 Sir Y.K. Pao took advantage of Jardine's vulnerable position to take control of one of its subsidiaries, Hong Kong and Kowloon Wharf. Pao and another prominent Chinese businessman, Li Ka-shing, were seen to pose a threat to Jardine's 'other half', Hongkong Land, and even to the Keswicks' control of the princely hong itself. Land and Jardine's exchanged shares to strengthen their defences against further takeover bids and the threat passed. Simon was sent to Hong Kong to straighten out the mess. He recruited new talent, paid off the hong's debts, and strengthened its corporate position. He also transferred the domicile of the parent holding company to Bermuda, a move which was likened by one commentator to 'the Pope abandoning the Vatican.' He was much criticized at the time but his example has been followed by other prominent companies anxious to safeguard their overseas assets from the higher political risk which the resumption of Chinese sovereignty will bring. For the time being, the hold of the Keswicks over Jardine's seems secure while the hong's market capitalization of over $5 billion make it Hong Kong's top company. The Swire family, ranked fifteenth in the list of Britain's richest people, still retains control of John Swire and Sons whose publicly quoted subsidiary, Swire Pacific, is now the central component of the Swire Group's interests in east Asia, Australia, and the United States. J.K. Swire, son of J. Swire, junior, was chairman of the parent company from 1946 to 1966 and honorary president of the Hong Kong-based airline, Cathay Pacific, one of Swire's most successful investments in recent years. In addition, he was chairman of the China Association from 1951 to 1955. His son, John A. Swire, was chairman of John Swire and Sons from 1966 to 1987 and director of Swire Pacific and Swire Properties. Another son, Sir Adrian, succeeded him as chairman.

The Hongkong and Shanghai Banking Corporation has very considerable assets and is in a position to pursue a more diversified expansion policy than any of the trading companies. Its interests include substantial holdings in a number of leading Hong Kong companies and it remains Hong Kong's premier banking group. The chairman, the Honourable William Purves, CBE, DSO, JP, is also a member of the Executive Council.

A number of Hong Kong's oldest established merchant companies came under the umbrella of the Inchcape Group, initially set up by the life president, the third Earl of Inchcape, in 1958 to co-ordinate the activities of the various businesses owned by the Inchcape family. The earl includes among his numerous directorships those of the P. & O. Steam Navigation Company and the Chartered Bank. The managing director of Inchcape (Hong Kong) is Viscount Errington. An interest in Gibb, Livingston was acquired by the Inchcape family in the 1920s. The company was sold to the Borneo Company in 1963 but the latter in turn merged with the Inchcape Group three years later. Gilman's became part of the Inchcape Group in 1968 and Dodwell's in 1972. All three remain active trading groups. Calbeck, MacGregor, the wine importing firm, passed under the control of Inchcape in 1975.

The core of Hongkong Land's interests remains its immensely valuable holdings in Central District which now total over 4 million square feet of space available for rent. Many of the leases were acquired in Sir Paul Chater's time. In recent years the company's properties have been vigorously redeveloped, completely changing the appearance of Central District. In 1972 the company took over the Dairy Farm group of supermarkets, restaurants, and food processing plants. There is a close, almost incestuous, relationship between Hongkong Land and Jardine, Matheson.

One recent chairman of Jardine's declared, 'We are just grocers. Grocers and merchants.' He was being a trifle ingenuous. Hong Kong was the creation of the taipans and today they continue to play a major part in its affairs. When Chairman Hua of the People's Republic of China visited Britain in 1979, a Keswick was among the guests at the dinner given in his honour. Judging by Hong Kong's economic progress in recent years, the latter-day taipans have lost little of the drive and enterprise of their predecessors. They may no longer have the ear of the Foreign Secretary and parliamentary seats rarely come the way of retired Hong Kong businessmen, yet, as Richard Hughes wrote in Hong Kong — Borrowed Place, Borrowed Time, 'the power, protocol and noblesse oblige remain.'

The prospects for the old-established expatriate hongs after 1997 seem reasonably good. The taipan of Swire's recently stated that 'China has gone out of its way to assure us that it is absolutely essential that British companies remain a substantial part of Hong Kong.' The survival of these hongs in British hands in the face of the meteoric post-war rise of Chinese entrepreneurs is partly explained by the fact that, in general, the latter have preferred to develop their own enterprises from the bottom up rather than attempt to take over established businesses. One who did develop predatory instincts was Li Ka-shing, who came to Hong Kong from China as the child of a poor family in 1939. Starting work as a salesman for a plastics company, by the 1950s he owned the largest plastic factory in the world and made a fortune, now estimated at between $1.5 and $2 billion, during the plastic flower boom. Property development and shrewd investments in the 1970s enabled him to buy a controlling share in Hutchison Whampoa, which had been badly hit in the mid-1970s recession, from the Hongkong Bank in 1979 for a relatively cheap $82 million. True to his reputation, though uncharacteristic of some Chinese tycoons, Li made good use of professional expatriate advisers and managers and appointed a former employee of Jardine's, Simon Murray, as the new chief executive. Parts of the conglomerate, John D. Hutchison, the original retailing group, and Hutchison-Boag Engineering, were sold to Inchcape in 1990 for $93 million. The alarm waves caused by Li's coup led Jardine's and Hongkong Land to close ranks but Li, who at one time controlled 10 per cent of Jardine's, avoided a direct confrontation, confining himself to the purchase of Hongkong Electric from the Jardine Group in 1985. Since then, Li has sought to expand his interests abroad, acquiring 5 per cent of Cable and Wireless and extensive interests in Canada.

The history of business in Hong Kong provides an interesting case-study of capitalism in microcosm. The colony of Hong Kong was established on Palmerston's 'barren rock' for the sole purpose of serving the needs of businessmen. From the start its civic affairs and social life were dominated by businessmen and to a large extent they have continued to be so dominated to this day. The influence of the taipans was tempered initially only by the desire of the Colonial Office to avoid subsidizing the colony from central funds. However, in the second half of the nineteenth century, the Colonial Office became increasingly concerned to ensure that Hong Kong was administered in accordance with the liberal and humanitarian sentiments which prevailed in Britain. The synthesis of these influences has produced a competitive, hard-working, money-oriented society whose leaders, with the exception of a few mavericks, would not claim to aspire to a philosophy higher than that of enlightened self-interest. This philosophy is thoroughly condoned by the pragmatic Chinese working population. The administrators' watchword of 'don't rock the boat' is echoed by the workers' cry of 'don't break the rice bowl'.

There are, of course, great contrasts of wealth and poverty in Hong Kong and the social services, although not as sketchy as some maintain, are more in accord with the principles of Samuel Smiles' Self Help than those of the Beveridge Report. None the less, the undeniable fact remains that, with all its warts, Hong Kong works. Its citizens enjoy relative freedom to voice their opinions and to carry on their lives as they wish. The ordinary man has little direct influence on the administration, but there are few states in the world where this is not the case. Moreover, by virtue of the fact that the present government is acutely conscious of being a colonial anachronism, its administrators take pains to avoid offending the susceptibilities of the general public. Materially, Hong Kong continues to flourish. Millionaires abound but the less well-off seek to emulate, not eliminate, them. Hong Kong has survived for nearly a hundred and fifty years partly as a result of peculiar historical circumstances but also because its inhabitants wished it to survive. All the indications are that the majority hope that it will continue to survive in the future.

It is true that a substantial number of Hong Kong's Chinese managerial and professional class fear that, even if China's officials are well-intentioned, Hong Kong's rare combination of a relatively honest and efficient administration, risk-taking and innovative enterprise, and freedom of thought under the rule of law will be 'destroyed by those who do not understand the underlying realities of life in Hong Kong.' Most of them have already got themselves foreign passports and it is likely that a greater or lesser number, depending on the state of affairs prevailing in China, will have departed with the British administrators by 1997. None the less, the most likely scenario is that, after some largely cosmetic adjustments in its lifestyle and administration to bring it more in line with those of China, Hong Kong will continue to prosper. Economic logic indicates that this prosperity will be based on the strengthening and development of its role as the design, marketing, and financial centre for the expanding industrial complex in south China. Optimists still hope that it will also serve as an example to show that industrial freedom and enterprise, together with an efficient *laissez-faire* administration, can flourish in a largely Chinese society.

1. However, the Bell-Irvings do appear in a current hunting directory. Captain and Mrs J. Bell-Irving of Lockerbie are listed as joint masters of the Dumfriesshire hounds.

2. Henry Keswick, Simon Keswick, J.A. Swire, Sir Adrian Swire, William Purves, Nigel Rich, the Earl of Inchcape, and Viscount Errington.

# Select Bibliography

## I LETTERS, NEWSPAPERS, AND JOURNALS

China Mail, 1876–1914.

China Repository, 1832–51.

Hong Kong Daily Press, 1870–8.

Journal of the Royal Asiatic Society, Hong Kong Branch, 1961–77.

Letters, 1820–54—in the possession of Charles Buchanan Jardine.

South China Morning Post, 1904–14.


## II BOOKS

Allen, C. G., and Donnithorne, A. G., Western Enterprise in Far East Development, London, 1954.

Beeching, J., The Chinese Opium Wars, London, 1975.

Braga, J. M., Hong Kong Business Symposium, Hong Kong, 1957.

—— 'A Seller of Sing Songs', Journal of Oriental Studies, v. VI, nos. 1–2, 1961/64.

Cameron, N., Hong Kong: The Cultured Pearl, Hong Kong, 1978.

Camplin, J., The Rise of the Plutocrats, London, 1978.

Cheng, Irene, Clara Ho Tung: A Hong Kong Lady, her Family and her Times, Hong Kong, 1976.

Clark, T. and Fletcher, G., *75 Not Out*, Hong Kong, 1978.

Coates, A., *Prelude to Hong Kong*, London, 1966.

—— *A Mountain of Light*, Hong Kong, 1977.

Collis, M., *Wayfoong*, London, 1965.

—— *Foreign Mud*, London, 1969.

Crisswell, C., and Briggs, T., *The Vanishing City*, Hong Kong, 1978.

Curzon, G. N., *Problems in the Far East*, London, 1894.

Des Voeux, Sir W., *My Colonial Service*, London, 1903.

Downing, C. T., *The Fan Qui in China*, 3 vols., London, 1838.

Drage, C., *Taikoo*, London, 1970.

Eitel, E. J., *The History of Hong Kong*, London, 1895.

Endacott, G. B., *A Biographical Sketch Book of Early Hong Kong*, Singapore, 1952.

—— *A History of Hong Kong*, Hong Kong, 1974.

Fairbank, J. K., *Trade and Diplomacy on the China Coast*, Harvard, 1964.

—— ed., *Cambridge History of China*, Vol. 10, Cambridge, 1978.

Gittins, Jean, *Eastern Windows—Western Skies*, Hong Kong, 1969.

Green, O. M., *The Foreigner in China*, London, 1942.

Greenberg, M., *British Trade and the Opening of China*, Cambridge, 1951.

—— *A Handbook to Hong Kong*, Hong Kong, 1893.

Harris, P., *Hong Kong: A Study in Bureaucratic Politics*, 1978.

Hughes, R., *Hong Kong—Borrowed Place, Borrowed Time*, Hong Kong, 1968.

Hunter, W. C., *The Fan Kwae in Canton before Treaty Days*, Shanghai, 1938.

Hyde, R. E., *Blue Funnel*, Liverpool, 1957.

—— *Far Eastern Trade 1860–1914*, London, 1973.

*Kelly's Handbook to the Titled, Landed and Official Classes*, London, 1963.

Knollys, H., *English Life in China*. London, 1885.

Le Fevour, E., *Western Enterprise in late Ch'ing China*, Cambridge, Mass., 1968.

Liu, Kwang-ching, *Anglo-American Steamship Rivalry in China 1862–1874*, Harvard, 1962.

Lubbock, B., *The Opium Clippers*, Glasgow, 1933.

Marriner, S., and Hyde, F., *The Senior, John Samuel Swire 1825–1898*, Liverpool, 1967.

Morse, H. B., *International Relations of the Chinese Empire*, London, 1918.

Oliphant, L., *Narrative of the Earl of Elgin's Mission to China and Japan*, London, 1859.

Pelcovits, N. A., *Old China Hands and the Foreign Office*, New York, 1948.

Pope-Hennessy, J., *Verandah*, London, 1964.

Roth, Cecil, *The Sassoon Dynasty*, London, 1941.

Sayer, G. R., *Hong Kong—Birth, Adolescence and Coming of Age*, Oxford, 1937.

—— *Hong Kong 1862–1919*, Hong Kong, 1975.

Smith, Albert, *To China and Back*, London, 1859; new edition Hong Kong, 1974.

Somers, G. V., *The Royal Hong Kong Jockey Club*, Hong Kong, 1975.

Stettler, J., ed., *The Peninsula's Anniversary 1928–78*, Hong Kong, 1978.

Steuart, J., *Jardine Matheson and Co 1832–1932*, Hong Kong, 1934.

Thomson, J., *The Straits of Malacca, Indo-China and China . . .*, London, 1875.

Wilson, D., *Hong Kong! Hong Kong!*, London, 1990.

Wright, A., *Twentieth Century Impressions of Hong Kong, Shanghai and other Treaty Ports of China*, London, 1908.

# Index